The Postmodern Turn

The Postmodern Turn

Essays in Postmodern Theory and Culture

IHAB HASSAN

OHIO STATE UNIVERSITY PRESS

Columbus

Library of Congress Cataloging-in-Publication Data

Hassan, Ihab Habib, 1925—
The postmodern turn.

Bibliography: p.
Includes index.
1. Literature, Modern—20th century—History and criticism. 2. Postmodernism. I. Title
PN771.H346 1987 809'.04 86-33320
ISBN 0–8142–0419–8
ISBN 0–8142–0428–7 (pbk.)

Printed by Bookcrafters, Inc., Chelsea, MI.

The paper in this book meets the guidelines for permanence and durability of the Committee on Production Guidelines for Book Longevity of the Council on Library Resources.

9 8 7 6 5 4 3 2

S

Contents

Acknowledgments

Sections of this work have appeared in articles or in chapters of my earlier books:

1. "The Literature of Silence," in *Encounter* 28, no. 1 (January 1967), and in *The Literature of Silence* (New York, 1967)
2. "POSTmodernISM: A Paracritical Bibliography," *New Literary History* 3, no. 1 (Fall 1971), and in *Paracriticisms: Seven Speculations of the Times* (Urbana, Ill., 1975)
3. "Culture, Indeterminacy, and Immanence: Margins of the (Postmodern) Age," in *Humanities in Society* 1, no. 1 (Winter 1977–78), and in *The Right Promethean Fire: Imagination, Science, and Cultural Change* (Urbana, Ill., 1980)
4. "Toward a Concept of Postmodernism" in *The Dismemberment of Orpheus: Toward a Postmodern Literature,* 2d ed., rev. (Madison, Wis., 1982)
5. "(   ): *Finnegans Wake* and the Postmodern Imagination," in *Paracriticisms*
6. "The Critic as Innovator: A Paracritical Strip in X Frames," in *Chicago Review* 28, no. 3 (Winter 1977), and in *The Right Promethean Fire*
7. "Parabiography: The Varieties of Critical Experience," *Georgia Review* 34, no. 3 (Fall 1980), and in Victor A. Kramer, ed., *American Critics at Work* (Troy, N.Y., 1984)
8. "Pluralism in Postmodern Perspective," in *Critical Inquiry* 12, no. 3 (1986)
9. "Making Sense: The Trials of Postmodern Discourse," was intended for Ralph Cohen, ed., *The Future of Literary Theory* (London and New York: Methuen, forthcoming). Difficulties with Methuen concerning "priority" of publication required me to withdraw the essay; it was kindly published by Ralph Cohen in *New Literary History* 18, no. 2 (Winter 1987)

I am grateful to the university presses of Chicago, Illinois, and Wisconsin, which hold the copyright of some chapters, for permission to reprint them. And I am particularly grateful to Danuta Zadworna and Giovanna Borradori for their help in compiling the bibliography in this volume.

Introduction

> First, you know, a new theory is attacked as absurd; then it is admitted to be true, but obvious and insignificant; finally, it is seen to be so important that its adversaries claim that they themselves have discovered it.—William James, *Pragmatism*

I

The essays in this volume turn on the question of postmodernism in the West, turn finally away from it. They span more than two decades. Thus they turn in time, reflecting their author's biography, recounting a short history of our epoch. Above all, the essays, chosen for this book with care, join here less to consolidate any statement on postmodernism than to review its questions, moot them once more—and thus, perhaps, welcome new horizons, another cultural moment.

Fastidious academics once shunned the word *postmodern* as they might shrink from the shadiest neologism. But now the term has become a shibboleth for tendencies in film, theater, dance, music, art, and architecture; in literature and criticism; in philosophy, theology, psychoanalysis, and historiography; in new sciences, cybernetic technologies, and various cultural life styles. Indeed, postmodernism has now received the bureaucratic accolade of the National Endowment for the Humanities in the form of Summer Seminars for College Teachers; and beyond that, it has penetrated the discourse of late Marxist critics who, only a decade ago, dismissed the term as another instance of the dreck, fads, and folderol of a consumer society.

No doubt the media's insidious chatter—that immanent white noise of postindustrial societies—has contributed much to the currency of postmodernism. But that currency also constitutes an act of self-apprehension by which a culture seeks to understand itself, presuming its uniqueness in history. Fashions often prove to be modes of obscure self-awareness as well as cultural desire. They beckon us to ourselves, somehow, under the twin aspects of our difference and solidarity with the past. Thus the fiction of the new becomes a tradition of novation—and the myth of a postmodernist breakthrough yields to international conferences on the subject.

This movement, this becoming, is precisely what the essays here want to articulate even if they remain themselves very much part of their moment. Though postmodernism may persist, like modernism itself, a fiercely contested category, at once signifier and signified, altering itself in the very process of signification, the effort to speak it can not be wholly vain. The effort, a nisus of unending discrimination, still merits our wakeful concern if only to adumbrate our cultural choices, our versions of historical reality, our images of ourselves—as we are, as we want to become. In our pluralist and dialogical universe, there may be no alternative to such transactions.

II

Written over twenty years, the essays selected here focus firmly on postmodernism but display different styles, different moods, some gay, later somber. (The owl of Minerva still flies by night when criticism paints its greys on greys.) I have not revised the essays, nor imposed on them a uniform system of references since the latter are integral to the tone of the texts. I have corrected only a few errors, excised redundancies, iterating only what the incremental theory of postmodernism requires. In short, I have preferred to admit my complicity with postmodernism, what we have come reluctantly to call postmodernism, without renouncing the exigencies of clarity and criticism.

It should be no surprise, therefore, that the organization of the book is nothing postmodern. Meant both as personal revaluation and general introduction, *The Postmodern Turn* presents itself in a sequence rigorously topical and, with one exception, chronological. Four sections, ten chapters, lead from initial concepts to theoretic elaborations, from prospective views to retrospective judgments. Reading the book as a whole, one may easily discern the warp and woof of themes, queries, names, a pattern that may be all we can perceive of postmodernism at this time.

The first, prelusive section contains but one chapter. It finds prefigurations of postmodernism in mannerism, romanticism, modernism, in a tradition of silence extending—through Henry Miller and Samuel Beckett, antipodal writers—to the present. But "silence" here is only metaphor: the head of Orpheus, dismembered, continues to sing, the words become second nature, art dissolved in life. Still, the metaphor betrays a certain distress of self and civilization, a certain revulsion of language, which provokes gestures of outrage and apocalypse—postures of the American sixties.

Three chapters in the next section assay the concept of postmodernism in various stages of its development. Chapter 2 contrasts modernism and postmodernism, without defining either, contending that the former is largely formalist/hierarchic, the latter antiformalist/anarchic. The paracritical style of the chapter deforms the page, hoping less to mime its subject than to suggest alternative critical discourses. But the essay conflates modernism with early avant-gardes too easily, and inflates the apocalyptic element of postmodern literature.

Chapter 3 offers a more ambitious, also antic, apprehension of postmodernism, perceiving Indeterminacy and Immanence (Indetermanence) as its ruling tendencies. The essay plays on analogies of postmodern art, science, and society, plays on its own margins with quotations, collages, counter-statements, doodles. Its conscious intent, though, is to explore not only the arts of indetermanence but also coherent hints of a posthumanist culture. Starting with the signal contrast between Matthew Arnold and Friedrich Nietzsche, the text discontinuously pursues a movement of the Western mind toward a different idea of the human, a problematic new gnosticism.

The following chapter, concluding this part of the book, returns to the received style of academe. Though brief, the chapter gives a quick history of the term *postmodernism,* discusses its ample difficulties, and, in admitting these, reaches for a workable concept by distinguishing between avant-garde, modern, and postmodern, and by drawing a tentative, a propadeutic, table of contrastive features. More than a decade after the earlier efforts to recognize postmodernism, the piece benefits from hindsight, enjoys the luxury of self-revision.

Critical theory fills the third section precisely because theory, puissant with new abractions, has clearly shaped postmodernism, a postmodernism wherein literature and criticism constantly blend. Thus the chapter on *Finnegans Wake,* a work proposed here as a "monstrous prophecy of our postmodernity," turns on a use of language that wavers between analysis and poesis, logic and myth. All the elements of postmodern literature crowd the "novel": dream, parody, play, pun, fragment, fable, reflexiveness, kitsch, the gnosis of some ironic Logos on the edge of pure silence or pure noise. Is not the *Wake* both augur and theory of a certain kind of literature?

Chapter 6 reviews the plight of innovative criticism in its current academic milieu. Paracritical levity barely masks vexed concern with the postmodern literary situation, in which (poststructuralist) novation quickly lapses into a (deconstructive) conformity of evasions. The essay takes an independent stance, at once personal and political. It refuses to evaluate the self in compliance with current demands, refuses as well to textualize existence. Both attitudes, symptomatic of postmodernism and its growing discontents, inform the last three chapters as well.

Defiantly, autobiography intersperses chapter 7 which implicates criticism—as desire, reading, writing/acting—in the critic's passional life. Postmodernism here is the tacit seduction, tempting us to acknowledge its cool versions of that life. But the chapter resists that seduction without reverting to humanist piety. Instead, it asks: what kind of self, in its society, is adequate to our postmodern world, a world caught between fragments and wholes, terror and totalitarianism of every kind? Inevitably, the question points to death as private, political, metaphysical facts.

The issue returns under the aegis of critical pluralism in chapter 8. Written in a style more sober than carnival—so much for the enervations of paracriticism—the chapter first renders eleven features of postmodernism; these, it argues, all serve to destabilize our cultural discourse. No cognitive, political, or libidinal code can now restrain the hesitancies of our knowledge. But a Jamesian pragmatism may permit us to act provisionally, consequently, on beliefs adequate to their circumstance. Such actions, in William James's pluralist universe, avoid the extremes of dogmatism and deferral, though pluralism itself could never become a stable sign.

Two chapters in the final section appraise postmodernism, its trials and prospects. Chapter 9 reviews the postmodern provocation in history, philosophy, literary theory. But the chapter also posits a cognitive imperative, a drive to "make sense," that postmodernism can not obviate. Still, *what* sense to make? Hints come from the debates between various social, textual, and pragmatic critics, from thinkers like Habermas, Lyotard, Rorty. In the end the debates engage fiduciary questions that William James long ago raised. Can his "willing nature" help us to traverse postmodernism in negotiations of pluralist praxis and belief?

And what lies beyond? Chapter 10 tries to answer the question retrospectively. It recalls the key issues of postmodern theory, observing shifts in approach, in critical apprehension, as the phenomenon itself comes of age. It remarks also how contending ideologies—neoconservative, neo-Marxist, poststructuralist, neopragmatist—vie to appropriate the life of postmodernism even as that life begins to wane. But what really is at stake? Once again, the chapter recaptures the triangular debate between Habermas, Lyotard, and Rorty, educing the major themes of their conflict. Such conflictual themes, exemplifying our indetermanences, may be as much as we can do now to conceptualize postmodernism. Yet even in theoretical conflict, an anxious consensus, perhaps just an assumption, begins to emerge about postmodernism. It is a pluralist assumption, waiting on further change.

Once more, what lies beyond postmodernism? We can ask, we can even answer, but no one truly knows. I would *hope* an interest in some new "fideology," less a science than pragmatics or maieutics of belief. I would hope an end to sterility.

III

All this, I realize, will satisfy no one who requires a more exact "definition" of postmodernism. But human actions trace no perfect circle or square; as historical events they escape axiomatic definition. Postmodernism, like any other movement—say romanticism, nearly as moot—is a complex of cultural actions. Such actions also resist sharp differentiation from other actions they assume. Thus any particular trait of postmodernism may find precursors in other eras, other movements. This, I suspect, is true of any single trait in any cultural movement.

Three reasons, at least, account for this peculiarity of our historical understanding. First, radically new, disjunctive events are rare. Norsemen, for instance, preceded Columbus in the "discovery" of America, and Egyptians could have preceded both. Newness, then, has some attributes of origins: it tends to recede, vanish, as we near it. (In this, Derrida was more right than Barthes.) Second, historical narrative demands a certain level of abstraction. It achieves continuity only at the expense of blurring the radical quiddity of things. Only thus, for instance, can we aver that the sublime "extends" from Longinus, through Burke, Wordsworth, and Emerson, to Lyotard. Third, any statement about "antecedents"—"X is not new; you can find it in Y"—conceals a triple interpretation: of X, of Y, and of a particular concept of newness. This compound interpretation, moreover, tips always toward the present. Thus, for instance, we perceive now—but did not perceive thirty years ago—postmodern features in *Tristram Shandy* precisely because our eyes have learned to recognize postmodern features. And so we propose *Tristram Shandy,* but not *Tom Jones,* as a "postmodern book."

Aristotelian definitions—man is a thinking biped, etc.—can hardly apply to our cultural histories. How, then, proceed without definitions? Conventionally, I think, pragmatically, as we have always done, by consuetude. *The Postmodern Turn* tilts that way: it clarifies by putting essential terms, ideas, contexts of postmodernism into wider play. The play is already familiar to us, all too familiar, as the "poststructuralist debate." But though postmodernism and poststructuralism share many interests, they finally resist conflation. Postmodernism appears larger, is international, in scope. Art, politics, technology, all of culture, fall within its compass, as do trends from Japanese architecture to Colombian magic realism. Hence the loose, baggy character of postmodernism, more kitschy than monstrous, so distressing to its critics.

Will these international tendencies ever coalesce into some coherent pattern? For the moment, the only pattern I can propose is the pattern that the essays selected here internally render. In this pattern I discern: indeterminacy and immanence; ubiquitous simulacra, pseudo-events; a conscious lack of mastery, lightness and evanescence everywhere; a new temporality, or rather intertemporality, a polychronic sense of history; a patchwork or ludic, transgressive, or deconstructive, approach to knowledge and authority; an ironic, parodic, reflexive, fantastic awareness of the moment; a linguistic turn, semiotic imperative, in culture; and in society generally, the violence of local desires diffused into a technology both of seduction and force. In short, I see a pattern that many others have also seen: a vast, revisionary will in the Western world, unsettling/resettling codes, canons, procedures, beliefs—intimating a posthumanism?

Is this not momentous? And if so, why should *The Postmodern Turn* finally turn away, as I have said, from postmodernism? Part of the answer is implied in the preceding pages, a larger part implied in the closing chapters of the book. But a more candid answer would require me to critique, even briefly, my own changing perception of that phenomenon we call postmodernism.

The phenomenon has proven more diverse than I originally expected, its cultural imbrications more complex. It justifies less technological optimism, less utopianism, than I first adduced, though the dream of technology and the possibility of utopia remain at its center, inviolate. It calls more, I now think, for political, indeed geopolitical, concern, though that concern should not reduce to rightist or leftist cant. It calls, rather, for a tough and limber pragmatism, inward with human desires, with the cunning of our beliefs. But postmodernism itself has also changed, taken, as I see it, a wrong turn. Caught between ideological truculence and demystifying nugacity, caught in its own kitsch, postmodernism has become a kind of eclectic raillery, the refined prurience of our borrowed pleasures and trivial disbeliefs. And yet, on some deeper level of its transformations, it still reaches for something larger, something other, which some call posthumanism.

In contesting Western discourse, then, the postmodernism revisionary will has also put itself on trial. It can no longer be taken at its own words, on its own terms, the terms of its own agonisms. *For the time being,* we can not, *must* not, choose between the One and the Many, Humanism and Deconstruction, Community and Dissemination. We can only reopen such terms to constant negotiations, perpetual transactions of desire, freedom, and justice, mediated by authorities we need as much to reestablish as to reinvent. Meanwhile, heterodox, heteromorph, heteroclite, and indeterminate withal, we live in one human universe and astonish each other with our assents. This is the provisional world, perdurable hope, of *The Postmodern Turn.*

Part I Prelude to Postmodernism

1 The Literature of Silence

I

The idea of an avant-garde in literature seems unduly naïve today. Inured to crisis, we have also lost the confident sense of direction. Which way is forward? Literature, turning against itself, aspires to silence, leaving us with uneasy intimations of outrage and apocalypse. If there is an avant-garde in our time, it is probably bent on discovery through suicide. Thus, the term anti-literature, like antimatter, comes to symbolize not merely an inversion of forms but will and energy turned inside out. Is the future, then, all vagrancy and disaster for all who profess the word?

Though I cannot believe that the word exhausts the possibilities of spirit, I must admit that disaster comes and goes in cunning rhythms. Mystics have always maintained that the way down is also the way out and that the end of things heralds a new beginning—negative transcendence, as we call it today, is a form of transcendence nevertheless. Therefore silence in literature does not necessarily augur the death of spirit.

The point to be made about the new literature is different: whatever is truly new in it evades the social, historical, and aesthetic criteria that gave an identity to the avant-garde in other periods. The force of evasion, or absence, in the new literature is radical indeed; it strikes at the roots and induces, metaphorically, a great silence. But the same force, moving up to the trunk and foliage, bursts into a great babel of noises. The most audible of these is the cry of outrage, the voice of apocalypse. Henry Miller and Samuel Beckett, both intimates of silence, are such obsessive babblers; between them, they sound all the notes of the new hollow speech. Their conjunction is therefore no mere conceit. Standing as mirror images of the contemporary imagination, they end by reflecting its peculiar assumptions. In old-fashioned parlance, they are the two masters of the avant-garde today.

II

But my discourse on Miller and Beckett may need some clarification of the components of silence. Let me begin with outrage. "Is art always an outrage—must it by its very nature be an outrage?" Lawrence Durrell, who had Miller in mind, once asked.[1] We can grant that art contains an element of danger and even subversion without conceding that all art is outrage. A particular genre of modern literature, however, seems to vindicate Durrell's view; it constantly touches on the experience that awes him. That experience is one of metaphysical revolt: Ahab striking the sun if it insulted him, or Ivan Karamazov returning his life-ticket to God. It is metaphysical revolt and at the same time metaphysical surrender, which is the desire for nothingness: "the cry of the mind exhausted by its own rebellion," as Albert Camus put it.[2] In outrage, then, the very being of man is put on trial. What ensues is a dialectic of violence, demonic action and demonic reaction compressed into a terrible unity that finally becomes a naught.

The violence I associate with the new literature is obviously of a special kind; it presupposes Dachau and Hiroshima but is not necessarily limited by them.[3] It is absurd in the sense that no meaning or value can be assigned to it. Its function is to turn men into things; under its pressure, the metamorphosis of the human form is downward, toward the worms of Beckett, the insect people and sentient ooze of Burroughs. It is not temporal but spatial, not historical but ontological, an inescapable part of the landscape. Indeed, as Frederick J. Hoffman argues in *The Mortal No,* this landscape of violence suggests a "total withdrawal of the humanly familiar from both assailant and victim. Moreover, the assailant and the victim are both part of the landscape."[4] This metaphor of violence as landscape or inscape is an extreme definition of outrage that my discussion will assume. We can begin to see such a landscape take shape in the surreal Broadway scenes of Miller's *Tropic* books, and we can see what is left of it, as violence recedes into death, in the empty spaces of Beckett's *Endgame* or *How It Is.* Over these scenes there always hangs a frightful stillness.

Precisely at this point, a reversal of motive may take place in the literature of silence; a new term may come into play. For if outrage is a response to the void, may it not also serve as an appeal to being, and thus beget its opposite, which is an invocation of apocalypse? The transformation is easy to see in Black literature where old-fashioned protest yields to modern outrage, and outrage requires apocalypse. Thus James Baldwin derives the title of his threatening book from a biblical epigraph: "God gave Noah the rainbow sign: No more water, *the fire next time.*" [Italics mine.] Apocalyptic violence, as D. H. Lawrence knew, can be conceived by the oppressed as retribution against their enemies, and even the millennium can be understood by them as an idea of power rather than of love.[5] In other types of recent literature, however, the feelings behind apocalyptic metaphors are more complex. Implied in them is something close to a total rejection of Western history and civilization. They also imply a rejection of human identity, the image of man as the measure of all things. "I want to be a machine," says Andy Warhol, and whether he speaks in earnest or in jest, he speaks for the cripples of Beckett, the satyrs of Miller, and the junkies of Burroughs. Indeed, the revulsion against the Western self strikes deeper than the repudiation of history and civilization. When such loathing fails to find consummation in orgiastic destruction, it may spend itself in Zen Buddhism, Pataphysics, or even Camp.

Revulsion against the self serves as a link between the destructive and visionary impulses of modern apocalypse; it prepares for rebirth. Thus D. H. Lawrence believes: "Start with the sun, and the rest will slowly, slowly happen."[6] The sun, however distant, is within view of the eye. Whitman, who is in some ways more prophetic of our mood, locates millennial perfection in the everlasting present:

> There was never more inception than there is now,
> Nor any more youth or age than there is now,
> And will never be any more perfection than there is now.[7]

Apocalypse is *now!* The term recovers its original sense, which is literally revelation; vision penetrates the perplexities of the moment to the heart of light. In current parlance this antinomian belief is sometimes called the alteration of consciousness, and traces of it may be recognized in the psychedelic experiments of Alpert and Leary, in the poetry of Ginsberg, in the Reichian view of orgasm advertised by Mailer, and in the psycho-mystic revelations of Norman O. Brown. The alteration of consciousness is also the constant hope of Miller throughout his apocalyptic harangues, and the object of parody in Beckett's Cartesian monologues, both of which project antithetical states of wordless perfection. Revelation is not confined, however, to shamanistic frenzy or unearthly trance. As Leslie Fiedler put it in *Waiting for the End:* "We can *see* a different world without firing a shot or framing a syllogism, merely by altering our consciousness; and the ways to alter it are at hand. . . ."[8] This is the dream of a revolution to end all revolutions—and perhaps all dreams.

Outrage and apocalypse, then, provide mirror images of the contemporary imagination, images that contain something vital and dangerous in our experience. They are also mirror images in the sense that Miller and Beckett reflect inverse worlds. For Beckett leaves us with a world so depleted of life that nothing short of a cataclysm can renew it; we are close to the absence of outrage. And Miller presents us with a chaotic world constantly on the verge of transformation; we are witness to the rage of apocalypse. What both worlds share is the degree of silence. For the human tongue is speechless in fright and ecstasy.

III

Yet if the new literature can be delimited by the extreme responses of outrage and apocalypse, other ideas help to maintain the silence at its center. Foremost among these, perhaps, is the idea of "absurd creation" which compels the author to deprecate and even to spurn his activity. "Creating or not creating changes nothing," Camus said. "The absurd creator does not prize his work. He could repudiate it."[9] Thus the imagination renounces its ancient authority, finding its apotheosis not in the romantic idea of the damned poet but in the ironic attitude of the wordless author binding a sheaf of blank pages.

When the writer deigns to put words to paper, he is apt to conceive antiliterature either as pure action or futile play. The view that art is action, we know, finds sanction in Jean-Paul Sartre's *What Is Literature?* To speak is to act, Sartre claims, and everything we name loses its innocence, becoming part of the world we live in. If art has value, it is because art declares itself as a public appeal. Likewise (in *The Myth of Sisyphus*), Camus extolls *savoir-vivre* over *savoir-faire.*[10] This view finds a strange and defiant conclusion in the action paintings of Pollock, who saw art not as a public appeal but as the process of creating art. This process is individual if not entirely private; its value redounds to the author more than to his audience. Miller's view is unexpectedly similar. For him writing is autobiography, and autobiography is therapy, which is a form of action upon the self. "We should look to the diary . . . ," Miller says, "not for the truth about things but as an expression of this struggle to be free of the obsession for truth." The struggle belongs mainly to the diarist or, when the action is directed outwards, to the poet; for Miller also says: "I do not call poets those who make verses, rhymed or unrhymed. I call that man poet who is capable of profoundly altering the world."[11]

For Beckett, however, writing is absurd play. In a certain sense, all his works may be thought of as a parody of Ludwig Wittgenstein's notion that language is a set of games, akin to the arithmetic of primitive tribes.[12] Beckett's parodies, which are full of self-spite, reveal a general tendency in antiliterature, one that Hugh Kenner describes brilliantly: "The dominant intellectual analogy of the present age is drawn not from biology, not from psychology (though these are sciences we are knowing about), but from general number theory."[13] Art in a closed field thus becomes an absurd game of permutations, like Molloy sucking stones at the beach; and "the retreat from the word"—the phrase is George Steiner's—reduces language to pure ratio.

Interestingly enough, the conceptions of literature as game and as action merge in another form of metaphoric silence: literary obscenity. The term is notoriously difficult to define except by court action; I use it here to refer mainly to works that connect obscenity with protest. It is easy to understand that in a culture given to sexual repression, protest may take the form, echo the ring, of obscenity. The literature that exposes this motive is thus a literature of revolt. Obscenity, however, is cruelly reductive; its terms, counters, and clichés are sharply limited. When the anger behind it is chilled, obscenity appears as a game of permutations, relying on few words and fewer actions. Surely this is the double impression we take from the writings of Sade: that his protest is monstrous and his game is finally numbing. Sade, considered by many today to be the first avant-gardist, projects a curious stillness; his obscene and repetitious violence muffles language. In bequeathing pornoaesthetics to literature, he also made it possible for Mailer, say, or for

Burroughs, to develop parodies of sexual violence. The sexual heroics of Miller are still too naïve to realize their full potential for self-parody; the excremental obsessions of Beckett, on the other hand, parody themselves and deny all love. In the game of parody as in the act of obscenity, antilanguage rules. Miller and Beckett, standing again in contrast, suggest the manner of genital and anal pornography.

But the literature of silence manages to deny the time-honored functions of literature in yet another way: it aspires to an impossible concreteness. The new literalism emerges in the *musique concrète* of Stockhausen, in Duchamp's to Rauschenberg's collages of found objects, in the environmental sculpture of Schwitters, and, under the combined influence of Schwitters and Apollinaire, in that hybrid form of verbal and visual effects, concrete poetry, which relies on the alphabet to make pictures. A less obvious aspiration to concreteness may be sensed in Truman Capote's *In Cold Blood.* Declining the appeal of fantasy, Capote pretends to adhere meticulously to fact and writes, as he claims, the first "nonfiction novel." In European literature, however, neoliteralism is sometimes linked not with reportage but with the phenomenology of Edmund Husserl. A difficult thinker who exerted considerable influence on men as different as Sartre and Heidegger, Husserl cannot be summarized without gross distortions. Yet it can be said that Husserl's philosophy defines a pure form of subjective consciousness that has no components and that can never become an object of experience. This form of consciousness, isolated by a series of "reductions," is not part of the common world of objects, feelings, or sensations. What we usually accept as the inmost self, the ego, must itself be "bracketed," or set aside, as an empirical unity subject to the final "transcendental reduction" which yields pure consciousness.[14] Stated crudely, then, the true self is unknowable and, perhaps like Beckett's antihero, unnamable.

How does this conclusion affect the novel? The old principles of causality, psychological analysis, and symbolic relations, principles on which the bourgeois novel once comfortably rested, begin to crumble. Beckett's *Molloy* may have been the first novel to be written in the new manner, though Sartre's *La Nausée* attracted wide attention. In Roquentin we see a character convinced of universal irrelevance; things have broken loose of words, and no connection between subject and object can be made. It remains for Alain Robbe-Grillet to reject the humanism of Sartre by rejecting his pan-anthropocentrism. If man desires to be alone, declining communion with the universe, if man proves, after all, not to be the answer to the eternal riddle of the Sphinx, then his fate can be neither tragic nor absurd. "Things are things, and man is only man," Robbe-Grillet argues happily. "Henceforth, we refuse all complicity with objects . . . We must refuse, that is, any idea of preestablished order."[15] It follows that the novelist can be only a literalist, naming the names or entertaining pure images. Without character, plot, metaphor, or meaning, without pretense of "interiorness," the French antinovels of Sarraute, Butor, and Robbe-Grillet aim, like the new cinema, at the effect of a silent reel. What Harold Rosenberg says seems as apposite to literature as to the visual arts: "All the French alchemists are after the same thing, the actuality which is always new—and which will come only forth out of silencing the existing rhetoric."[16]

Silence in the new literature is also attained through radical irony—a term I apply to any statement that contains its own ironic denial. The Cretan who claimed all Cretans were liars may serve as an example; the machine of Tinguely, which has no function but to destroy itself, serves as another. Radical irony, in other words, requires not a collage of found objects, but an empty canvas. Its modern origins may be traced back to some of the major figures of our century, notably Kafka and Mann. Kafka came close to rendering the experience of blank and frozen spaces. And Mann prized the voice of consummate irony, rising only to cancel itself in self-parody, which as Mann came to believe, held the only hope of art. Erich Heller is therefore right in noting: "Art tragically laments the loss of its own mystery in *Doctor Faustus,* and gaily reports it to the cosmic police in *Felix Krull.*"[17] This trend finds still earlier precedents among the German Romantics and the French Symbolists. In recent times, however, radical irony has increased in sophistication. Heidegger's idea of "the mystery of oblivion" and Blanchot's view of literature as a form of "forgetfulness" suggest a theoretical development of irony.[18] More concretely, Mailer's *An American Dream* frankly burlesques, and actually denies, the novel form by transforming it into pop art. And Nathalie Sarraute's *The Golden Fruits* is a novel about a novel called *The Golden Fruits* which cancels itself, by drifting into oblivion, during the act of reading. This reflexive technique was probably developed by Beckett; it was certainly perfected by him. The conclusion of his latest novel, *How It Is,* is that the book is really about *"How It*

Wasn't." Such legerdemain is not frivolous; for the paradox of art employing art to deny itself is rooted in the power of human consciousness to view itself both as subject and object. Within the mind is the Archimedean point; when the world becomes intolerable, the mind lifts itself to nirvana or drops into madness. Or it may resort to radical irony in order to reveal art at the end of its tether. Thus in Beckett, literature rigorously unmakes itself, and in Miller, literature pretends, erratically, to be life. What is harder to discern in radical irony is that it disguises genuine aggressions against art. Through it, the artist makes his last devotions to the Muse, and through it he desecrates her too. This ambivalence is obvious in both Miller and Beckett.

Finally, literature strives for silence by accepting chance and improvisation; its principle becomes indeterminacy. By refusing order, order imposed or discovered, this kind of literature refuses purpose. Its forms are therefore nontelic; its world is the eternal present.[19] We are invited to regain our original innocence, for error and revision, now irrelevant, are forever banished. Like the stepping stones in a Zen garden, random literature seems to celebrate things as they are. This impression is confirmed by the writings of John Cage, who is as much a composer as a poet, and who, more than Satie, has shocked his public into a sacramental awareness of random composition. This is what Cage says in *Silence:* "Our intention is to affirm this life, not to bring order out of a chaos nor to suggest improvements in creation, but simply to wake up to the very life we're living, which is so excellent once one gets one's mind and one's desires out of its way and lets it act of its own accord."[20] Traces of this attitude may be found throughout the works of Henry Miller, and in the poetry of Ginsberg, the novels of Kerouac, and the later stories of J. D. Salinger. Unlike Cage, however, these authors seem superficial in adapting their spiritual life to the practice of literature. Miller, for instance, likes to pose as a garrulous raconteur, despite all his affection for Tao and Milarepa. Whatever appears random in his work can be ascribed less to design than to disposition. Many years ago Dadaists and Surrealists came close to the dismemberment of literary forms with less spiritual *chic.* Perhaps this is also true, in our time, of random authors like Raymond Queneau, Marc Saporta, and William Burroughs. In *Cent Mille Milliards de Poèmes,* Queneau has constructed a "poetry machine," ten overlapping pages of fourteen-line sonnets, each line of which can be read in every possible combination with all other lines;

the result takes two hundred million years to "read." In *Number 1* Saporta invites the reader to create his own book each time he sits down to a set of inscribed cards. His "shuffle novel" is a stratagem that proposes chance as a legitimate part of the literary experience. And Burroughs, who believes that to speak is to lie, attempts to evade mendacity through "The Cut Up Method of Brion Gysin." Harking back to the Dadaist antics of Tristan Tzara, Burroughs explains:

> Method is simple: Take a page or more or less of your own writing or from any writer living or dead. Any written or spoken words. Cut into sections with scissors or switch blade as preferred and rearrange the sections. Looking away. Now write out the result. . . .
>
> Applications of cut up method are literally unlimited cut out from time limits. Old word lines keep you in old word slots. Cut your way out. Cut paper cut film cut tape. Scissors or switch blade as preferred. Take it to cut city.[21]

Dadaist collage, Zen Buddhism, or even Neumann's theory of games seem equally valid in freeing man from the word habit. Burroughs, who has something in common with Beckett, ends by sharing with the latter the jerky rhythms of a subtracting machine. The machine has one purpose: to operate on language, and subtract thereof all meaning.

Clearly, the silence at the center of antiliterature is loud and various. Whether it is created by the shock of outrage or of apocalypse, whether it is enhanced by the conception of literature as pure action or pure play, and of the literary work itself as a concrete object, a blank page, or a random array, is perhaps finally irrelevant. The point is this: silence develops as the metaphor of a new attitude that literature has chosen to adopt toward itself. This attitude puts to question the peculiar power, the ancient excellence, of literary discourse—and challenges the assumptions of our civilization.

IV

It is rather puzzling that this attitude has failed, on the whole, to make an impression on English and American critics. The sensible, practical outlook of the former and the laborious formalism that still engages the latter may partially account for their antipathy. Moreover, antiliterature tends to unsettle critics with a firm humanistic bent and to repel others, Marxists or Socialists, who are committed to a certain idea of realism.

French critics, who can be as doctrinaire or provincial as any others, manage to remain the exception. Sartre reflected at length in *What Is Literature?* on the Dadaist and Surrealist crisis of language at the beginning of our century; a decade later, he wrote the introduction to Nathalie Sarraute's *Portrait d'un inconnu* and spoke of "d'oeuvres vivaces et toutes négatives qu'on pourrait nommer des anti-romans."[22] Thus a new term was given to the vocabulary of mid-century. In *Le Livre à venir,* Maurice Blanchot identified Rousseau as the first culprit in the tradition of silence, "acharné à écrire contre l'écriture," and saw literature approaching "l'ère sans parole" which, like some works of Beckett and Miller, can be understood only as incessant sound.[23] Thus, according to Blanchot, literature moves toward its essence, which is disappearance. Likewise, the theme of Roland Barthes' *Le Degré zéro de l'écriture* is absence. "La modernité commence avec la recherche d'une littérature impossible," Barthes proposes; the conclusion to this search is the Orphic dream: "un écrivain sans Littérature."[24] And Claude Mauriac, who was perhaps the first to include Miller and Beckett in the same critical study, notes in *The New Literature:* "After the silence of Rimbaud, the blank page of Mallarmé, the inarticulate cry of Artaud, aliterature finally dissolves in alliteration with Joyce. . . . For Beckett . . . words all say the same thing."[25] Obviously, the spirit of French lucidity cannot bring itself to rail at silence in literature.

But I suspect that lucidity may no longer be wholly adequate to the ambitions of criticism. We increasingly feel that criticism should do more than clarify; it should also possess wisdom of the senses and of the spirit. We want it to endanger itself, as literature does, and to testify to our condition. We even hope that it can sustain the burden of revelation. This hope has led me to suggest that criticism may have to become apocalyptic before it can compel our sense of relevance. In the very least, it will have to entertain some sympathy for the metaphors of apocalypse in order to test the intuitions of antiliterature. This is evident in a rare piece of American criticism that attempts precisely this task. In "The New Mutants," Leslie Fiedler shows that he understands the complex alliances that the literary imagination now makes with silence, with obscenity, with madness, and even with those post-sexual states akin to mystical trance. He also knows that crucial for our time is "the sense in which literature first conceived the possibility of the future . . . and then furnished that future in joyous or terrified anticipation, thus preparing all of us to inhabit it."[26]

V

Antiliterature may strain toward the future but the critical mind still seeks the reassurances of history. Does the literature of silence recall the dismemberment of Orpheus, first among singers, and also reverse that original biblical miracle, which witnessed the transformation of the Word into Flesh? And must the human race, after coming a long way through the passages of prehistory, now succumb to a wordless dream? Quite the contrary. The new literature may be extreme, and its dream apocalyptic and outrageous. But it is conceived in the interests of life; and life, we know, sometimes progresses through violence and contradictions.

In one version of the myth, Orpheus was torn by the Maenads at the behest of Dionysos; in another version, he was killed by them in a fit of uncontrollable jealousy, for since the death of his wife Eurydice, Orpheus preferred the company of young men to women. One thing is clear: Orpheus, that supreme maker, was the victim of an inexorable clash between the Dionysian principle, represented by the Maenads, and the Apollonian ideal which he, as poet, venerated. Orpheus is dismembered; but his head continues to sing, and where his limbs are buried by the Muses, the nightingales warble sweeter than anywhere else in the world. The myth of Orpheus may be a parable of the artist at certain times. The powers of Dionysos, which civilization must repress, threaten at these times to erupt with a vengeance. In the process energy may overwhelm order; language may turn into a howl, a cackle, a terrible silence; form may be mangled as ruthlessly as the poor body of Orpheus was. Yet the haunting question remains, now as on that wild day in the hills of Thrace: must not the head of the poet be severed in order that he may continue to sing? Let me put the question even more bluntly: must not life overwhelm art periodically to insure the health, the prevalence, of man? Must not words aspire to stillness?

There is some evidence of this in literary history, in earlier premonitions of hush and dismemberment. In *Strains of Discord,* for instance, Robert Martin Adams aptly defines a structure that may be the antecedent of current antiforms. "Open form," he says, is a structure of meanings that "include a major unresolved conflict with the intent of displaying its unresolvedness. . . . On the left flank, it is divided by an indefinite, quantitative line from perverse or general formlessness and indeterminacy; on the right, by an equally indefinite, quantitative line from a form which impresses us as pre-eminently closed, even though it has open elements."[27] An earnest typologist, taking his cue from Northrop Frye, may wish to claim that just as literature seems to have developed from the mythical to the ironic modes, so do literary forms seem to develop from closed to open to antiforms. The distinction between closed and open forms becomes apparent when we contrast Sophocles' *Oedipus the King* with Euripides' *The Bacchae.* Adams is right in perceiving that although *Oedipus* manages to resolve its conflicts and to induce a state of partial repose in the audience, *The Bacchae* leaves its audience in a state of unreleased anguish. As a closed form, *Oedipus* expresses a conservative and religious view of the world and a collective sense of experience; as an open form, *The Bacchae* conveys a radical and skeptical view of the world and an individual sense of experience. By extrapolating boldly on this curve, we may say that as an antiform, Beckett's *Waiting for Godot* implies an ironic and perhaps a nihilistic view of the world and a sense of experience that is entirely private.

But we need not adhere to a strict typology in order to realize that between *The Bacchae* and *Waiting for Godot* a great number of works in Western literature reveal a growing sense of disruption, an increasing capacity for distortion. Consider, in drama alone, the sequence suggested by the following plays: Shakespeare's *Hamlet,* Goethe's *Faust,* Büchner's *Woyzeck,* Maeterlinck's *Blue Bird,* Strindberg's *A Dream Play,* Jarry's *Ubu Roi,* Pirandello's *Six Characters in Search of An Author,* Genet's *The Blacks,* and Ionesco's *The Killer.* Dramatic form seems to move from unresolved tensions to symbolic elusiveness, from the latter to surreal or expressionistic contortion, and finally comes to rest in absurdity. The movement of form toward antiform, despite large and irrefutable exceptions throughout history, applies not only to drama; it can be observed in Western art generally.

It is probably fair to say that the three major phases of that development were marked by the emergence of Mannerism, Romanticism, and Modernism. Mannerism was the formal dissolution of the Renaissance style. It was, as Wylie Sypher suggests in *Four Stages of Renaissance Style,* a sign of strain and irresolution. In Mannerist art "the psychological effect diverges from the structural logic." Here is Sypher's definition of what we mean by an open form:

> Behind the technical ingenuities of mannerist style there usually is a personal unrest, a complex psychology that agitates the form and the phrase. When we examine the strains within the mannerist structure in painting, architecture, and poetry, we inevitably become aware of the scourge—or the quicksand—within the mannerist temperament. Mannerism is experiment with the techniques of disproportion and disturbed balance; with zigzag, spiral shuttling motion; with space like a vortex or alley; with oblique or mobile points of view and strange—even abnormal—perspectives that yield approximations rather than certainties.[28]

Is not this precisely the feeling we have about Shakespeare's later plays, Jacobean drama, and metaphysical poetry, as well as the paintings of Titian, Tintoretto, and El Greco?

The Romantics went further toward unsettling literary forms, haunted as they were by the vague *Stimmung,* the craving for the infinite. *Faust* stands at the very threshold of the period, an amalgam of pagan and Christian influences, which it transmuted, both in structure and theme, into a plea for life's outrageous contradictions—only the dazzling genius of Goethe could keep such a drama in artistic control. The dark company of Romantic heroes—Faust, Endymion, Alastor, Don Juan, Julien Sorel, Manfred, Axel—were forever threatening to break out from the mold that contained them, in proud insurrection against their makers. The Self had erupted in literature, and so had the dream and the unconscious. Novalis and Nerval, Hoffmann and Poe, Kleist and Büchner, Coleridge and Keats carried language into the midnight terrain of the soul, or else they cultivated that notorious romantic irony that served to incorporate in every statement its own negative. At other times Romanticism denied itself the possibilities of harmony or resolution by the perversity of its own spirit. It explored sadism, demonism, cabalism, necrophilia, vampirism, and lycanthropy, reaching for a definition of man where no human definition could obtain. It is no wonder that Goethe thought Romanticism to be a form of disease, and Hugo identified it with the grotesque. I am aware, of course, that I am emphasizing the nocturnal impulse of the movement. But that was precisely the impulse from which a large part of modern literature derived its energy. It was also the impulse, the agony if you wish, that helped to destroy the classic forms of literature. Mario Praz says in *The Romantic Agony,* "The essence of Romanticism comes to consist in that which cannot be described. . . . The Romantic exalts the artist who does not give a material form to his dreams—the poet ecstatic in front of a forever blank page, the musician who listens to the prodigious concerts of his soul without attempting to translate them into notes. It is romantic to consider concrete expression as a decadence, a contamination."[29] Here, then, is the beginning of silence, a literature without words—or to be more precise, a literature that disdains all but the most primitive and magical use of language. The French Symbolists, who are the direct ancestors of the modern movement, exemplify this trend clearly. Mallarmé's sonnets devised the syntax of self-abolition; Rimbaud's *Illuminations* scrambled the denotation of language in an effort to derange the senses; and Lautréamont's *Maldoror* opened the way for Surrealism. It may well be, as Norman O. Brown claims, that in late Romanticism Dionysos reentered the consciousness of literature.[30] It is more certain that in Romanticism the dual retreat from language became evident: first, in the ironic and self-effacing manner of Mallarmé and, second, in the indiscriminate and surrealistic manner of Rimbaud. In one, language aspires to Nothing; in the other, it aspires to All. The correlative of the first is Number, and the correlative of the second Action. In the former, literature moves, as we have noted Blanchot say, toward its disappearance. This is perhaps the strain of Mallarmé, Kafka, and Beckett. In the latter, literature strains, as Gaston Bachelard believes, toward a monstrous reintegration of the self in "la vie ardente."[31] This is the strain of Rimbaud and Lautréamont, at times of Lawrence, at times of Miller. Both strains find their source in a kind of terror. (Both are therefore contained in an earlier avant-gardist, Sade, who knew that outrage and prayer lie close to the center of literature.[32]) The two strains lead finally to silence, the disruption of all connections between language and reality.

With Modernism organized chaos reigns; or as Yeats put it in one of his apocalyptic moods:

> the center cannot hold;
> Mere anarchy is loosed upon the world,
> The blood-dimmed tide is loosed. . . . [33]

It is impossible to convey in a few paragraphs the extent of disintegration and reintegration in the major works of our century. Joyce, who was one of the few still to believe in language, believed that words could substitute for the world and ended in *Finnegans Wake* with a Cyclopeian pun. Kafka calmly established the frightening indeterminacy of which literature is capable and showed that love or terror may finally inhibit language from exercising its powers. With Marinetti, Futurism veered toward another extreme; with pick and axe, literature became the imaginary sacker of cities. Marinetti pretended to stand on the promontory of the centuries, and declaimed to the air. Dadaism and Surrealism have yet to be fully assessed. These two movements, which turned inside out all pieties of life and art, could still prove the challenge every writer of our time must meet; for though they spoke outlandishly in no language we ordinarily speak, they spoke for life and increase. The writers who began publishing between the two world wars seemed on the whole less ambitious. Yet it was possible for R. W. B. Lewis to distinguish the generation of Malraux, Silone, Camus, and Graham Greene from earlier generations that held the aesthetic experience to be supreme, and say, in *The Picaresque Saint,* that for the younger writers "the chief experience has been the discovery of what it means to be a writer and alive." Lewis concluded: "Criticism, examining this world, is drawn to the more radically human considerations of life and death, and of the aspiring, sinful nature of man."[34] In the literature of our own time, which Frank Kermode has rightly characterized as more "schismatic" than earlier types of modernist literature, the dismemberment of Orpheus continues with zeal.[35] Literature moves toward antiliterature and in so doing reinvents forms that become progressively crazy and disruptive: neopicaresque, black burlesque, grotesque, gothic, nightmarish science fiction. In the end, the antiforms of outrage and apocalypse blend in silence.

VI

History does not prove reassuring after all. In 1938 Antonin Artaud published a book, later translated as *The Theatre and Its Double,* in which he said: "And if there is still one hellish, truly accursed thing in our time, it is our artistic dallying with forms, instead of being like victims burnt at the stake, signalling through the flames."[36] Orpheus is not only dismembered; his limbs become incandescent. History brings us to the threshold of our moment and leaves us with scorching questions. Why should the disaffection with our civilization drive literature to such extreme measures, forcing upon it a fiery silence?

Until a black Synopticon of our maladies is compiled, the question can be answered only obliquely. Perhaps the clue is still in the myth of

Orpheus, and in the undying struggle between Apollo and Dionysus. Freud offers powerful insights into the subject. In *Civilization and Its Discontents,* he shows that society rests on instinctual repression. This much we always suspected. What we do not always realize is that every act of renunciation in our lives prepares the way for further renunciations. But the matter does not end there. Freud goes on to argue that civilization, in its innermost dynamic, *requires more and more repression.*[37] The psychic toll of this process is compounded. Its implications for literature are crucial. In a shocking and important book, *Life Against Death,* Norman O. Brown begins where Freud ends. Arguing that all sublimation entails a certain degree of negation of the life instincts, Brown concludes thus: "The negative moment in sublimation is plain in the inseparable connection between symbolism (in language, science, religion, and art) and abstraction. Abstraction, as Whitehead has taught us, is a denial of the living organ of experience, the living body as a whole. . . . "[38] The logic then—and I do not know if it is quite as relentless as both Brown and Freud make it out to be—is that repression begets civilization, civilization begets more repression, more repression begets abstraction, and abstraction begets death. We are moving along the road of pure intelligence, which, as Ferenczi thought, is a principle of madness. Is any salvation for the race possible? Brown offers this:

> The human ego must face the Dionysian reality, and therefore a great work of self-transformation lies ahead of it. For Nietzsche was right in saying that the Apollonian preserves, the Dionysian destroys, self-consciousness. As long as the structure of the ego is Apollonian, Dionysian experience can only be bought at the price of ego-dissolution. Nor can the issue be resolved by a "synthesis" of the Apollonian and the Dionysian ego. Hence the late Nietzsche preaches Dionysus. . . . The work of constructing a Dionysian ego is immense; but there are signs that it is already under way. If we can discern the Dionysian witches' brew in the upheavals of modern history—in the sexology of de Sade and the politics of Hitler—we can also discern in the romantic reaction the entry of Dionysus into consciousness.[39]

For the neo-Freudians, then, the problem is repression and abstraction, and the solution is the construction of a Dionysian ego. In their view language ultimately becomes "the natural speech of the body," a phrase adopted from Rilke.

But the fact that Brown cites Nietzsche is also relevant; for Nietzsche is indeed the crucial figure in the intellectual history of our time. He is the ancestor of both Freudians and Existentialists, and he is the living mediator between the two movements. His analysis of Western civilization offers, therefore, a parallel argument to Freud's, and one that is perhaps even more compelling. For Nietzsche, the root of evil in the modern world is not simply repression, which is wholly instinctual, but also nihilism, which acknowledges the conscious human drive to meaning. From the depths of the nineteenth century he proclaimed God dead, and he saw that the crisis of modern man was a crisis of values. "Why has the advent of nihilism become necessary?" Nietzsche asks in *The Will to Power.* And he answers: "because nihilism represents the ultimate logical conclusion of our great values and ideals—because we must experience nihilism before we can find out what values these 'values' really had. We require, at some time, new values."[40] For him, as for contemporary Existentialists, the fundamental problem is obviously one of meaning. (Unlike most of them, however, Nietzsche was a "utopian"; his solution rested on the affluence of life in the Superman.) In that Nietzschean view, the ideal of language becomes action, becomes gesture, since the creation of meaning is less a verbal than a vital process. A Christian like Nikolai Berdyaev may state the question differently: "The inner apocalypse of history is a revelation of the results of not realizing in history the Kingdom of God, i.e., Meaning."[41] But the question, we discover, is still one of meaning.

Secularism, *acedia,* guilt, and nihilism may be merely the symptoms of a deeper absence of meaning. Man is losing his inner space, as Herbert Marcuse says in *One Dimensional Man;* his unique world is squashed. No wonder that language, which is traditionally man's largest repository of private as well as public meaning, should be held in discount. Nor do the prophets and utopians of our time offer to redeem the word. By minimizing the role of sublimation in the future, they also minimize the role of language. The human Dionysus or the Superman to come is not a loquacious creature. The modern revolt against verbal discourse may be thus seen, at bottom, as a revolt against authority and abstraction: the civilization that Apollo sponsored has become totalitarian, and the tools he gave man to live by have become machines fueled on abstractions. Because all meaning is ultimately rooted in the flesh—assertions may be regarded as affirmations of the body—meaninglessness is a correlative of abstraction. Ironically, the revolt against language in literature reflects, but also parodies, the retreat from the word in technocracy. This is a point George Steiner misses in an otherwise important article, "The Retreat from the Word," in which he says:

> Until the seventeenth century, the sphere of language encompassed nearly the whole of experience and reality; today, it comprises a narrower domain. It no longer articulates, or is relevant to, all major modes of action, thought, and sensibility. Large areas of meaning and praxis now belong to such non-verbal languages as mathematics, symbolic logic, and formulas of chemical or electronic relation. Other areas belong to the sub-languages or anti-languages of non-objective art and *musique concrète.* The world of words has shrunk.[42]

Yet it is too easy to blame all our ills on the death-of-God or on technology. A younger generation of theologians, which includes Altizer, Hamilton, and Van Buren, has made of the death-of-God a challenging occasion for cultural and spiritual affirmations. And there are prophets of technology, like Marshall McLuhan and Buckminster Fuller, who see marvelous possibilities in "the global village" that our earth has become under the influence of the new science and of electronics. Still, even McLuhan realizes that we must face terrible dangers in the transition from the visual culture of the printed word to the "total" culture of electric technology; we may revert to an oral, tribal culture. This is what he says in *The Gutenberg Galaxy:* "Terror is the normal state of any oral society, for in it everything affects everything all the time." Meantime: "Our most ordinary and conventional attitudes seem suddenly twisted into gargoyles and grotesques. Familiar institutions and associations seem at times menacing and malignant."[43] Whatever its causes may prove to be and whatever forms it may take, silence emerges as a literary attitude and thus a fact of our time.

1. Lawrence Durrell and Alfred Perles, *Art and Outrage: A Correspondence About Henry Miller* (New York, 1961), 9.
2. Albert Camus, *The Rebel* (New York, 1956), 91.
3. The literature of total terror has become abundant. An introduction to the possibilities of outrage may be found in Bruno Bettleheim, *The Informed Heart* (New York, 1960); Erich Fromm, *Escape From Freedom* (New York, 1941); Frederick J. Hoffman, *The Mortal No* (Princeton, N.J., 1964); and Eugen Kogon, *The Theory and Practice of Hell* (New York, 1946).
4. Hoffman, *The Mortal No,* 181.
5. D. H. Lawrence, *Apocalypse* (Florence, 1931), 37f., 93.
6. Ibid., 308.

7. Walt Whitman, *The Portable Walt Whitman*, ed. Mark Van Doren (New York, 1945), 63.

8. Leslie Fiedler, *Waiting for the End* (New York, 1964), 167.

9. Albert Camus, *The Myth of Sisyphus* (New York, 1959), 72.

10. Jean-Paul Sartre, *What is Literature?* (New York, 1965), chapters 2 and 3. Camus, *The Myth of Sisyphus*, 73.

11. Henry Miller, *The Cosmological Eye* (New York, 1939), 271; and *The Time of the Assassins* (New York, 1956), 38f.

12. Ludwig Wittgenstein, *The Blue and Brown Books* (Oxford, 1958), 81f.

13. Hugh Kenner, "Art in a Closed Field," in *Learners and Discerners*, ed. Robert Scholes (Charlottesville, Va., 1964), 122.

14. See Edmund Husserl, *Ideas* (London, 1931).

15. Alain Robbe-Grillet, "Old 'Values' and the New Novel," *Evergreen Review* 3 (Summer 1959), 100, 116.

16. Harold Rosenberg, *The Tradition of the New* (New York, 1961), 90.

17. Erich Heller, *The Ironic German* (London, 1958), 185.

18. Geoffrey Hartman, "Maurice Blanchot," in *The Novelist as Philosopher*, ed. John Cruickshank (New York, 1962), 151.

19. A discussion of indeterminacy, with particular reference to art and music, may be found in Leonard B. Meyer, "The End of the Renaissance," *Hudson Review* 16 (Summer 1963).

20. John Cage, *Silence* (Middletown, Conn., 1961), 95.

21. William Burroughs, "The Cut Up Method of Brion Gysin," in *A Casebook on the Beat*, ed. Thomas Parkinson (New York, 1961), 105f.

22. Jean-Paul Sartre, introduction to Nathalie Sarraute, *Portrait d'un inconnu* (Paris, 1956), 7.

23. Maurice Blanchot, *Le Livre à venir* (Paris, 1959), 55, 265.

24. Roland Barthes, *Le Degré zéro de l'écriture* (Paris, 1953), 58, 12.

25. Claude Mauriac, *The New Literature* (New York, 1959), 12.

26. Leslie Fiedler, "The New Mutants," *Partisan Review* (Fall 1965), 506f. A perceptive rebuttal of Fiedler is attempted by Frank Kermode, "Modernisms Again," *Encounter* (April 1966).

27. Robert Martin Adams, *Strains of Discord* (Ithaca, N.Y., 1958), 13, 16.

28. Wylie Sypher, *Four Stages of Renaissance Style* (Garden City, N.Y., 1955), 116.

29. Mario Praz, *The Romantic Agony* (New York, 1956), 14f.

30. Norman O. Brown, *Life Against Death* (Middletown, Conn., 1959), 172.

31. Gaston Bachelard, *Lautréamont* (Paris, 1963), 154.

32. D. A. F. de Sade, "Idée sur les Romans," *Les Crimes de l'amour* (Paris, 1961), 15, 28.

33. William Butler Yeats, *The Collected Poems* (New York, 1957), 184.

34. R. W. B. Lewis, *The Picaresque Saint* (New York, 1959), 9.

35. This statement has been elaborated in conversation with the author and in an unpublished lecture, "Radical Elements in Modernist Literature," delivered by Frank Kermode at Rutgers University, Summer 1965.

36. Antonin Artaud, *The Theatre and Its Double* (New York, 1958), 13.

37. Sigmund Freud, *Civilization and Its Discontents* (London, 1955), 114f.

38. Brown, *Life Against Death*, 172.

39. Ibid., 175f.

40. Friedrich Nietzsche, quoted by Walter Kaufmann, ed., *Existentialism from Dostoyevsky to Sartre* (New York, 1956), 110.

41. Nikolai Berdyaev, *The Fate of Man in the Modern World* (Ann Arbor, Mich., 1961), 24.

42. George Steiner, "The Retreat from the Word," *Kenyon Review* 23 (Spring 1961), 203.

43. Marshall McLuhan, *The Gutenberg Galaxy* (Toronto, 1965), 32, 279.

Part II Concepts of Postmodernism

2

POSTmodernISM: A Paracritical Bibliography

I. Change

Dionysus and Cupid are both agents of change. First, *The Bacchae,* destruction of the city, then *The Metamorphoses,* mischievous variations of nature. Some might say that change is violence, and violence is continuous whether it be Horror or High Camp. But sly Ovid simply declares:

> My intention is to tell of bodies changed
> To different forms; the gods, who made the changes,
> Will help me—or I hope so—with a poem
> That runs from the world's beginning to our own days.

To our own days, the bodies natural or politic wax and wane, *carpen perpetuam.* Something warms Galatea out of ivory; even rock turns into spiritual forms. Perhaps love is one way we experience change.

How then can we live without love of change?

> Evolution has its enemies, that quiet genius Owen Barfield knows. In *Unancestral Voices* he calls them by name: Lucifer and Ahriman. Most often they coexist in us. Lucifer preserves the past utterly from dissolution. Ahriman destroys the past utterly for the sake of his own inventions.

a. Thus in one kind of history, chronicles of continuity, we deny real change. Even endings become part of a history of endings. From schism to paradigm; from apocalypse to archetype. Warring empires, catastrophe and famine, immense hopes, faraway names—Cheops, Hammurabi, David, Darius, Alcibiades, Hannibal, Caesar—all fall into place on numbered pages.

Yet continuities, "the glory that was Greece, the grandeur that was Rome," must prevail in Story, on a certain level of narrative abstraction, obscuring change.

b. Thus, too, in another kind of history, we reinvent continually the past. Without vision, constant revision, the Party chronicles of *Nineteen Eighty-Four.* Or individually, each man dreams his ancestors to remake himself. The Black Muslim takes on a new name, ignoring the deadly dawn raids, cries of Allah among slave traders, journeys across Africa in Arab chains.

Yet relevances must persist in Story, on a certain level of fictional selectivity, veiling change.

Behind all history, continuous or discrete, abstract or autistic, lurks the struggle of identity with death. Is history often the secret biography of historians? The recorded imagination of our own mortality?

> Thou, silent form, dost tease us out of thought
> As doth eternity: Cold Pastoral.

II. Periods

When will the Modern Period end?

Has ever a period waited so long? Renaissance? Baroque? Neo-Classical? Romantic? Victorian? Perhaps only the Dark Middle Ages.

When will Modernism cease and what comes thereafter?

What will the twenty-first century call us? and will its voice come from the same side of our graves?

Does Modernism stretch merely to stretch out our lives? Or, ductile, does it give a new sense of time? The end of periodicization? The slow arrival of simultaneity?

If change changes ever more rapidly and the future jolts us now, do men, more than ever, resist both endings and beginnings?

> Childhood is huge and youth golden. Few recover. Critics are no exception. Like everyone else, they recall the literature of their youth brilliantly; they do not think it can ever tarnish.

> "Let us consider where the great men are
> Who will obsess the child when he can read."

So Delmore Schwartz wrote, naming Joyce, Eliot, Pound, Rilke, Yeats, Kafka, Mann. He could have added: Proust, Valéry, Gide, Conrad, Lawrence, Woolf, Faulkner, Hemingway, O'Neill. . . .

A walker in the city of that literature will not forget. Nor will he forgive. How can contemporaries of Ellison, Pinter, or Grass dare breathe in this ancestral air? Yet it is possible that we will all remain Invisible Men until each becomes his own father.

III. Innovation

All of us devise cunning ceremonies of ancestor worship. Yet there is a fable for us in the lives of two men: Proteus and Picasso, mentors of shapes. Their forms are self-transformations. They know the secret of Innovation: Motion.

Masters of possibility, ponder this. They used to say: the kingdom of the dead is larger than any kingdom. But the earth has now exploded. Soon the day may come when there will be more people alive than ever lived.

When the quick are more populous than all the departed, will history reverse itself? End?

We resist the new under the guise of judgment. "We must have standards." But standards apply only where they are applicable. This has been the problem with the Tradition of the New (Harold Rosenberg).

Standards are inevitable, and the best of these will create themselves to meet, to *create,* new occasions. Let us, therefore, admit standards. But let us also ask how many critics of literature espouse, even selectively, the new, speak of it with joyous intelligence? Taking few risks, the best known among them wait for reviewers to clear the way.

Reaction to the new has its own reasons that reason seldom acknowledges. It also has its rhetoric of dismissal.

a. The Fad
 –"It's a passing fashion, frivolous; if we ignore it now, it will quietly go away."

–This implies permanence as absolute value. It also implies the ability to distinguish between fashion and history without benefit of time or creative intuition. How many judgments of this kind fill the Purgatorio of Letters?

b. The Old Story

–"It's been done before, there's nothing new in it; you can find it in Euripides, Sterne, or Whitman."

–This implies prior acquaintance, rejection on the basis of dubious similitude. It also implies that nothing really changes. Therefore, why unsettle things, re-quire a fresh response?

c. The Safe Version

–"Yes, it seems new, but in the same genre, I prefer Duchamp; he really did it better."

–This implies a certain inwardness with innovation. The entrance fee has been paid, once and forever. Without seeming in the least Philistine, one can disdain the intrusions of the present.

d. The Newspeak of Art

–"The avant-garde is just the new academicism."

–This may imply that art which seems conventional can be more genuinely innovative: this is sometimes true. It may also imply mere irritation: the oxymoron as means of discreditation.

About true innovation we can have no easy preconceptions. Prediction is mere extrapolation, the cool whisper of RAND. But prophecy is akin to madness, or the creative imagination; its path, seldom linear, breaks, turns, disappears in mutations or quantum jumps.

Therefore, we cannot expect the avant-garde of past, present, and future to obey the same logic, assume the same forms. For instance, the new avant-garde need not have a historical consciousness, express recognizable values, or endorse radical politics. It need not shock, surprise, protest. The new avant-garde may not be an "avant-garde" at all: simply an agent of yet-invisible change.

Note: Consult Renato Poggioli, *The Theory of the Avant-Garde* (Cambridge, Mass., 1968).

And yet everything I have said here can lend itself to abuse. The rage for change can be a form of self-hatred or spite. Look deep into any revolutionary.

Look also into extremes of the recent avant-garde. Vito Hannibal Acconci creates his "body sculptures" by biting, mutilating, himself in public. Rudolph Schwarzkogler slowly amputates his penis, and expires. In a world no longer linear, we must wonder: which way is forward? which way is life? Action often acquires the logic of the boomerang.

IV. Distinctions

The change in Modernism may be called Postmodernism. Viewing the former with later eyes, we begin to discern fringe figures closer to us now than the great Moderns who "will obsess the child" someday.

Thus the classic text of Modernism is Edmund Wilson's *Axel's Castle: A Study in the Imaginative Literature of 1870–1930* (1931). Contents: Symbolism, Yeats, Valéry, Eliot, Proust, Joyce, Stein.

Thus, forty years later, my alternate view, *The Dismemberment of Orpheus: Toward a Postmodern Literature* (1971). Contents: Sade, 'Pataphysics to Surrealism, Hemingway, Kafka, Existentialism to Aliterature, Genet, Beckett.

Erratum: Gertrude Stein should have appeared in the latter work, for she contributed to both Modernism and Postmodernism.

But without a doubt, the crucial text is

F

K I

A N

W e N

S E

N G

A

If we can arbitrarily state that literary Modernism includes certain works between Jarry's *Ubu Roi* (1896) and Joyce's *Finnegans Wake* (1939), where will we arbitrarily say that Postmodernism begins? A year earlier than the *Wake?* With Sartre's *La Nausée* (1938) or Beckett's *Murphy* (1938)? In any case Postmodernism includes works by writers as different as **B**arth, arthelme, ecker, eckett, ense, lanchot, orges, recht, urroughs, utor.

Query: But is not *Ubu Roi* itself as Postmodern as it is Modern?

V. Critics

The assumptions of Modernism elaborated by formalist and mythopoeic critics especially, by the intellectual culture of the first half of the century as a whole, still define the dominant perspective on the study of literature.

Exception: Karl Shapiro's *Beyond Criticism* (1953), *In Defence of Ignorance* (1960). Too "cranky" and "cantankerous" for academic *biens pensants?*

In England as in America, the known critics, different as they may seem in age, persuasion, or distinction, share the broad Modernist view: Blackmur, Brooks, Connolly, Empson, Frye, Howe, Kazin, Kermode, Leavis, Levin, Pritchett, Ransom, Rahv, Richards, Schorer, Tate, Trilling, Warren, Wellek, Wilson, Winters, etc.

No doubt there are many passages in the writings of these critics—of Leavis, say, or of Wilson—which will enlighten minds in every age. Yet it was Herbert Read who possessed the most active sympathy for the avant-garde. His generosity of intuition enabled him to sponsor the new, rarely embracing the trivial. He engaged the Postmodern spirit in his anarchic affinities, in his concern for the prevalence of suffering, in his sensuous apprehension of renewed being. He cried: behold the Child! To him, education through art meant a salutation to Eros. Believing that the imagination serves the purpose of moral good, Read hoped to implicate art into existence so fully that their common substance became as simple, as necessary, as bread and water. This is a sacramental hope, still alive though mute in our midst, which recalls Tolstoy's *What*

Is Art? I can hardly think of another critic, younger even by several decades, who might have composed that extraordinary romance, *The Green Child.*

The culture of literary criticism is still ruled by Modernist assumptions. This is particularly true within the academic profession, excepting certain linguistic, structuralist, and hermeneutic schools. But it is also true within the more noisy culture of our media. *The New York Review of Books, Time* (the literary sections), and *The New York Times Book Review* share a certain aspiration to wit or liveliness, to intelligence really, concealing resistance to the new. All the more skeptical in periods of excess, the culture of the Logos insists on old orders in clever or current guises, and, with the means of communication at hand, inhibits and restrains.

> *Self-Admonition:* Beware of glib condemnations of the media. They are playing a national role as bold, as crucial, as the Supreme Court played in the Fifties. Willful and arbitrary as they may be in their creation of public images—which preempt our selves—they are still custodians of some collective sanity. Note, too, the rising quality of the very publications you cited. [This was written in 1971.]

VI. Bibliography

Here is a curious chronology of some Postmodern criticism:

1. George Steiner, "The Retreat from the Word," *Kenyon Review* 23 (Spring 1961). See also his *Language and Silence* (New York, 1967), and *Extraterritorial* (New York, 1971).
2. Ihab Hassan, "The Dismemberment of Orpheus," *American Scholar* 23 (Summer 1963). See also his *Literature of Silence* (New York, 1967).
3. Hugh Kenner, "Art in a Closed Field," in *Learners and Discerners*, ed. Robert Scholes (Charlottesville, Va., 1964). See also his *Samuel Beckett* (New York, 1961; Berkeley and Los Angeles, 1968), and *The Counterfeiters* (Bloomington, Ind., 1968).
4. Leslie Fiedler, "The New Mutants," *Partisan Review* 32 (Fall 1965). See also his "The Children's Hour; or, The Return of the Vanishing Longfellow," in *Liberations*, ed. Ihab Hassan (Middletown, Conn., 1971), and *Collected Essays* (New York, 1971).
5. Susan Sontag, "The Aesthetics of Silence," *Aspen*, nos. 5 & 6 (1967). See also her *Against Interpretation* (New York, 1966), and *Styles of Radical Will* (New York, 1969).

6. Richard Poirier, "The Literature of Waste," *New Republic,* 20 May 1967. See also his "The Politics of Self-Parody," *Partisan Review* 35 (Summer 1968), and *The Performing Self* (New York, 1971).
7. John Barth, "The Literature of Exhaustion," *Atlantic Monthly,* August 1967. See also his *Lost in the Funhouse* (New York, 1968).

And here are some leitmotifs of that criticism: the literary act in quest and question of itself; self-subversion or self-transcendence of forms; popular mutations; languages of silence.

VII. ReVisions

A revision of Modernism is slowly taking place, and this is another evidence of Postmodernism. In *The Performing Self,* Richard Poirier tries to mediate between these two movements. We need to recall the doctrines of formalist criticism, the canons of classroom and quarterly in the last three decades, to savor such statements:

> Three of the great and much used texts of twentieth-century criticism, *Moby Dick, Ulysses, The Waste Land,* are written in mockery of system, written against any effort to harmonize discordant elements, against any mythic or metaphoric scheme. . . . But while this form of the literary imagination is radical in its essentially parodistic treatment of systems, its radicalism is in the interest of essentially conservative feelings.
>
> * * *
>
> The most complicated examples of twentieth-century literature, like *Ulysses* and *The Waste Land,* the end of which seems parodied by the end of *Giles [Goat-Boy* by Barth], are more than contemptuous of their own formal and stylistic elaborateness.

Certainly some profound philosophic minds of our century have concerned themselves with the disease of verbal systems: Heidegger, Wittgenstein, Sartre. And later writers as different as John Cage, Norman O. Brown, and Elie Wiesel have listened intently to the sounds of silence in art or politics, sex, morality, or religion. In this context the statements of Poirier do not merely display a revisionist will; they strain toward an aesthetic of Postmodernism.

We are still some way from attaining such an aesthetic; nor is it clear that Postmodern art gives high priority to that end. Perhaps we can start by revisioning Modernism as well as revising the pieties we have inherited about it. In *Continuities* Frank Kermode cautiously attempts that task. A critic of great civility, he discriminates well between types of modernism—what he calls "palaeo- and neo-modern" correspond perhaps to Modern and Postmodern—and takes note of the new "anti-art," which he rightly traces back to Duchamp. But his preference for continuities tempts him to assimilate current to past things. Kermode, for instance, writes: "Aleatory art is accordingly, for all its novelty, an extension of past art, indeed the hypertrophy of one aspect of that art." Does not this statement close more possibilities than it opens? There is another perspective of things that Goethe described: "The most important thing is always the contemporary element, because it is most purely reflected in ourselves, as we are in it." I think that we will not grasp the cultural experience of our moment if we insist that the new arts are "marginal developments of older modernism," or that distinctions between "art" and "joke" are crucial to any future aesthetic.

Whether we tend to revalue Modernism in terms of Postmodernism (Poirier) or to reverse that procedure (Kermode), we will end by doing something of both since relations, analogies, enable our thought. Modernism does not suddenly cease so that Postmodernism may begin: they now *coexist.* New lines emerge from the past because our eyes every morning open anew. In a certain frame of mind, Michelangelo or Rembrandt, Goethe or Hegel, Nietzsche or Rilke, can reveal to us something about Postmodernism, as Erich Heller incidentally shows. Consider this marvelous passage from *The Artist's Journey to the Interior:*

> Michelangelo spent the whole of his last working day, six days before his death, trying to finish the Pietà which is known as the "Pietà Rondanini." He did not succeed. Perhaps it lies in the nature of stone that he had to leave unfinished what Rembrandt completed in paint: the employment of the material in the service of its own negation. For this sculpture seems to intimate that its maker was in the end determined to use only as much marble as was necessary to show that matter did not matter; what alone mattered was the pure inward spirit.

Here Michelangelo envisions, past any struggle with the obdurate material of existence, a state of gnostic consciousness to which we may be tending. Yet can we justifiably call him Postmodern?

Where Modern and Postmodern May Meet: or, *Make Your Own List*

1. Blake, Sade, Lautréamont, Rimbaud, Mallarmé, Whitman, etc.
2. daDaDA

3. SURrealism
4. KAFKA
5. Finnegans Wake
6. The Cantos
7. ? ? ?

VIII. Modernism

This is no place to offer a comprehensive definition of Modernism. From Apollinaire and Arp to Valéry, Woolf, and Yeats—I seem to miss the letters X and Z—runs the alphabet of authors who have delivered themselves memorably on the subject; and the weighty work of Richard Ellmann and Charles Feidelson, Jr., *The Modern Tradition,* still stands as the best compendium of that "large spiritual enterprise including philosophic, social, and scientific thought, and aesthetic and literary theories and manifestoes, as well as poems, novels, dramas."

Expectations of agreement, let alone of definition, seem superlatively naive. This is true among stately and distinguished minds, not only rowdy critical tempers. Here, for instance, is Lionel Trilling, "On the Modern Element in Modern Literature":

> I can identify it by calling it the disenchantment of our culture with culture itself . . . the bitter line of hostility to civilization that runs through it [modern literature]. . . . I venture to say that the idea of losing oneself up to the point of self-destruction, of surrendering oneself to experience without regard to self-interest or conventional morality, of escaping wholly from the societal bonds, is an "element" somewhere in the mind of every modern person.

To this, Harry Levin counters in "What Was Modernism?"[1]:

> Insofar as we are still moderns, I would argue, we are the children of Humanism and the Enlightenment. To identify and isolate the forces of unreason, in a certain sense, has been a triumph for the intellect. In another sense, it has reinforced that anti-intellectual undercurrent which, as it comes to the surface, I would prefer to call post-modern.

Yet the controversy of Modernism has still wider scope, as Monroe K. Spears, in *Dionysus and the City,* with bias beneath his Apollonian lucidity, shows. Released as energy from the contradictions of history, Modernism makes contradiction its own.

For my purpose, let Modernism stand for X: a window on human madness, the shield of Perseus against which Medusa glances, the dream of some frowning, scholarly muse. I offer, instead, some rubrics and spaces. Let readers fill them with their own queries or grimaces. We value what we choose.

a. *Urbanism:* Nature put in doubt, from Baudelaire's *"cité fourmillante"* to Proust's Paris, Joyce's Dublin, Eliot's London, Dos Passos' New York, Döblin's Berlin. It is not a question of locale but of presence. The sanatorium of *The Magic Mountain* and the village of *The Castle* are still enclosed in an urban spiritual space. Exceptions, Faulkner's Yoknapatawpha or Lawrence's Midlands, recognize the City as pervasive threat.

____

____

____

b. *Technologism:* City and Machine make and remake one another. Extension, diffusion, and alienation of the human will. Yet technology does not feature simply as a theme of Modernism; it is also a form of its artistic struggle. Witness Cubism, Futurism, Dadaism. Other *reactions* to technology: primitivism, the occult, Bergsonian time, the dissociation of sensibility, etc. (See Wylie Sypher, *Literature and Technology.*)

____

____

____

c. *"Dehumanization"*: Ortega y Gasset really means Elitism, Irony, and Abstraction (*The Dehumanization of Art*). Style takes over; let life and the masses fend for themselves. "Poetry has become the higher algebra of metaphor." Instead of Vitruvian man, Leonardo's famous image of the human measure, we have Picasso's beings splintered on many planes. Not less human, just another idea of man.

____

____

____

Elitism:	Aristocratic or crypto-fascist: Rilke, Proust, Yeats, Eliot, Lawrence, Pound, d'Annunzio, Wyndham Lewis, etc.
Irony:	Play, complexity, formalism. The aloofness of art but also sly hints of its radical incompleteness. *Dr. Faustus* and *Confessions of Felix Krull.* Irony as awareness of Nonbeing.
Abstraction:	Impersonality, sophistical simplicity, reduction and construction, time decomposed or spatialized. Thus Mondrian on Reductionism: "To create pure reality plastically, it is necessary to reduce natural forms to the *constant elements* of form and natural colour to *primary colour.*" Gabo on Constructivism: "It has revealed a universal law that the elements of a visual art such as lines, colours, shapes, possess their own forces of expression, independent of any association with the external aspects of the world. . . ." The literary equivalent of these ideas may be "spatial time." (See Joseph Frank, "Spatial Form in Modern Literature," in *The Widening Gyre.*)
An Addendum:	There is more to "dehumanization" than "another idea of man"; there is also an incipient revulsion against the human, sometimes a renewal of the sense of the superhuman. Rilke's "Angels." Lawrence's "Fish":

And my heart accused itself
Thinking: I am not the measure of creation
This is beyond me, this fish.
His God stands outside my God.

d. *Primitivism:* The archetypes behind abstraction, beneath ironic civilization. An African mask, a beast slouching toward Bethlehem. Structure as ritual or myth, metaphors from the collective dream of mankind. Cunning palimpsests of literary time and space, knowing palingenesis of literary souls. Also Dionysus and the violent return of the repressed. (See Northrop Frye, *The Modern Century.*)

e. *Eroticism:* All literature is erotic but Modernist sex scratches the skin from within. It is not merely the liberation of the libido, a new language of anger or desire; love now becomes an intimate of disease. Sadomasochism, solipsism, nihilism, anomie. Consciousness seeks desperately to discharge itself in the world. A new and darker stage in the struggle between Eros and Thanatos. (See Lionel Trilling, "The Fate of Pleasure," in *Beyond Culture.*)

f. *Antinomianism:* Beyond law, dwelling in paradox. Also discontinuity, alienation, *non serviam!* The pride of art, of the self, defining the conditions of its own grace. Iconoclasm, schism, excess. Beyond antinomianism, toward apocalypse. Therefore, decadence and renovation. (See Nathan A. Scott, Jr., *The Broken Center.*)

g. *Experimentalism:* Innovation, dissociation, the brilliance of change in all its aesthetic shapes. New languages, new concepts of order. Also, the Word beginning to put its miracle to question in the midst of an artistic miracle. Poem, novel, or play henceforth can never really bear the same name.

In those seven rubrics, I seek not so much to define Modernism as to carry certain elements which I consider crucial, carry them forward toward Postmodernism.

IX. The Unimaginable

The unimaginable lies somewhere between the Kingdom of Complacence and the Sea of Hysteria. It balks all geographies; bilks the spirit of the traveler who passes unwittingly through its space-realm; boggles time. Yet anyone who can return from it to tell his tale may also know how to spell the destiny of man.

I know the near-infinite resources of man, and that his imagination may still serve as the teleological organ of his evolution. Yet I am possessed by the feeling that in the next few decades, certainly within half a century, the earth and all that inhabits it may be wholly other, perhaps ravaged, perhaps on the way to some strange utopia indistinguishable from nightmare. I have no language to articulate this feeling with conviction, nor imagination to conceive this special destiny. To live from hour to hour seems as maudlin as to invoke every hour the Last Things. In this feeling I find that I am not alone.

The litany of our disasters is all too familiar, and we recite it in the name of that unholy trinity, Population, Pollution, Power (read genocide), hoping to appease our furies, turn our fate inside out. But soon our minds lull themselves to sleep again on this song of abstractions, and a few freak out. The deathly dreariness of politics brings us ever closer to death. Neither is the alteration of human consciousness at hand. And the great promise of technology? Which technology? Fuller's? Skinner's? Dr. Strangelove's and Dr. No's? Engineers of liberation or of control? The promise is conditional on everything that we are, in this our ambiguous state.

Truly, we dwell happily in the Unimaginable. We also dwell at our task: Literature. I could learn to do pushups in a prison cell, but I cannot bring myself to "study literature" as if the earth were still in the orbit of our imagination. I hope this is Hope.

X. Postmodernism

Postmodernism may be a response, direct or oblique, to the Unimaginable that Modernism glimpsed only in its most prophetic moments. Certainly it is not the Dehumanization of the Arts that concerns us now; it is rather the Denaturalization of the Planet and the End of Man. We are, I believe, inhabitants of another Time and another Space, and we no longer know what response is adequate to our reality. In a sense we have all learned to become minimalists—of that time and space we can call our own—though the globe may have become our village. That is why it seems bootless to compare Modern with Postmodern artists, range "masters" against "epigones." The latter are closer to "zero in the bone," to silence or exhaustion, and the best of them brilliantly display the resources of the void. Thus the verbal omnipotence of Joyce yields to the impotence of Beckett, heir and peer, no less genuine, only more austere. Yet moving into the void, these artists sometimes pass to the other side of silence. The consummation of their art is a work that, remaining art, pretends to abolish itself (Beckett, Tinguely, Robert Morris), or else to become indistinguishable from life (Cage, Rauschenberg, Mailer). Duchamp coolly pointed the way.

Nihilism is a word we often use, when we use it unhistorically, to designate values we dislike. It is sometimes applied to the children of Marcel Duchamp.

When John Cage, in "HPSCHD" for instance, insists on Quantity rather than Quality, he does not surrender to nihilism—far, far from it—he requires:

- affluence and permission of being, generosity
- discovery in multitude, confusion of prior judgment

–mutation of perception, of consciousness, through randomness and diversity
Cage knows how to praise Duchamp: "The rest of them were artists. Duchamp collects dust."

I have not defined Modernism; I can define Postmodernism less. No doubt, the more we ponder, the more we will need to qualify all we say. Perhaps elisions may serve to qualify these notes.

Modernist Rubrics	*Postmodernist Notes*
a. Urbanism	—The City and also the Global Village (McLuhan) and Spaceship Earth (Fuller). The City as Cosmos. Therefore, Science Fiction. —Meanwhile, the world breaks up into untold blocs, nations, tribes, clans, parties, languages, sects. Anarchy and fragmentation everywhere. A new diversity or prelude to world totalitarianism? Or to world unification? —Nature recovered partly in ecological activism, the green revolution, urban renewal, health foods, etc. —Meanwhile, Dionysus has entered the City: prison riots, urban crime, pornography, etc. Worse, the City as holocaust or death camp: Hiroshima, Dresden, Auschwitz.
b. Technologism	—Runaway technology, from genetic engineering and thought control to the conquest of space. Futurists and Technophiles vs. Arcadians and Luddites. —All the physical materials of the arts changed. New media, art forms. The problematics of the book as artifact. —Boundless dispersal by media. The sensuous object becoming "anxious," then "de-

defined" (Rosenberg). Matter disappearing into a concept?

—The computer as substitute consciousness, or as extension of consciousness? Will it prove tautological, increasing reliance on prior orders? Or will it help to create novel forms?

c. "Dehumanization"

—Antielitism, antiauthoritarianism. Diffusion of the ego. Participation. Art becomes communal, optional, anarchic. Acceptance.

—At the same time, Irony becomes radical, self-consuming play, entropy of meaning. Also comedy of the absurd, black humor, insane parody and slapstick, Camp. Negation.

—Abstraction taken to the limit and coming back as New Concreteness: the found object, the signed Brillo box or soup can, the nonfiction novel, the novel as history. The range is from Concept Art (abstract) to Environmental Art (concrete).

—Warhol's wanting to be a machine, Cioran's ambivalent temptation to exist. Humanism yields to infrahumanism or posthumanism. But yields also to a cosmic humanism, as in Science Fiction, as in Fuller, Castaneda, N. O. Brown, Ursula LeGuin.

"Dehumanization," both in Modernism and Postmodernism, finally means the end of the old Realism. Increasingly, Illusionism takes its place, not only in art but also in life. The media contribute egregiously to this process in Postmodern society. In *Act and the Actor Making the Self,* Harold Rosenberg says: "History has been turned inside out; writing takes place in advance of its occurrence, and every statesman is an author in embryo." Thus the Illusionism of politics matches that of Pop Art or Neo-Realism. An Event need never have happened.

The end of the old Realism also affects the sense

of the Self. Thus "Dehumanization," both in Modernism and Postmodernism, requires a revision of the literary and authorial Self evidenced:

in Modernism—by doctrines of Surrealism (Breton), by ideas of impersonality in art (the masks of Yeats, the tradition of Eliot), by modes of hyperpersonality (the stream of consciousness of Joyce, Proust, Faulkner, Nin, or the allotropic ego of Lawrence). (See Robert Langbaum, *The Modern Spirit,* 164–84.)

In Postmodernism—by authorial self-reflexiveness, by the fusion of fact and fiction (Capote, Wolfe, Mailer), phenomenology (Husserl, Sartre, Merleau-Ponty), Beckett's fiction of consciousness, varieties of the *nouveau roman* (Sarraute, Butor, Robbe-Grillet), and the linguistic novel of *Tel Quel* (Sollers, Thibaudeau). (See Vivian Mercier, *The New Novel,* 3–42.)

d. Primitivism

—Away from the mythic, toward the existential. Beat and Hip. Energy and spontaneity of the White Negro (Mailer).

—Later, the post-existential ethos, psychedelics (Leary), the Dionysian ego (Brown), Pranksters (Kesey), madness (Laing), animism and magic (Castaneda).

—The Hippie movement. Woodstock, rock music and poetry, communes. The culture of *The Whole Earth Catalog.* Pop.

—The primitive Jesus. The new Rousseauism and Deweyism: Human Potential movement, Open Classroom (Goodman, Rogers, Leonard).

e. Eroticism	—Beyond the trial of *Lady Chatterley's Lover.* The repeal of censorship. Grove Press and *Evergreen Review.* —The new sexuality, from Reichian orgasm to polymorphous perversity and Esalen body consciousness. —The homosexual novel (Burroughs, Vidal, Selby, Rechy). From feminism to lesbianism. Toward a new androgyny? —Camp and comic pornography. Sex as solipsist play.
f. Antinomianism	—The Counter Cultures, political and otherwise. Free Speech Movement, S.D.S., Weathermen, Church Militants, Women's Lib, J.D.L., Black, Red, and Chicano Power, etc. Rebellion and Reaction! —Beyond alienation from the whole culture, acceptance of discreteness and discontinuity. Evolution of radical empiricism in art as in politics or morality. —Counter Western "ways" or metaphysics, Zen, Buddhism, Hinduism. But also Western mysticism, transcendentalism, witchcraft, the occult. (See "Primitivism" above.) —The widespread cult of apocalyptism, sometimes as renovation, sometimes as annihilation—often both.
g. Experimentalism	—Open, discontinuous, improvisational, indeterminate, or aleatory structures. End-game strategies and neosurrealist modes. Both reductive, minimalist forms and lavish extravaganzas. In general, antiformalism. (See Calvin Tomkins, *The Bride and the Bachelors.)* —Simultaneism. Now. The impermanence of art (scupture made of dry ice or a hole in Cen-

tral Park filled with earth), the transcience of man. Absurd time.

—Fantasy, play, humor, happening, parody, "dreck" (Barthelme). Also, increasing self-reflexiveness. (See Irony under "Dehumanization" above.)

—Intermedia, the fusion of forms, the confusion of realms. An end to traditional aesthetics focused on the "beauty" or "uniqueness" of the art work? Against interpretation (Sontag).

In *Man's Rage for Chaos,* Morse Peckham argues "that art is a disjunctive category, established by convention, and that art is not a category of perceptual fields, but of role-playing." And in *The Art of Time,* Michael Kirby says: "Traditional aesthetics asks a particular hermetic attitude or state of mind that concentrates on the sensory perception of the work. . . . [Postmodern] aesthetics makes use of no special attitude or set, and art is viewed just as anything else in life." When art is viewed like "anything else in life," Fantasy is loosened from its "objective correlatives"; Fantasy becomes supreme.

Is this why Postmodern art, viewed in a Modernist perspective, creates more anxiety than it appeases? Or is the tendency toward a new gnosticism?

XI. Alternatives

The reader, no doubt, will want to judge for himself how much Modernism permeates the present and how much the latter contains elements of a new reality. The judgment is not always made rationally; self-love and the fear of dissolution may enter into it as much as the conflict of literary generations. Yet it is already possible to note that whereas Modernism—excepting Dada and Surrealism—created its own forms of artistic Authority precisely because the center no longer held, Postmodernism has tended toward artistic Anarchy in deeper complicity with things falling apart—or has tended toward Pop.

Speculating further, we may say that the Authority of Modernism—artistic, cultural, personal—rests on intense, elitist, self-generated orders in times of crisis, of which the Hemingway Code is perhaps the starkest exemplar, and Eliot's Tradition or Yeats's Ceremony is a more devious kind. Such elitist orders, perhaps the last of the world's Eleusinian mysteries, may no longer have a place amongst us, threatened as we are, at the same instant, by extermination and totalitarianism.

Yet is the Anarchy or Pop of Postmodernism, or its Fantasy, a deeper response, somehow more inward with destiny? Though my sympathies are in the present, I cannot believe this to be entirely so. True, there is enhancement of life in certain anarchies of the spirit, in humor and play, in love released and freedom of the imagination to overreach itself, in a cosmic consciousness of variousness as of unity. I recognize these as values intended by Postmodern art, and see the latter as closer, not only in time, but even more in tenor, to the transformation of hope itself. Still, I wonder if any art can help to engender the motives we must now acquire; or if we can long continue to value an art that fails us in such endeavor.

1. More accurately, the quotation appears in a note preceding the essay. See Harry Levin, *Refractions* (New York, 1966), 271–73.

3 Culture, Indeterminacy, and Immanence: Margins of the (Postmodern) Age

The Argument:

The play of indeterminacy and immanence is crucial to the episteme of postmodernism, a term that may have now outlived its awkward use. Between shifting margins and maieutic fragments, the argument concerning this age of "indetermanence" proceeds in seven orderly parts:

I. Anarchy or Indeterminacy?
II. The Question of Epistemes
III. The New Science
IV. Of Herrings: Red, Silver, and Purple
V. The Cultural Evidence of Our Time
VI. In the Arts
VII. Human and Inconclusive

The Counter argument:

This text is itself an inconclusive fiction of our time. The present remains always concealed from us, and true prophecy requires madness, unseemly on this occasion. Indeterminacy and immanence are as ageless as language; "indetermanence" is a barbarism; and epistemes are diversions from the imperative of our world, just praxis. Less maieutic than mystical or sophistical, the argument is itself marginal.

I. Anarchy or Indeterminacy

We are enjoined to reflect upon the order and disorder of knowledge in our time. But I also wonder about our time, the margin of our mortality, and how we shall name ourselves as we die to meet posterity half way. Uncouthly, do we say: we are children of the Postmodern Age? Yet why ponder the question? What, after all, is in a name? Partly our presence, our hope in part. Call it parturition and play. We always raise our voices to invoke ancestors whom we then proceed to remake.

The order of knowledge is founded on exclusions, Michel Foucault asserts. The task is to expose (include?) these exclusions. *L'Ordre du discours* (Paris, 1971).

I call upon Matthew Arnold and Friedrich Nietzsche, who have been summoned so often they no longer come bearing the odor of clay.

Think of "Lucy," three and a half feet tall, not *Homo sapiens* but *Homo erectus* nonetheless, lying more than three million years on the Afar plain. Gracile hominid, was she mother of us all? They say not. She looked curiously at our "true ancestors" as they began to walk the earth. Thus, with every turn of the page, our "ancestors" recede; and the fiction of origins meets the fiction of differences. From paleontology to grammatology.

Arnold has nearly preempted the concept of culture among academic Anglophiles of our day. His work, *Culture and Anarchy,* certainly casts a shadow on my subject, which I may seek to dispel in vain. Culture for Arnold—we know this all too well—was an "inward operation," a fruitful and passionate "curiosity," a "general intelligence" in "pursuit of our total perfection by means of getting to know . . . the best which has been thought and said in the world." It demanded civility of the "best self," harmony "in developing all sides of our humanity," and in "developing all parts of society" as well. In these dicta, "harmony," "totality," and "perfection" are key. Their absence leaves us open to anarchy or, worse still, harsh morality; at both, Arnold thought, Americans tended to excel.

Culture and Anarchy, ed. Ian Gregor (Indianapolis and New York, 1971), 5–8.

I have American culture particularly in mind. Is it given more than ever to either transcendent Hebraism or plain anarchy? Or is it transmuting itself into something Arnold would scarcely recognize, something indeterminate, immanent, rich and strange? For indeterminacy surely need not deny an ideal of harmonious perfection; nor is strangeness

"From Maine to Florida, and back again, all America Hebraises," Amold complains (p. 15). This was in 1869. What might he think of Southern California today?

sometimes but the action of an immanent future in our lives. Arnold wrote: "So that, for the sake of the present, but far more for the sake of the future, the lovers of culture are unswervingly and with a good conscience the opposers of anarchy." The difficulty has become this: how to recognize "anarchy," which like "nihilism" can simply serve as objurgation of the New.

(p. 17)

How much of our intellectual rhetoric is mainly magical or apotropic?

Yet there is another case, and it is flamboyantly made by Nietzsche. No sweetness and light here; instead, the hammer and dying sparks off the anvil. I quote at some length:

The Will to Power, ed. Walter Kaufmann (New York, 1967), 13, 39, 149, 163, 181, 199, 267, 283, 291, 309, 380, 418, 548.

> What we find here is still the *hyperbolic naïveté* of man: positing himself as the meaning and measure of the value of things.
>
> *
>
> The period of clarity: one understands that the old and the new are basically opposite . . . that all the old ideals are hostile to life (born of decadence and agents of decadence, even if in the magnificent Sunday clothes of morality).
>
> *
>
> *My chief proposition: there are no moral phenomena, there is only a moral interpretation of these phenomena. This interpretation itself is of extramoral origin.*
>
> *
>
> *Play-acting* as a consequence of the morality of "free will". . . . Personal perfection as conditioned by will, as consciousness, as reasoning with dialects, is a caricature, a kind of self-contradiction—A degree of consciousness makes perfection impossible—Form of *play-acting.*

So many features of postmodernism are implicit in these chips and shavings of 1883–88. For instance:

a. the decenterment of man

*

It seems to me [why this sudden access of modesty?] important that one should get rid of the all, the unity, some force, something unconditioned; otherwise one will never cease regarding it as the highest court of appeal and baptizing it "God."

*

The "subject" is only a fiction: the ego of which one speaks when one censures egoism does not exist at all.

*

"There are only *facts* "—I would say: No, facts are precisely what there is not, only interpretations. . . . Insofar as the word "knowledge" has any meaning, the world is knowable; but it is *interpretable* otherwise, it has no meaning behind it, but countless meanings.—"Perspectivism."

*

Language depends on the most naïve prejudices.

Now we read disharmonies and problems into things because we think *only* in the form of language—and thus believe in the "eternal truth" of "reason". . . .

We cease to think when we refuse to do so under the constraint of language ["the prison house of language" in other translations]; we barely reach the doubt that sees this limitation as a limitation.

*

Parmenides said, "one cannot think of what is not";—we are at the other extreme, and say, "what can be thought of must certainly be a fiction."

b. the vitality of the new

c. hermeneutics

d. the demystification of reason

e. the refusal of unity

f. the empty subject

g. fact-fiction, perspectivism

h. the liminality of language

i. thinking in fictions

j. the denial of origins

k. the energetics of value

l. ludic arts, the metaphysics of play

m. the collapse of being and becoming, a new ontology

We tend to forget that Nietzsche's contemporary, William James, may also prove a source of postmodern

*

Knowledge is referring back: in its essence a *regressus in infinitum.* That which comes to a standstill (at a supposed *causa prima,* at something unconditioned, etc.) is laziness, weariness. . . .

tendencies. For instance: "The mind is at every stage a theatre of simultaneous possibilities." Or even Ralph Waldo Emerson: "But man thyself, and all things unfix, dispart, and flee."

*

Value is the highest quantum of power that a man is able to incorporate—a man: not mankind! . . . mankind is merely the experimental material, the tremendous surplus of failures: a field of ruins.

*

The world as a work of art that gives birth to itself. . . . "Play," the useless—as the ideal of him who is overfull of strength, as "childlike."

*

The new world-conception. —The world exists; it is not something that becomes, not something that passes away . . .—it maintains itself in both. It lives on itself: its excrements are its food.

No doubt, some will judge this catena of musings half demented and in any case rebarbative, though I admit to a certain pleasure that two great Europeans, near contemporaries—Nietzsche went mad within a year of Arnold's death—should perceive the human condition so differently. Against Arnold's hope for a universal culture, and for a criticism founded upon "a centre of taste and authority," Nietzsche speaks with irony, poetry, and truculence to exalt a perspectivism so radical as to appear to beggar nihilism itself.

Walter Kaufmann: "The publication of *The Will to Power* as Nietzsche's final and systematic work blurred the distinction between his works and his notes and created the false impression that the aphorisms in his books are of a kind with these disjointed jottings" (p. xix).

There are, of course, many Nietzsches. One is the German Nietzsche, slayer of God, herald of the

"Among all the thinkers of the nineteenth century he [Nietzsche]

Overman, Dionysian psychologist, prophet of the transvaluation of all values, of whom Freud, Spengler, Heidegger, Jaspers, and Wittgenstein were acutely aware, as were Rilke, George, Kafka, Mann, Musil, Benn, and Ernst Jünger. But there is now another Nietzsche, French Nietzsche, perhaps less modern than postmodern, magus of deconstruction, geometer of decenterment, philosopher of language. Georges Bataille and Pierre Klossowski have written about him, and more recently, Jacques Derrida, Gilles Deleuze, Jean-François Lyotard, Henri Lefebvre, and Michel Foucault, among many others.

Whatever avatar of Nietzsche we choose to invoke, we must now acknowledge a radical countertradition that redefines for us both culture and anarchy, one that Arnoldians can only find dismaying. Yet the task, of course, is to avoid the tendency of one tradition to lapse into nihilistic chic and the other into pious beneficence—to avoid, that is, the strut and shuffle of our intellectual performances.

is, with the possible exceptions of Dostoyevsky and Kierkegaard, the only one who would not be too amazed by the amazing scene upon which we now move. . . . Much, too much, would strike him as *déjà vu:* yes, he had foreseen it; and he would understand. . . ." Erich Heller, *The Artist's Journey into the Interior* (New York, 1968), 173. Nietzsche himself cried: "Oh grant madness, you heavenly powers! Madness that at last I may believe in myself . . . ," *Ibid,* 197.

Contrast Norman O. Brown's "Apocalypse: The Place of Mystery in the Life of the Mind," *Harper's,* May 1961, with Lionel Trilling's *Mind in the Modern World* (New York, 1972).

Maieutic

How is belief suspended, desire delayed, affect shunted or contained? Perhaps through Imagination, through all its evasions and tropes. Yet Nietzsche claims: "It is our needs that interpret the world; our drives and their For and Against. Every drive is a kind of lust to rule . . . " (p. 267). Lust to rule: what then is an academic conference? A colosseum of ideas or gladiatorial show, with Andabates, Retiariuses, Mirmillons, Samnites, and Thracians, vying for victory, or if they fall, hoping for a swarm of thumbs pointing heavenward? And the outcome of all this: what can it be? "Clarification," as we all half hope and half of that half half believe? Or is there an ontology of conferences, more precisely an onto-erotics and onto-politics, a presence anyway that shapes and gently mocks all our epistemes?

II. The Question of Epistemes

Nietzsche's radical perspectivism, not merely his skepticism, challenged the grounds on which philosophy, from Plato to Hegel, had sought to build. Nature, language, and mind, no longer congruent, defied the articulations of a sovereign code. This view has now become banal. Yet the question remains: is such indeterminacy itself part of a new episteme?

Les Mots et les choses (Paris, 1966), 219–21, 313.

In *The Order of Things,* Michel Foucault identifies three major *"épistémès"* of Western history; the last, beginning early in the nineteenth century, is the "modern." Two modern forms of reflection arise: science, which explores the relation of logic to ontology, and history, which explores that of signification to time. But the decisive trait is this: putting in doubt the reciprocities of being and meaning, modernism finally generates a self-reflexive discourse, a radically intransitive language, which can only affirm its own "precipitous existence," its ludic "dispersal." We call that language modern literature.

In our quotidian and comfortable humanism, "ought we not to remember that we are bound to the back of a tiger?" Foucault asks (p. 333). The tiger of an emergent posthumanism?

The dispersal of language—shall we say its near immanence?—marks for Foucault the "disappearance" of man, not literally, to be sure, but as a particular idea, a concrete figuration of history. This "disappearance" turns out to be yet another Nietzschean prophecy, its realization coming nearer every day. The prophecy fulfills itself in a field of lexical play; for as Foucault says:

(pp. 394 ff.)

> In the interior of language experienced and traversed as language, in the play of its possibilities stretched to their extreme point, what announces itself is that man has "come to an end," and that in reaching the summit of all possible speech, he arrives not at the very heart of himself, but at the edge of what limits him: in that region where death

> prowls, where thought is extinguished, where the promise of the origin indefinitely recedes.

Referring to Artaud, to Roussel, to Bataille, Blanchot, and Kafka, Foucault hints at yet another summit, at a luminous transformation still to come. There where the episteme of modernism begins to dissolve and the human face explodes beneath its masks in laughter, Foucault envisions the return of some unspeakable power in language and wonders: "is this not the sign that the whole of this configuration is now about to topple, and that man is in the process of perishing as the being of language continues to shine ever brighter upon our horizon?" Thus the being of all our languages seems to summon the future immanence of mind.

Foucault is a materialist, yet his vision here seems concordant with Teillhard de Chardin's. Foucault, however, senses that behind the apparent logophilia of every culture hides a profound logophobia, an obscure fear of "the great buzz, chaotic and continuous, of discourse." *L'Ordre du discours,* 53.

But we need to pause: where does Foucault's argument precisely rest? I put it for him baldly: the modern episteme, starting early in the nineteenth century, has nearly run out its course; during its movement, the dispersal of discourse, the indeterminacy of knowledge, the disappearance of man occur gradually; we may be approaching now a new logos, a new immanence of language. For Foucault, then, the moment of dispersal has been two centuries in the making; and what literary historians call Romanticism, Victorianism, Modernism, and Postmodernism are all subsumed by it. But this is macrohistory, and metahistory as well. For Michel Foucault could have scarcely performed his dazzling archaeology of knowledge were he not writing with a hindsight that, say, Gibbon, Michelet, Henry Adams, or Spengler could not possess. Where Arnold saw anarchy, Foucault sees indeterminacies betokening another order of discourse. Thus his concept of dispersal is itself part of the postmodern ethos. Whether a valid episteme of postmodernism, a new organizing principle of cul-

Again, Nietzsche may be here an exception. Yet modernity itself is always complex. As Paul de Man says: "Modernity invests its trust in the power of the present moment as an origin, but discovers that, in severing itself from the past, it has at the same time severed itself from the present. Nietzsche's text [*The*

Use and Abuse of History] leads him irrevocably to this discovery. . . ." *Blindness and Insight* (New York, 1971), 149.

ture and mind, can be enunciated at this time is still moot.

But the time has surely come to probe the term indeterminacy itself, which so far has remained indeterminate, before it congeals into yet another critical slogan.

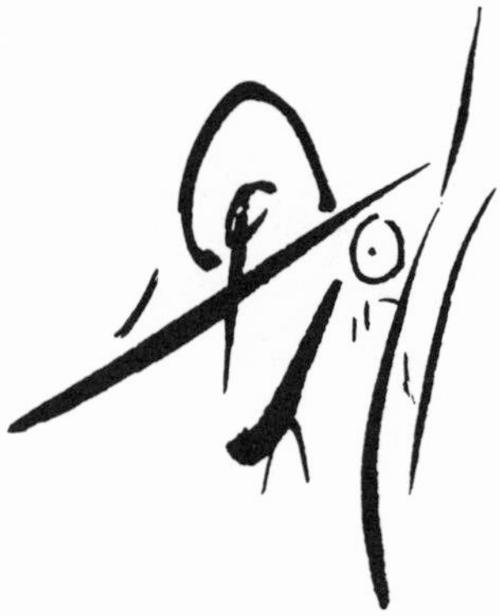

Maieutic

All thought hardens; abstract thought hardens absolutely. Even metaphor becomes archetype, neotype, stereotype; and "deconstruction" may soon provide a base more solid than the one on which the tomb of Lenin rests. Is there a permanent revolution in language? We call it poetry. But what is the place and play of poesis in criticism? And what if that poesis should prove too thin even for critical discourse? Must we thus choose between critical ideology and critical doggerel? Perhaps we require a form for the critic's SUFFERING: for there is fluency in pain when its sources are in gravity and grace. Yet this may seem too fierce an exigency to put in the way of criticism. Might we not also ask: what are the PLEASURES of the critical text? Poesis, suffering, pleasure: how do we acknowledge their presence in the shapes of our critical discourse?

III. The New Science

I wish to acknowledge here an excellent paper: Teresa Ebert's "The Tolerance of Ambiguity."

Science, according to Foucault, is one of the two modes of "reflection"—the other being history—that marks the emergence of the modern episteme in the nineteenth century. But the science of our century is sufficiently distinctive to warrant epistemological demarcations of its own, which Husserl somewhat adversely began in *The Crisis of European Sciences and Transcendental Phenomenology* late in the thirties.

We may consider 1905 as a turning point. In that year Albert Einstein published his paper on the Special Theory of Relativity. Events are always perceived with reference to a particular frame; in another system of coordinates, the "same" events are not the same. As Einstein succinctly put it: "There is no absolute motion." Nor is there absolute time or space. A moving clock ticks slower, a moving rod measures shorter, as their speeds approach the constant speed of light *in vacuo* (c). But the theory, which assumes the transformations of Maxwell and Lorentz, is no mere legerdemain. It has led to a new un-

Out of My Later Years (New York, 1950), 41.

$$\ell = \sqrt{1 - \frac{v^2}{c^2}}$$

derstanding of space, time, and motion; obviated the concept of absolute simultaneity; clarified the equations of electromagnetism; unified the laws of conservation of momentum and of energy; and, as we all devastatingly know, proven the equivalence of mass and energy.

$$t = \frac{1}{\sqrt{1 - \frac{v^2}{c^2}}}$$

In 1915 Einstein formulated the General Theory of Relativity, which reckoned with gravity and inertial systems as elements of a unified field: "according to that theory, the physical properties of space are affected by ponderable matter." The theory also dispensed with Euclidean geometry, adopting instead "curved" or Riemannian space. "The fundamental concepts of the 'straight line,' the 'plane,' etc., thereby lose their precise significance in physics," Einstein notes. Much, much more was, of course, at stake, including the "singularities" of black holes in space. Suffice it now to say that with both theories Einstein forced the universe of Galileo and Newton to reveal an entirely different face.

$E = mc^2$

Essays in Science (New York, 1934), 52, 58.

Einstein also wrote: "There is no place in this new kind of physics both for the field and matter, for the field is the only reality." Quoted by Fritjof Capra, *The Tao of Physics* (Boulder, Colorado, 1975), 211.

Still, as Einstein thought, God does not "play dice with the universe." The witticism was a serious reproach to the

To which Niels Bohr responded: "Nor is it our business to prescribe to God how he should run the world." Werner

Heisenberg, *Physics and Beyond* (New York, 1971), 81.

new theoreticians of quantum physics, most particularly to Niels Bohr and Werner Heisenberg, authors of the "Copenhagen interpretation." For Heisenberg had published in 1927 his famous paper on the Uncertainty Principle: either the momentum of a particle or its position could be precisely determined, not both, thus betraying the ineluctable complicity of observer and observed, measuring system and field of measurement. That same year Bohr formulated his Principle of Complementarity: since light seemed to behave both as waves and as quanta of particles, logical contradictions in certain phenomena could be heuristically viewed under the aspect of complementarity. The mathematical formalism of these principles, which I have rendered in a few ill-chosen words, has an awesome elegance, though their philosophical implications are to this day in passionate debate.

Werner Heisenberg: "What we observe is not nature in itself but nature exposed to our method of questioning. . . . In this way quantum theory reminds us, as Bohr has put it, of the old wisdom that . . . in the drama of existence we are ourselves both players and spectators." *Physics and Philosophy* (New York, 1962), 58.
W. B. Yeats: "How can we know the dancer from the dance?" "Among School Children."
N. B. When Bohr was knighted, he chose as his *motto: contraria sunt complementa.* He had also visited China in 1937, and been struck by *t'ai chi.*

Certain features of the new physics, however, seem provisionally clear. As a non-iconic science, physics now dispenses with geometric models to describe subatomic events. As a largely non-verbal disci-

Einstein to Jacques Hademard: "The words of the language, as they are written or spoken,

pline, it avoids both the ambiguities and conceptual constraints of natural languages. Instead of discrete objects, the new science also speaks of probabilities, tendencies to exist, thus blurring the ontological lines of being. As Heisenberg put it:

do not seem to play any role in my mechanism of thought." And Mozart in a letter of doubtful authenticity: "Nor do I hear in my imagination the parts *successively,* but I hear them, as it were all at once (*gleich alles zusammen*)." Quoted in Brewster Ghiselin, ed., *The Creative Process* (New York, 1952), 43.

> The new experiments have taught us that we can combine the two seemingly conflicting statements: "Matter is infinitely divisible" and "There are smallest units of matter," without running into logical difficulties.

Across the Frontiers (New York, 1974), 115.

Causality proves to be a concept of dubious use, and continuity in "matter waves" appears merely nominal. Thus electrons may "jump" from one "orbit" to another without traveling through intervening spaces. As for objectivity, that too seems a fiction transposed from classical concepts, useful only if the object is distinguished not from a subject but from the rest of the universe. Mechanism, determinism, materialism recede before the flux of consciousness, a kind of noetic Heraclitean fire. There is fright as well as elation in this recognition, to which Heisenberg attests:

Zeno's paradox? No, simply the probability function Ψ explains the quirk. There are also quarks, neutrinos, and other ghosts of matter with "charm," "resonance," or "strangeness," that populate our cloud chambers.

Physics and Beyond, 61.

At first, I was deeply alarmed. I had the feeling that, through the surface of atomic phenomena, I was looking at a strangely beautiful interior, and felt almost giddy at the thought that I now had to probe this wealth of mathematical structures nature had so generously spread out before me.

EXCURSUS ON GÖDEL'S PROOF

EVEN THE "WEALTH OF MATHEMATICAL STRUCTURES" HAVE THEIR LIMITS. THREE YEARS AFTER HEISENBERG'S PAPER ON UNCERTAINTY, KURT GÖDEL DEMONSTRATED THAT EVERY LOGICAL STRUCTURE MUST BE PART OF A LARGER AND "STRONGER" STRUCTURE; NONE CAN BE COMPLETE. AS STROTHER B. PURDY PUTS IT: "WITH THE LIMITATIVE THEOREMS OF KURT GÖDEL (1930) AND ALONZO CHURCH (1936) IT BECAME CLEAR THAT THE UNSOLVABILITY OF CERTAIN PROBLEMS, THE UNANSWERABILITY OF CERTAIN QUESTIONS, BASIC TO THE NATURE OF MATHEMATICS, HAD TO BE FORMALLY RECOGNIZED. IN THESE AREAS, MATHEMATICS SEEMS NOW MORE LIKE A GAME OF HUMAN INVENTION THAN AN UNCOVERING OF REALITY" [*THE HOLE IN THE FABRIC* (PITTSBURGH, 1977), 5]. THUS THE INCOMMENSURABILITY OF MIND AND THE WHOLE OF REALITY IS SUGGESTED. RECOGNIZING THE THEOLOGICAL AURA OF THE ARGUMENT, JEAN PIAGET WHIMSICALLY NOTES: "BUT GOD HIMSELF HAS, SINCE GÖDEL'S THEOREM, CEASED TO BE MOTIONLESS. HE IS THE LIVING GOD, MORE SO THAN HERETOFORE, BECAUSE HE IS UNCEASINGLY CONSTRUCTING EVER 'STRONGER' SYSTEMS" [*STRUCTURALISM* (LONDON, 1968), 141].

ALL THIS, I SUSPECT, HARDLY ACCORDS WITH ARNOLD'S SENSE OF DIVINITY. MORE TO OUR POINT: SINCE THE IDEAL OF A STRUCTURE OF ALL POSSIBLE STRUCTURES SEEMS UNREALIZABLE, KNOWLEDGE MUST REMAIN *FINALLY INDETERMINATE.*

In such rarefied realms of reason, a humanist, modern *or* postmodern, gasps for breath. We need to return to our primary concern: contemporary culture and its singular indeterminacies. Granting that we inhabit neither a Newtonian nor a Laplacian universe, how then can the new sciences contribute to a definition of postmodernism?

The question must be answered by admitting first its obduracies. Scientific concepts, we are cautioned, should not be confused with cultural metaphors and literary tropes. Nor is there unanimity among scientists themselves concerning the implications of their discoveries. Against the instrumentalism of Bohr, Einstein to the end clung to his realism, while Schrödinger stood uneasily in between. We encounter another difficulty when we coerce mathematical forms to yield philosophical statements about the nature of reality; the former tend to vanish, leaving behind only an abstract grin. (In this regard the ingenious efforts of Carl Friedrich von Weizsäcker to modify classical logic and so corre-

Schrödinger's Cat Paradox:

"Imagine a cat confined in a chamber containing the following 'torture device' which cannot be operated by the cat itself. A Geiger counter with a very tiny amount of radioactive substance is placed in the chamber, so that in an hour *perhaps* one of the atoms decays. . . . If an atom decays, then

late verbal and mathematical patterns proved inconclusive.) Finally, we need to recall that science, however tolerant of ambiguity, can not easily renounce the premise of immanence on which it rests. "Quantum theory forces us to see the universe not as a collection of physical objects, but rather as a complicated web of relations between the various parts of a unified whole," writes a contemporary physicist, thus echoing the organicism of Whitehead, so masterfully expressed in *Science and the Modern World* half a century before.

Capra, *The Tao of Physics,* 138.

Yet in these same perplexities may lie some answer to our initial query: how can the paradoxes of physics contribute to an understanding of contemporary culture? For however alien quasars or quarks may seem to humanists—and I find them no more so than certain social structures we inhabit—it is now clear that science, through its technological extensions, has become an inalienable part of our lives. More, the new Prometheus, quite as in the adamantine days of Zeus, assays nothing less than the unification of

the counter reacts and, by a relay mechanism, triggers a hammer which releases a pellet of cyanide. On leaving the system alone for an hour one would say that the cat is alive *if* no atom has decayed in the meanwhile, while the first atomic decay would have poisoned it. The function of the whole system would express this situation by containing in itself the fact of the living and the dead cat mixed or smeared out in equal parts. . . . the indeterminacy which is originally restricted to the atomic realm becomes a macroscopic sentient indeterminacy which can only be decided by direct observation." Erwin Schödinger, quoted in Jagdish Mehra, *The Quantum Principle* (Dodrecht, Holland and Boston, 1974), 72 ff. But should it be a black, ginger, or Siamese cat?

mind. The project is not altogether mythical; its evidence is equivocally in our midst. Of this we can be more certain: the epistemological concerns of science must concern us all the more in that scientists themselves, defying difficulties I have noted, insist on philosophizing, speaking not in mathematics but in natural languages. Even Heisenberg admits:

Physics and Philosophy, 201 ff.

> We know that any understanding must be based finally upon the natural language because it is only there that we can be certain to touch reality, and hence we must be skeptical about any skepticism with regard to this natural language and its essential concepts. . . . In this way modern physics has perhaps opened the door to a wider outlook on the relation between the human mind and reality.

In brief, relativity, uncertainty, complementarity, and incompleteness are not simply mathematical idealizations; they are concepts that begin to constitute our cultural languages; they are part of a new order of knowledge founded on both indeterminacy and immanence. In them we witness signal examples of

"In the order of mental things, there seem to be certain very mysterious relations between *the desire and the event*. . . . That is because the mind when reduced to its own sole substance does not have the power to *finish,* and absolutely cannot bind itself by itself." Paul Valéry, in Ghiselin, ed., *The Creative Process,* 101. Also: "a literary object

the "dispersal of discourse." In them and in other *Gedankenexperimente*—concept science seems to have preceded concept art—we may also discover models for our own historical moment. Admittedly, current analogies between science, culture, and sundry artistic and spiritual phenomena can prove too facile. Yet it is possible to be at once too rigorous and too timorous in exploring the cognitive possibilities of homologies. The semiotician Umberto Eco has put it thus:

never reaches the end of its many-faceted determinacy." And: "Thus it is perhaps one of the chief values of literature that by its very indeterminacy it is able to transcend the restrictions of time and written word and to give to people of all ages and backgrounds the chance to enter other worlds and so enrich their own lives." Wolfgang Iser, "Indeterminacy and the Reader's Response in Prose Fiction," in J. Hillis Miller, ed., *Aspects of Narrative* (New York, 1971), 10, 45.

Quoted and translated from *Opera aperta* by Teresa de Lauretis, "Semiosis Unlimited," *Journal for Descriptive Poetics and Theory of Literature* 2 (1977), 367 ff.

> An analogy ceases to be undue when it is posited as a starting point for further verification: the problem now consists in reducing the various phenomena (esthetic and otherwise) to more rigorous *structural models* and to identify in them not analogies, but rather similarities of structure, structural *homologies.*

Such homologies may help us better to define not only a cultural episteme but also the inadequacies of other models, including those of science itself, which is now as fully charged with promise as with menace.

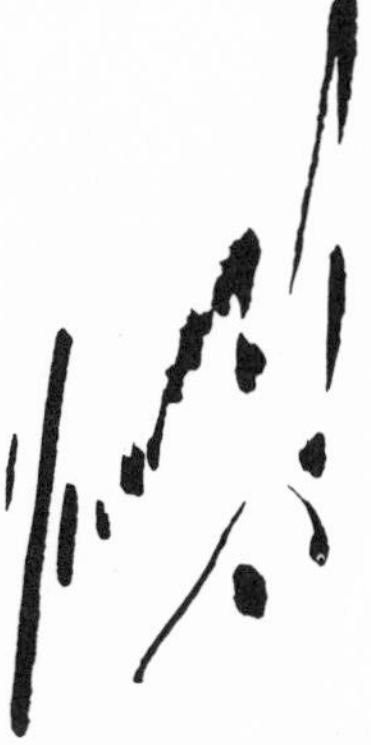

Maieutic

This solemn excursion into science, where precisely does it lead us? Toward an acceptance of immanence and *indeterminacy, holism* and *idiomorphism, integration* and *chance, totality and freedom? Physicists and biologists find such terms compatible; and so should humanists who live with the enabling contradictions of Imagination.*

Why then must critics choose between naïve scholarship and obsessive deconstruction, presence and play, "cognitive belief" and "cognitive atheism" (E. D. Hirsch)? Either humanism, with all its weary assumptions, or else dreary language games? Humanism speaks of "man," "values," "excellence," and the "critical intelligence" quite as if these could be legislated by the National Endowment for the Humanities. Deconstruction, calling happily upon the Sophists, ends by "troping" every "trope" and "demystifying" all "texts" in an ironic regress ad nauseam. *On the one hand, mental sloth, sometimes even "bad faith" (Jean-Paul Sartre); on the other, sterility, a "science" without true "gaiety" (Friedrich Nietzsche). What is finally missing in both?* Poesis, *intuition, some sense of the numinous?*

Consider Nietzsche again, our genius of this time-place: was he not both *overcomer and ironist, and "artistic Socrates" (Walter Kaufmann)? And how is culture itself founded? In his proleptic essay, "Truth and Falsity in an Ultramoral Sense," Nietzsche says:*

> *There are ages when the rational and the intuitive man stand side by side, the one full of fear of the intuition, the other full of scorn for the abstraction; the latter just as irrational as the former is inartistic. Both desire to rule over life. . . . Whenever intuitive man, as for instance in the earlier history of Greece, brandishes his weapons more powerfully and victoriously than his opponent, there under favorable conditions, a culture can develop and art can establish her rule over life.*
> (The Philosophy of Nietzsche, *ed. Geoffrey Clive [New York, 1965], 514ff.)*

A "culture can develop." Has the time come to defy our own "belatedness" (Harold Bloom) and to remake ourselves by that power that made our science and our poetry in the first and still present place?

IV. Of Herrings: Red, Silver, and Purple

We are approaching determinedly the problematic of postmodernism. There are certain problems, however, that I should like to clarify at the outset, and others that I intend to bracket or ignore in this context (Turn to pp. 87–90 below).

Maieutic

Decidedly, Postmodernism is but a poor name for our desire, insufficient for the life we want to hold and bequeath. How, then, shall we call our time? The Age of Indeterminacy? The Age of Immanence? The Age of Indetermanence? Or, bluntly, the Atomic Age?

V. The Evidence of Our Time

What evidence may we expect from our (postmodern) culture? Perhaps only evidence circumstantial: social bric-a-brac, intellectual *bricolage,* bright shards of a disestablished imagination, all jangling their peculiar themes and variations. I should like to hazard seven related themes, in advertence to that cultural jangle:

a. *Indeterminacy.* As in scientific so in cultural thought, indeterminacy fills the space between the will to unmaking (dispersal, deconstruction, discontinuity, etc.) and its opposite, the integrative will. Cultural indeterminacy, however, reveals itself with greater cunning and valency; choice, pluralism, fragmentation, contingency, imagination are only a few of its ambiguous aspects, as I shall presently have occasion to show.

b. *Process and Change.* In a technological world, all is flux; the time machine is the postindustrial machine itself, which accelerates both life and death. At its worst, process may transform the Logos into "instrumental reason"; we become "one-dimensional" (Herbert Marcuse). At its best, process permits change, surprise, innovation; it declares the openness of Being to Time (Martin Heidegger). Yet this metaphysical intuition rarely penetrates our polity. There, objects and even institutions become merely ephemeral; and in an "age of sensation" (Herbert Hendin), people seek satisfactions without commitment. Reification becomes suspect. Futurology on the rise (Herman Kahn & Co.) makes teleology obsolete. Thus process, more than any consensual goal or form of change, may come to be the sole source of value in history.

c. *The Diffractions of the Self.* From "loss of self" (Wylie Sypher), through the "Dionysian ego" (Norman O. Brown) and the "divided self" (R. D. Laing), to "protean man" (Robert Jay Lifton) and the "deconstructed self" (Leo Bersani), the identity of the individual is diffracted. Some practice the "mythotherapy" of changing masks (John Barth); a few emulate the old ways of the "new mutants" (Leslie Fiedler), surrendering themselves to orgiastic states of sex, psychedelics, and madness; many more cultivate the "new narcissism" (Peter Marin), vanishing quietly in their own silvered refractions. Such are the "games people play" (Eric Berne). Yet throughout contemporary arts, the ludic diffractions of the self generate brilliant new structures.

d. *The Displacements of Desire.* Desire has been liberated in all its violent and multifarious forms. Other ages may have been as explicit in their sensuality; none has so keenly understood the immanence of desire or so thoroughly made it into an object of reflection. Indeed, desire has become a kind of privileged theoretical discourse, an essential chatter of our culture. Neo- and post-Freudians, here as abroad, (Sandor Ferenczi, Wilhelm Reich, Melanie Klein, Jacques Lacan, Gilles Deleuze, Félix Guattari, Jean-François Lyotard, etc.) have helped to disseminate the languages of desire, perhaps even to encode them in the flesh. In America, such recent notions as "surplus repression" and "repressive desublimation" (Herbert Marcuse), "polymorphous perverse sexuality" (Norman O. Brown), "the erotics of texts" (Susan Sontag), and the "psychology of fragmentary and *dis*continuous desires" (Leo Bersani) may suggest the tropisms of love, its displacements in our personal and cultural lives.

e. *The Immanence of Media.* It may have begun with Gutenberg; it certainly will not end with McLuhan. The "work of art in an age of mechanical reproduction" (Walter Benjamin) and the "museum without walls" (André Malraux) presage larger tendencies in "mass culture" and "mid-cult" (Robert Warshaw, Dwight Macdonald), and point to "Voyager 1" (Carl Sagan), carrying the sounds of Bach, Beethoven, and Chuck Berry into the cosmic void. Closer at hand, media shape all our daily facts. These, in fact, dissolve into frames, events, "images" (Daniel Boorstin); or as in Watergate, they may vanish forever between public "mis-speakings" and private tapes. History itself is staged, more like a happening than a performance, before its own facts; the "politics of illusion" (Harold Rosenberg) prevail. From radio astronomy to the dispositions of our most secret heart, the immanence of media now effects the dispersal of the Logos.

f. *The Marriage of Earth and Sky.* Religion and science, myth and technology, intuition and reason, popular and high cultures, female and male archetypes (or stereotypes) begin to modify and inform one another; everywhere we may witness attempts to "cross the border, close the gap" (Leslie Fiedler). Beyond the "two cultures" (C. P. Snow, F. R. Leavis), beyond "mystics and mechanists" (William Irwin Thompson), beyond "arcadians and technophiles" (Ihab Hassan), lineaments of a new consciousness begin to emerge. Hence the un-"silent spring" of ecology (Rachel Carson), the "new alchemists" (John Todd and William McLarney), ideological or visionary "androgyny" (Carolyn Heilbrun, June Singer), the "Tao of physics" (Fritjof Capra), and perhaps even a "unitary sensibility" (Susan Sontag), calling for an epistemological shift in the order of our knowledge.

g. *The New Gnosticism, or the Dematerialization of Existence.* Here we encounter the most speculative stage in the dispersal of the Logos. Nature turns into "history" (Karl Marx), culture turns into "symbolic languages" (Lewis Mumford, Ernst Cassirer), and now languages begin to turn into "non-sensory communication" (José Delgado). This "gnostic tendency" (Ihab Hassan) assumes the increasing "etherealization" (Arnold Toynbee) or "ephemeralization" (Buckminster Fuller) or "conceptualization" (Ervin Laszlo) of existence. Mental constructs—Nietzsche would say "fictions"—become the primary resource of the earth;

they are our knowledge. Mind insists on encompassing more mind in itself, on apprehending more and more of reality im-mediately. In this, the physicist (Gerald Feinberg), the mystic (Teilhard de Chardin), and the fabulator (Olaf Stapledon, Arthur Clarke, Alfred Bester, Theodore Sturgeon, Ursula LeGuin, Samuel Delany, etc.) seem to be of one imagination compact. Yet we must ask: how problematic will this extension of consciousness prove, how demonic or simply illusory?

Throughout these seven themes, the play of indeterminacy and immanence may be constantly inferred, if not always heard or seen. But are these themes mere abstractions, figures in our own imaginary carpet? Not entirely so. I now return to the first of these themes, indeterminacy itself, to show how many versions of it our culture sustains in its optative, contingent, and manifold moods. Here are twelve versions of cultural indeterminacy, in the guise of a catalogue *déraisonné:*

Item: Society invites secession. Races, sexes, classes, languages, age groups make their claims and counter claims; values collide with values. Terrorism and totalitarianism, anarchy and bureaucracy, coexist. Between them, pluralism in America can still thrive. But Daniel Bell takes a gloomier view. Discord between the three realms of society—economy, polity, and culture—engender perilous contradictions. For Bell, "modernism is exhausted and the various kinds of post-modernism . . . are simply the decomposition of the self in an effort to erase individual ego." [*The Cultural Contradictions of Capitalism* (New York, 1976), 29.]

Item: In religion, both ecumenism and esotericism flourish. Zen Buddhism, Yoga, Tantrism, Hari-Krishna, Transcendental Meditation, the Arica and Naropa Institutes, Pythagoreanism, Sufism, Teilhardism, Kabalism, Hassidism, Gnosticism, Anthroposophy, Shamanism, Black and White Magic, Alchemy, Astrology, Spiritualism, Psychedelism, all besiege our shy souls. Churches admit women to the priesthood while Fundamentalists rage. Perhaps it is all summarized by David L. Miller, who quotes Nietzsche ("In polytheism man's free-thinking and many-sided thinking has a prototype set up: the power to create for himself new and individual eyes . . .") and who proclaims the joyous rebirth of many gods and goddesses. [*The New Polytheism* (New York, 1974), 1.]

Item: Gods and goddesses of the secular psyche are also reborn in their multitudes: Esalen, Gestalt Psychology, the Human Potential Movement, est. More significantly, Abraham Maslow probes the farther reaches of human nature; and James Hillman exposes the unitary myth of analysis, calling for a polytheistic psychology. Before them, we know, Norman O. Brown wrote poetically ("Everything is metaphor; there is only poetry") to free the body from the tyranny of genital organization, and to extol the openness of brokenness, though Brown also unfashionably assumed the oneness of all things: "To heal is to make whole." [*Love's Body* (New York, 1966), 266, 80.]

Item: Man's rage for chaos, Morse Peckham speculates, may be a biological mechanism meant to counter the social need to impose order and closure. "To use an old expression," he says, "the drive to order is also a drive to get stuck in the mud." Art serves to resist this tendency, offering itself as a playful and disjunctive means of adaptation. "Art is the exposure to the tensions and problems of a false [imaginary] world so that man may endure exposing himself to the tensions and problems of the real world." [*Man's Rage for Chaos* (Philadelphia and New York, 1965), xi, 314.]

Item: A philosopher of science, Paul Feyerabend, argues that "science is an essentially anarchistic enterprise: theoretical anarchism is more humanitarian and more likely to encourage progress than its law-and-order alternatives." Learned, lucid, and antic, Feyerabend thinks of himself as a neo-Dadaist "prepared to initiate joyful experiments even in those domains where change and experimentation seem to be out of the question." [*Against Method* (London, 1975), 17, 21.]

Item: Taking his cue from Leibniz, who believed that ours is only one among an infinitude of possible words, a mathematical prodigy of our times, Saul Kripke, has extended the boundaries of modal logic to distinguish between *kinds* of true statements in various "possible world semantics." Thus even the most formal modes of thought seem to entertain the optative mood; and mathematical logicians, like Kripke, challenge the orthodoxies of analytical philosophy. [Taylor Branch, "New Frontiers in American Philosophy," *New York Times Magazine,* 14 August 1966.]

Item: Originality in every field is now perceived as a tense tolerance of ambiguity, a tendency toward complexity and asymmetry. Frank Barron, who has devised many ingenious experiments for the study of creativity, notes: "Originality, then, flourishes where suspension [of disunity] is at a minimum and where some measure of disintegration is tolerable in the interests of a higher level of integration which may yet be reached." [*Creativity and Personal Freedom* (New York, 1968), 212.]

Item: In critical theory today, the central debate concerns the "limits of pluralism": the accent is on "the critic as innovator." [*Critical Inquiry* 3, nos. 3 & 4 (Spring and Summer 1977) and 4, no. 1 (Autumn 1977); and the *Chicago Review* 28, no. 3 (Winter 1977).] Psychoanalytic critics also speak of a "third phase" of analysis, which risks intimacy and incompleteness in order to restore individual interpretation. As Norman N. Holland put it: "There can be as many readings as there are readers to write them. Can be and should be." ["Literary Interpretation and the Three Phases of Psychoanalysis," *Critical Inquiry,* 3, no. 2 (Winter 1976), 233.] In general, antithetical critics, deconstructionists, critifictioneers, and paracritics (who shall all remain nameless) vie with one another in outrageousness while traditionalists glower and moderates wearily seek to reaffirm the "responsibilities" of criticism.

Item: In fact as in fiction, in society as in literature, fact and fiction jostle and blend; hence Capote's "non-fiction" novel, Styron's "meditation on history," Mailer's "history as biography," and the "new journalism" of Tom Wolfe, among countless others. This has led Mas'ud Zavarzadeh to theorize about a "fictual" genre which refuses "totalization," integration: "a zone of experience where the factual is not secure or unequivocal but seems preternaturally strange and eerie, and where the fictional seems not all that remote and alien, but bears uncanny resemblance to daily experiences." [*The Mythopoeic Reality* (Urbana, Ill., 1977), 56.]

Item: Nowadays, historians would rather serve Calliope than Clio. According to Hayden White, history is compounded of poetics and metaphysics: "The dominant tropological mode and its attendant linguistic protocol comprise the irreducibly 'metahistorical' basis of every historical work." [*Metahistory* (Baltimore, 1973), xi; see also Angus Fletcher, ed., *The Literature of Fact* (New York, 1976), and *New Literary History,* 8, no. 1 (Autumn 1976).] So much for the new rhetoricians of time.

Item: The rhetoricians of space are architects, and they too speak of new "languages" far removed from the austere style, sharp, and pure, and linear, of high modernism. Charles Jencks says this of postmodern architecture: "The present situation tolerates opposite approaches. . . . If there is a single direction, I prefer the reader will discover that it is pluralistic: the idea that an architect must master several styles and codes of communication and vary these to suit the particular culture for which he is designing. I have called this 'adhocism' in the past, and I use the term 'radical eclecticism' here." *The Language of Post-Modern Architecture* (New York and London, 1977), 7.] Indeed, as Jencks goes on to show, architecture has become witty edifices of various subcultures and "semiotic groups."

Item: Even semiotics, science of all signs, sign of our times, opens itself to the full ambiguities of social reality and recognizes the continual shifts of semantic fields within a culture. Such shifts, despite the regularity of linguistic codes, can become creative, altering the rules of the semiotic game. Indeed, Umberto Eco perceives the semiotic project itself under the aspect of a kind of indeterminacy. The project, he says, "will not be like exploring the sea, where a ship's wake disappears as soon as it has passed, but more exploring a forest where cart-trails or footprints do modify the explored landscape, so that the description the explorer gives of it must also take into account the ecological variations that he has produced." [Umberto Eco, *A Theory of Semiotics* (Bloomington, Ind., 1976), 29.]

No doubt, the variations of these cultural themes are countless, composed in our minds as the mind becomes part of what it comprehends. Some may seem vestiges of the Sixties, that prodigal decade now lost to us in its rhetoric and our own constraints. Yet in the end I believe indeterminacy to be neither a fashionable nor a factitious term but rather a decisive element in the new order of our knowledge. And on the other side of it lies immanence. This is vividly manifest in the arts.

Maieutic

Is there not as much control, manipulation, torture, in our world as there is choice or indeterminacy in it? And this conjunction of indeterminacy and immanence, was it not in the mind of the great Romantics as well? There is a celebrated letter of 21 December 1817 in which a young poet reflects: "and at once it struck me what quality went to form a Man of Achievement, especially in Literature. . . . I mean Negative Capability, that is, when a man is capable of being in uncertainties, mysteries, doubts, without irritable reaching after fact and reason." What, then, has changed since Keats's time?

Perhaps our sense of immanence has become at once more semiotic and more technological; and our sense of indeterminacy, no longer the possession of a few, has become almost a decree of our cultural consciences. What else can such current titles as The Age of Discontinuity, The Age of Uncertainty, The Age of Anxiety, *or* The De-Definition of Art *mean? Why else should Charles Olson, in his fumid essay on* The Special View of History, *claim that Negative Capability is "crucial to post-Modern man"?*

The ambiguities of Empson, the paradoxes of Brooks, once described the style of a mannerist literature from a modernist perspective. Do indeterminacy and immanence now suggest our very concepts of self and world, language and reality, from another (postmodernist) vantage?

VI. IN THE ARTS

Virginia Woolf knew exactly when human character changed and modernism began: "In or about December, 1910." I confess to a vaguer sense of beginnings. When did the arts of indetermanence start? Whenever that may have been, (postmodernism) in the arts is now widely viewed and reviewed, not only in avant-garde mag-

For instance: *Trema,* 1 (1976); *Amerikastudien,* 22, no. 1 (1977); *Kritikon Litterarum,* 2 (1973) and 5 (1976), which include essay reviews by Manfred Pütz

azines, but also in academic journals, both here and abroad.

Consider indeterminacy first: as in culture generally, indeterminacy in the arts has many guises. It may be called different things, from negative capability to parataxis. And it takes innumerable artistic forms: collages, montages, aleatory music, happenings, computer and topological art, earth art and body art, kinetic and process art, concept art, minimalism, concrete poetry, found objects and ready mades, auto-destructive sculpture, absurdist, uncanny, and fantastic modes, partial, discontinuous, decreative, ludic, or self-relexive forms of every kind, and many more. All these "arts" tend, by diverse means, to delay closures, frustrate expectations, promote abstractions, sustain a playful plurality of perspectives, and generally shift the grounds of meaning on their audiences.

and Hartwig Isernhagen respectively.

"But today we do, indeed, find ourselves in a period in which the primary quality of the 'men of achievement'—of a Beckett, a Robbe-Grillet, a Grass, a Burroughs, a Godard—appears to be a Negative Capability, for they represent, generally, a firm disinclination to transfigure or to try to subdue or resolve what is recalcitrantly indeterminate and ambiguous in the human scene of our time. . . . " Nathan A. Scott, Jr., *Negative Capability* (New Haven, 1969), xiv. John Cage is also crucial here.

*

On black humor and the "metaphysics of multiplicity": "This new Pyrrhonism I have called . . . radical sophistication." Max Schulz, *Radical Sophistication* (Athens, Ohio, 1969), viii.

*

"Antiformal imperatives of absurd time." William Spanos, *Existentialism* 2, p. 169.

*

"Chance as a supplement to necessity and necessity as the determinant of chance. Their interplay would be the game." Jacques Ehrmann, "Introduction: Games, Play, Literature," *Yale French Studies,* no. 41 (1968), 5.

*

On game theory and the systems approach to literature: "We call potential literature the research into forms, into new structures which can be utilized by writers as they wish." Raymond Queneau in *OULIPO* (Paris, 1973), 38.

*

"The change . . . is the sundering of art from artist—the complete and disciplined absence from the work of art as

we experience it of any qualities or patterns which were intended by the artist." Louis Mink, "Art without Artists," in Ihab Hassan, ed., *Liberations* (Middletown, Conn., 1971), 80.

*

"Modernism seems to stress the relationship between the creative sensibility and the work of art, between addresser and message, postmodernism that between message and addressee." Gerhard Hoffmann, Alfred Hornung, Rüdiger Kunow, " 'Modern,' 'Postmodern,' and 'Contemporary,' " *Amerikastudien,* 22, no. 1 (1977), 40.

*

"What the innovative artists and thinkers of this era have rebelled against is the very principle of a syntactically organized vision, the consciousness that requires the organization of reality into relationships of subordination and domination. . . . Paratactical conventions try to resist any impulse to the hierarchical arrangement of images and perceptions and, as the roots of the word parataxis indicate, sanction their 'arrangement together, side by side'."
And again:
"The paratactical style is an intrinsically *communal* style, rather than a *societal* one; it is inherently democratic and egalitarian rather than aristocratic and elitist, and it is possible that the rebirth of parataxis in art and thought in this century does not represent the fall back into myth or the advent of a new totalitarianism so much as the demand for a change of consciousness that will finally make a unified humanity possible."
Hayden White, "The Culture of Criticism," in *Liberations,* ed. Hassan, 67, 69.

Indeterminacy, then, has its own protocols and prepossessions in the arts. It favors paratactical styles; and, in the curious rhetoric of current

French criticism, it tends to valorize metonymy over metaphor, syntagmatic over paradigmatic modes, play over presence, child over parents in a "displaced parental space."

The crucial statement here is: "For the displacement of origins, of parents, the reliance on play rather than a hierarchy of symbolic meaning, the joyous acceptance of absence rather than a morose and negative theology, language our only 'seigneur,' not even language as code but language as play, as joy—all these attitudes amount to a demystifying phrase: nothing more than human." Michel Benamou, "Displacements of Parental Space: American Poetry and French Symbolism," *Boundary 2*, 5, no. 2 (Winter 1977), 483.

And for nearly everyone—which is always suspect—the crucial poetic unparents are: Stevens, Pound, Williams. Thus for Joseph Riddel, from Pater to Son is Paterson, or simply Language. *The Inverted Bell* (Baton Rouge, 1974), Ch. 1, esp. 83 ff.

At the far limit of indeterminacy, however, the figurative state of silence—variously expounded by George Steiner, Susan Sontag, and me—reigns. Silence begins as "experiment" in literature, its urge to question and contest itself; and it moves through self-parody and self-subversion, radical irony, to the edges of speech. There, on the dark margins of consciousness, literature wants to consume or transcend itself wholly—in vain. And precisely there, on the margins of silence, the dream of immanence teases literature, teases all art, back into waking. As in *Finnegans Wake.*

"*Finnegans Wake* intentionally opens itself to the free play of language. . . . How will we read this curious(ity shop) of signs that is also a museyroom, a public house, a dreamspace? . . . And what is *it* that We and Thou had out? That meaning is dialogic? That first- and second-person, text and reader, dissolve—as Shem and Shaun into HCE, Issy in ALP, and ALP finally into HCE—into one intersubjectivity reading itself endlessly, or into one intertextuality expanding perpetually: into all-read-I?" Charles Caramello, "Postface," in Michel Benamou and Charles Caramello, eds., *Performance in Postmodern Culture* (Madison, Wis., 1977), 222.

Immanence is indeed implicit in the farthest reaches of dispersal, the dispersal of signs, the extension of consciousness. It has become, quite unmetaphysically, the quality of all expanding semiotic systems, including literature. Concerning the latter, Charles Altieri has argued persuasively that Coleridge and Wordsworth presage the symbolist and immanentist modes respectively; and it is immanence now that constitutes the ground of (postmodern) poetics.

"Postmodern poets have been seeking to uncover the ways man and nature are unified, so that value can be seen as the result of immanent processes in which man is as much object as he is agent of creativity."
And:
"While incarnation for the moderns exemplified the union of form and significant value on an otherwise empty and chaotic natural world, God for the con-

temporaries [postmodernists] manifests itself as energy, as the intense expression of immanent power."
Finally:
Distrusting symbolism and hence mediation—"postmodern poetics are radically Protestant"—"the postmoderns seek to have the universal concretized, to see the particular as numinous, not as representative." Charles Altieri, "From Symbolist Thought to Immanence: The Ground of Postmodern American Poetics," *Boundary* 2, 1, no. 3 (Spring 1973), 608, 610, 611.

Yet the point could be stated generally to include the other (postmodern) arts. In a society increasingly oriented toward systems rather than objects, art must often utilize transparent elements of these systems; it must shape, alter, or simply make visible the flow of communicable experience. Thus it becomes the negentropy of informational schemes rather than masterpieces crafted for the ages.

"In other words, if we extend the meaning of software to cover the entire art information processing cycle, then art books, catalogs, interviews, reviews, advertisements, sales, and contracts are all software extensions of art, and as such legitimately embody the work of art. The art object is, in effect, an information 'trigger.' " Jack Burnham, *Great Western Salt Works* (New York, 1974), 28.

The conception of art as an immanent system or field betokens the crescive power of abstractions in every domain of culture, and once again recalls the overweening project: to generalize the condition of language

and of art till the
ment itself be-
mense signifier,
begins to speak.
kinds of art—say
art of Newton
rison or the ritual
pien and Michael
suous and even
become part of
a vaguely pan-
sonal, vision. In
hermetic and
proaches to art
congruent. Thus,
Hebrew letters of
vah, in Kabala,
staggering com-
human sign sys-
the laws of crea-
on Kabalistic,
chemical lore,
a startling case
between esoteric
works of Marcel
tic or furtive as
analogies seem,
champ's serene
admixture of in-
immanence, dis-
pervasive erotic-
focus of an "aes-
difference."

human environ-
comes an im-
till dumb matter
Yet in many
the ecological
and Helen Har-
art of Daryl Sa-
Hinton—sen-
sensual actions
a sacramental,
theist and imper-
still other cases,
systematic ap-
prove uncannily
for instance, the
the *Sepher Yetzi-*
constitute in their
binations all
tems as well as
tion. Drawing
gnostic, and al-
Burnham makes
for analogies
wisdom and the
Duchamp. Cryp-
some of these
they hint at Du-
enigma: a unique
determinacy and
junctive wit and
ism, held in the
thetics of in-

Coincidentally, Susan Sontag emphasizes the gnostic and Kabalistic influences on Artaud. See her *Antonin Artaud: Selected Writings* (New York, 1976), xiv–liii. Artaud and Duchamp, our precursors: two numinous artists, one convulsive, the other cool, masters of fragments, waiters upon the All.

"In essence, *The Large Glass* defines the means by which the powers of the Hebrew letters may be established whereas the Ready-mades use the powers of the letters in producing art yet to be made."
Also:
"Within the lore of cabalistic literature various permutations of the four elements represent *bound forms,* that is, they possess a mathematical and psychic cohesiveness that makes it impossible to separate or isolate the parts of language or artistic forms. . . .
Duchamp deals with this."
And:
"So in the hermetic scheme followed by Duchamp, the notion of feeling the presence of God in an icon is vastly infe-

rior to sensing the presence of God in everything—just as witnessing the presence of God in perspective is a degraded form of iconization."
Finally:
"Hence by using the principles of classification devised by the Cabalists, we find the Bride divided into various 'living substances.'

FIRE:	Art involving complementarity
AIR:	Art using indeterminacy
WATER:	Art employing causality or implication
EARTH:	Art concerned with the principles of true physical and spiritual orientation."

Burnham, *Great Western Salt Works,* 75, 79, 93, 115.

So much for Marchand du Sel, author of *Salt Seller,* who may or may not have known of the alchemical triangle, in which Salt rejoins Mercury and Sulphur—the volatile, dispersing principle and the fixed, indrawing principle—at the apex of androgynous wisdom. Yet how representative of our poetics can Duchamp, can the occult as system, really be?

"Many postmodern fictions serve as 'esoteric writing' waiting to be deciphered, as if in terms of an initiatory rite: to read them, we must have mastered Seeing, which in turn enables us to transcribe our reading on to the world-text." Campbell Tatham, "Mythotherapy and Postmodern Fictions," in *Performance,* 153.

*

"Beyond its direct portrayal of the mind-in-creation, Kabbalah offers both a model for the processes of poetic influence, and maps for the problematic pathways of interpretation. More audaciously than any developments in recent French criticism, Kabbalah is a theory of *writing,* but this is a theory that denies the absolute distinction between writing and inspired speech, even as it denies human distinctions between presence and absence." Harold Bloom, *Kabbalah and Criticism* (New York, 1975), 52.

If nothing else, our moment engenders too many metaphors and systems, and these may help us to escape enslavement by the system of another. I confess to a richer sympathy for Kabala than Deconstruction, though none is compelled to chose one or the other. But the larger point here is this: whatever our philosophic persuasion may be, and whatever our attitude to Duchamp, we may still observe how the arts of indetermanence trace both center and circumference in our culture, how they continually play between self-reflexiveness and self-surrender.

Some names, alphabetically: A. R. Ammons, David Antin, John Ashbery, John Barth, Donald Barthelme, Christine Brooke-Rose, John Cage, Christo, Merce Cunningham, Jasper Johns, Allan Kaprow, Robert Morris, Alwin Nikolais, Nam June Paik, Thomas Pynchon, Robert Rauschenberg, Michael Snow, Robert Wilson, Andy Warhol, LaMonte Young, etc.

Maieutic

Though the ironic geomancy of Duchamp cannot represent all our arts, let alone our culture in its various parts, his figure of the artist persists as a figura *in our midst. But now we may ask: is it not a mark of vexation or self-indulgence that we invoke science and the occult in such fits and starts?*

This is indeed the risk of indetermanence: it invites recuperation, cooptation by ideologies of every sort. At once underdefined and overextended, it may give to need or whimsy too great a scope. Yet need is also desire, a kind of hope. How shall we live with indetermanence, then, which is the epistemic equivalent of our violence, and still make of our disorders new knowledge?

VII. Human and Inconclusive

"Man is the measure of all things." "Many the wonders but nothing walks stranger than man." "What a piece of work is man." The human measure has not changed much since Protagoras and Sophocles and Shakespeare—and yet it has altogether changed.

Consider the simple idea of measure: a meter. Sealed in its vacuum glass case, the platinum-iridium meter at Sèvres has served for more than a century as the standard of length. Now the standard is a spectrum wave length of light, the orange-red line of Krypton 86. Here is dematerialization of a kind. But we need to reckon further with Duchamp's "canned chance": three lengths of string, one meter each, allowed to fall freely from a meter's height on strips of dark blue canvas, to which they are carefully glued. Thus Duchamp provides us with three versions of an ideal length; of if you prefer, with a "work of art" entitled *3 Standard Stoppages*, courtesy of the Katherine S. Dreier Bequest. Perhaps everything I have tried to say about indetermanence lurks here, around these meters made of metal, gas, and curling string.

Let me now move to end. We may be living in liminal times, at the threshold of changes in the human measure more profound than we imagine; or we may be simply living through the ordinary nightmare of history from which there is no awakening.

Arthur C. Clarke: "For the one fact about the future of which we can be certain is that it will be utterly fantastic." [*Profiles of the Future* (New York, 1972), xv.] Kenneth E. Boulding: "The twentieth century marks the middle period of a great transition in the state of the human race. It may properly be called the second great transition in the history of mankind." [*The Meaning of the Twentieth Century* (New York, 1965), 1.] N.B.: Clarke's and Boulding's works were first published in 1963 and 1964, respectively.

The openness of our time to time, its vulnerability to the future, has been noted by many authors, from futurologists like Alvin Toffler to poets like David Antin. Some, like Willis W. Harman of the Stanford Research Institute, go so far as to say: "As we grappled with the significance of contemporary revolutionary forces, we began to feel that the crucial gap is not between generations, nor between liberals and conservatives, but between those who anticipate a continuation of present trends and those who insist that a drastic change must occur." [*The Futurist* 11, no. 1 (February 1977), 8.]

Artists, though fewer in literature than in other arts, have also sensed this ending of a phase in Western history. This has led Leonard B. Meyer to say: "Man is no longer to be the measure of all things, the center of the universe . . . for these radical empiricists, *the Renaissance is over* . . . . Whether the Renaissance is over for the rest of us—for our culture generally—only the future will tell. But whether it is over or not, the merit of considering the art and aesthetic of radical empiricism seriously is that it challenges us to discover and make explicit the grounds for belief and values which we unconsciously take for granted." [*Music, the Arts, and Ideas* (Chicago, 1967), 83ff.] Meyer first published this essay in 1963; he saw then the indeterminacy, not the immanence.

But there is no doubt that rancorous afflictions are visited upon humanists across the nation, around the world. Whence these miseries? Others more informed than I on the sociology or economics of the Humanities may know the facts. I had it in mind only to note a certain cultural ethos, a certain epistemological shift, which I thought pertinent to the anxious order of our knowledge. I mean the order of indetermanence, a term finally no less uncouth than postmodernism itself, which I hoped to displace by a more precise token of our historical energies.

The cardinal question of course remains: how in practice to found a human or posthuman vision—call it inconclusively human—or an anxious order of knowledge? Predictably, I have no answer, though I have some urgent hunches and guesses. We may begin by acknowledging the realities of change if only to challenge them, remembering always that true challenges require self-exposure. We may also insist on a larger scope for our moral and intellectual ambitions. Humanists once prided themselves on taking the entire human universe, with all its wonder, cruelty, and crankiness, as province to their imagination. How many still do or can?

Walter Kaufmann: "In their serious work, scholastics prefer to address only those who agree with them on essentials. As a result we are losing a whole dimension of discourse." And: "Those who really wish to work on the frontiers of knowledge must cross the frontiers of their departments." [*The Future of the Humanities* (New York, 1977), 42, 43.]

Arthur Schopenhauer was more scornful: "He who holds a professorship may be said to receive his food in the stall; and this is the best way with ruminant animals"; then goes on to say: "It is precisely minds of the first order that will never be specialists. For their very nature is to make the whole of existence their problem. . . ." [*The Art of Literature* (Ann Arbor, Mich., 1960), 40, 42.]

Concomitantly, we may restore our sense of an audience, of a human *other* to which we address our speech, if only to transgress against expectations, if only to cry, "No, do not understand me too easily." This is to say that humanists may honor the responsive intelligence, and honor true style against jargon and babbling sophistication. At the same time, we may remain mindful, without brutalizing our own minds, of the imperatives of action in our lives, of the conflicting demands, say, of justice and freedom. What silent ideologies constitute the culture of indetermanence, and to what praxis or commitment are we then drawn? Finally, we may learn to dream.

What does it mean for humanists to dream? Perhaps it means to confess human desire and so transmute it into life's still uncreated forms. Grandiose dream! More modestly, it may mean to acknowledge imagination, the power of sympathy, acknowledge our own hope and gall. Yeats, we recall, rebuked the scholars: "Bald heads forgetful of their sins." But humanists are scholars and more than scholars: they know what turbulence it takes to make the spirit whole. Though knowledge is rightfully their primary call, humanists on a transhumanized earth may, like artists, mediate between culture and desire, history and hope. And who is there to say that in some penultimate scheme, the human urge to Know—so profound, mysterious, and possibly mad—may not be a version of what Gnostics long ago called Love?

4 Toward a Concept of Postmodernism

The strains of silence in literature, from Sade to Beckett, convey complexities of language, culture, and consciousness as these contest themselves and one another. Such eerie music may yield an experience, an intuition, of postmodernism but no concept or definition of it. Perhaps I can move here toward such a concept by putting forth certain queries. I begin with the most obvious: can we really perceive a phenomenon, in Western societies generally and in their literatures particularly, that needs to be distinguished from modernism, needs to be named? If so, will the provisional rubric "postmodernism" serve? Can we then—or even should we at this time—construct of this phenomenon some probative scheme, both chronological and typological, that may account for its various trends and counter-trends, its artistic, epistemic, and social character? And how would this phenomenon—let us call it postmodernism—relate itself to such earlier modes of change as turn-of-the-century avant-gardes or the high modernism of the twenties? Finally, what difficulties would inhere in any such act of definition, such a tentative heuristic scheme?

I am not certain that I can wholly satisfy my own questions, though I can assay some answers that may help to focus the larger problem. History, I take it, moves in measures both continuous and discontinuous. Thus the prevalence of postmodernism today, if indeed it prevails, does not suggest that ideas or institutions of the past cease to shape the present. Rather, traditions develop, and even types suffer a seachange. Certainly, the powerful cultural assumptions generated by, say, Darwin, Marx, Baudelaire, Nietzsche, Cézanne, Debussy, Freud, and Einstein still pervade the Western mind. Certainly those assumptions have been reconceived, not once but many times—else history would repeat itself, forever same. In this perspective postmodernism may appear as a significant revision, if not an original *épistémè,* of twentieth-century Western societies.

Some names, piled here pell-mell, may serve to adumbrate postmodernism, or at least suggest its range of assumptions: Jacques Derrida, Jean-François Lyotard (philosophy), Michel Foucault, Hayden White (history), Jacques Lacan, Gilles Deleuze, R. D. Laing, Norman O. Brown (psychoanalysis), Herbert Marcuse, Jean Baudrillard, Jürgen Habermas (political philosophy), Thomas Kuhn, Paul Feyerabend (philosophy of science), Roland Barthes, Julia Kristeva, Wolfgang Iser, the "Yale Critics" (literary theory), Merce Cunningham, Alwin Nikolais, Meredith Monk (dance), John Cage, Karlheinz Stockhausen, Pierre Boulez (music), Robert Rauschenberg, Jean Tinguely, Joseph Beuys (art), Robert Venturi, Charles Jencks, Brent Bolin (architecture), and various authors from Samuel Beckett, Eugène Ionesco, Jorge Luis Borges, Max Bense, and Vladimir Nabokov to Harold Pinter, B. S. Johnson, Rayner Heppenstall, Christine Brooke-Rose, Helmut Heissenbüttel, Jürgen Becker, Peter Handke, Thomas Bernhardt, Ernst Jandl, Gabriel García Márquez, Julio Cortázar, Alain Robbe-Grillet, Michel Butor, Maurice Roche, Philippe Sollers, and, in America, John Barth, William Burroughs, Thomas Pynchon, Donald Barthelme, Walter Abish, John Ashbery, David Antin, Sam Shepard, and Robert Wilson. Indubitably, these names are far too heterogenous to form a movement, paradigm, or school. Still, they may evoke a number of related cultural tendencies, a constellation of values, a repertoire of procedures and attitudes. These we call *postmodernism.*

Whence this term? Its origin remains uncertain, though we know that Federico de Onís used the word *postmodernismo* in his *Antología de la poesía española e hispanoamericana* (1882–1932), published in Madrid in 1934; and Dudley Fitts picked it up again in his *Anthology of Contemporary Latin-American Poetry* of 1942.[1] Both meant thus to indicate a minor reaction to modernism already latent within it, reverting to the early twentieth century. The term also appeared in Arnold Toynbee's *A Study of History* as early as D. C. Somervell's first-volume abridgement in 1947. For Toynbee, Post-Modernism designated a new historical cycle in Western civilization, starting around 1875, which we now scarcely begin to discern. Somewhat later, during the fifties, Charles Olson often spoke of postmodernism with more sweep than lapidary definition.

But prophets and poets enjoy an ample sense of time, which few literary scholars seem to afford. In 1959 and 1960, Irving Howe and Harry Levin wrote of postmodernism rather disconsolately as a falling off from the great modernist movement.[2] It remained for Leslie Fiedler and myself, among others, to employ the term during the sixties with premature approbation, and even with a touch of bravado.[3] Fiedler had it in mind to challenge the elitism of the high modernist tradition in the name of popular culture. I wanted to explore the impulse of self-unmaking which is part of the literary tradition of silence. Pop and silence, or mass culture and deconstruction, or Superman and Godot—or as I shall later argue, immanence and indeterminacy—may all be aspects of the postmodern universe. But all this must wait upon more patient analysis, longer history.

Yet the history of literary terms serves only to confirm the irrational genius of language. We come closer to the question of postmodernism itself by acknowledging the psychopolitics, if not the psychopathology, of academic life. Let us admit it: there is a will to power in nomenclature, as well as in people or texts. A new term opens for its proponents a space in language. A critical concept or system is a "poor" poem of the intellectual imagination. The battle of the books is also an ontic battle against death. That may be why Max Planck believed that one never manages to convince one's opponents—not even in theoretical physics!—one simply tries to outlive them. William James described the process in less morbid terms: novelties are first repudiated as nonsense, then declared obvious, then appropriated by former adversaries as their own discoveries.

I do not mean to take my stand with the postmoderns against the (ancient) moderns. In an age of frantic intellectual fashions, values can be too recklessly voided, and tomorrow can quickly preempt today or yesteryear. Nor is it merely a matter of fashions; for the sense of supervention may express some cultural urgency that partakes less of hope than fear. This much we recall: Lionel Trilling entitled one of his most thoughtful works *Beyond Culture* (1965); Kenneth Boulding argued that "postcivilization" is an essential part of *The Meaning of the 20th Century* (1964); and George Steiner could have subtitled his essay, *In Bluebeard's Castle* (1971), "Notes Toward the Definition of Postculture." Before them, Roderick Seidenberg published his *Post-Historic Man* exactly in mid-century; and most recently, I have myself speculated, in *The Right Promethean Fire* (1980), about the advent of a posthumanist era. As Daniel Bell put it: "It used to be that the great literary modifier was the word *beyond*. . . . But we seem to have exhausted the beyond, and today the sociological modifier is *post*."[4]

My point here is double: in the question of postmodernism, there is a will and counter-will to intellectual power, an imperial desire of the mind, but this will and desire are themselves caught in a historical moment of supervention, if not exactly of obsolescence. The reception or denial of postmodernism thus remains contingent on the psychopolitics of academic life—including the various dispositions of people and power in our universities, of critical factions and personal frictions, of boundaries that arbitrarily include or exclude—no less than on the imperatives of the culture at large. This much, reflexivity seems to demand from us at the start.

But reflection demands also that we address a number of conceptual problems that both conceal and constitute postmodernism itself. I shall try to isolate ten of these, commencing with the simpler, moving toward the more intractable.

1. The word postmodernism sounds not only awkward, uncouth; it evokes what it wishes to surpass or suppress, modernism itself. The term thus contains its enemy within, as the terms romanticism and classicism, baroque and rococo, do not. Moreover, it denotes temporal linearity and connotes belatedness, even decadence, to which no postmodernist would admit. But what better name have we to give this curious age? The Atomic, or Space, or Television, Age? These technological tags lack theoretical definition. Or shall we call it the Age of Indetermanence (indeterminacy + immanence) as I have half-antically proposed?[5] Or better still, shall we simply live and let others live to call us what they may?

2. Like other categorical terms—say poststructuralism, or modernism, or romanticism for that matter—postmodernism suffers from a certain *semantic* instability: that is, no clear consensus about its meaning exists among scholars. The general difficulty is compounded in this case by two factors: (a) the relative youth, indeed brash adolescence, of the term postmodernism, and (b) its semantic kinship to more current terms, themselves equally unstable. Thus some critics mean by postmodernism what others call avant-gardism or even neo-avant-gardism, while still others would call the same phenomenon simply modernism. This can make for inspired debates.[6]

3. A related difficulty concerns the *historical* instability of many literary concepts, their openness to change. Who, in this epoch of fierce misprisions, would dare to claim that romanticism is apprehended by Coleridge, Pater, Lovejoy, Abrams, Peckham, and Bloom in quite the same way? There is already some evidence that postmodernism, and modernism even more, are beginning to slip and slide in time, threatening to make any diacritical distinction between them desperate.[7] But perhaps the phenomenon, akin to Hubble's "red shift" in astronomy, may someday serve to measure the historical velocity of literary concepts.

4. Modernism and postmodernism are not separated by an Iron Curtain or Chinese Wall; for history is a palimpsest, and culture is permeable to time past, time present, and time future. We are all, I suspect, a little Victorian, Modern, and Postmodern, at once. And an author may, in his or her own life time, easily write both a modernist and postmodernist work. (Contrast Joyce's *Portrait of the Artist as a Young Man* with his *Finnegans Wake.*) More generally, on a certain level of narrative abstraction, modernism itself may be rightly assimilated to romanticism, romanticism related to the enlightenment, the latter to the renaissance, and so back, if not to the Olduvai Gorge, then certainly to ancient Greece.

5. This means that a "period," as I have already intimated, must be perceived in terms *both* of continuity *and* discontinuity, the two perspectives being complementary and partial. The Apollonian view, rangy and abstract, discerns only historical conjunctions; the Dionysian feeling, sensuous though nearly purblind, touches only the disjunctive moment. Thus postmodernism, by invoking two divinities at once, engages a double view. Sameness and difference, unity and rupture, filiation and revolt, all must be honored if we are to attend to history, apprehend (perceive, understand) change both as a spatial, mental structure and as a temporal, physical process, both as pattern and unique event.

6. Thus a "period" is generally not a period at all; it is rather both a diachronic and synchronic construct. Postmodernism, again like modernism or romanticism, is no exception; it requires *both* historical *and* theoretical definition. We would not seriously claim an inaugural "date" for it as Virginia Woolf pertly did for modernism, though we may sometimes woefully imagine that postmodernism began "in or about September, 1939." Thus we continually discover "antecedents" of postmodernism—in Sterne, Sade, Blake, Lautréamont, Rimbaud, Jarry,

Tzara, Hofmannsthal, Gertrude Stein, the later Joyce, the later Pound, Duchamp, Artaud, Roussel, Bataille, Broch, Queneau, and Kafka. What this really indicates is that we have created in our mind a model of postmodernism, a particular typology of culture and imagination, and have proceeded to "rediscover" the affinities of various authors and different moments with that model. We have, that is, reinvented our ancestors—and always shall. Consequently, "older" authors can be postmodern—Kafka, Beckett, Borges, Nabokov, Gombrowicz—while "younger" authors need not be so—Styron, Updike, Capote, Irving, Doctorow, Gardner.

7. As we have seen, any definition of postmodernism calls upon a fourfold vision of complementarities, embracing continuity and discontinuity, diachrony and synchrony. But a definition of the concept also requires a dialectical vision; for defining traits are often antithetical, and to ignore this tendency of historical reality is to lapse into single vision and Newton's sleep. Defining traits are dialectical and also plural; to elect a single trait as an absolute criterion of postmodern grace is to make of all other writers preterites.[8] Thus we can not simply rest—as I have sometimes done—on the assumption that postmodernism is antiformal, anarchic, or decreative; for though it is indeed all these, and despite its fanatic will to unmaking, it also contains the need to discover a "unitary sensibility" (Sontag), to "cross the border and close the gap" (Fiedler), and to attain, as I have suggested, an immanence of discourse, an expanded noetic intervention, a "neo-gnostic im-mediacy of mind."[9]

8. All this leads to the prior problem of periodization itself, which is also that of literary history conceived as a particular apprehension of change. Indeed, the concept of postmodernism implies some theory of innovation, renovation, novation, or simply change. But which one? Heraclitean? Viconian? Darwinian? Marxist? Freudian? Kuhnian? Derridean? Eclectic?[10] Or is a "theory of change" itself an oxymoron best suited to ideologues intolerant of the ambiguities of time? Should postmodernism, then, be left—at least for the moment—unconceptualized, a kind of literary-historical "difference" or "trace"?[11]

9. Postmodernism can expand into a still larger problem: is it only an artistic tendency or also a social phenomenon, perhaps even a mutation in Western humanism? If so, how are the various aspects of this phenomenon—psychological, philosophical, economic, political—joined or

disjoined? In short, can we understand postmodernism in literature without some attempt to perceive the lineaments of a postmodern society, a Toynbeean postmodernity, or future Foucauldian *épistémè,* of which the literary tendency I have been discussing is but a single, elitist strain?[12]

10. Finally, though not least vexing, is postmodernism an honorific term, used insidiously to valorize writers, however disparate, whom we otherwise esteem, to hail trends, however discordant, which we somehow approve? Or is it, on the contrary, a term of opprobrium and objurgation? In short, is postmodernism a descriptive as well as evaluative or normative category of literary thought? Or does it belong, as Charles Altieri notes, to that category of "essentially contested concepts" in philosophy that never wholly exhaust their constitutive confusions?[13]

No doubt, other conceptual problems lurk in the matter of postmodernism. Such problems, however, can not finally inhibit the intellectual imagination, the desire to apprehend our historical presence in noetic constructs that reveal our being to ourselves. I move, therefore, to propose a provisional scheme that the literature of silence, from Sade to Beckett, seems to envisage, and do so by distinguishing, tentatively, between three modes of artistic change in the last hundred years. I call these avant-garde, modern, and postmodern, though I realize that all three have conspired together to create that "tradition of the new" that, since Baudelaire, brought "into being an art whose history regardless of the credos of its practitioners, has consisted of leaps from vanguard to vanguard, and political mass movements whose aim has been the total renovation not only of social institutions but of man himself."[14]

By avant-garde, I mean those movements that agitated the earlier part of our century, including 'Pataphysics, Cubism, Futurism, Dadaism, Surrealism, Suprematism, Constructivism, Merzism, de Stijl—some of which I have already discussed in this work. Anarchic, these assaulted the bourgeoisie with their art, their manifestoes, their antics. But their activism could also turn inward, becoming suicidal—as happened later to some postmodernists like Rudolf Schwartzkogler. Once full of brio and bravura, these movements have all but vanished now, leaving only their story, at once fugacious and exemplary. Modernism, however, proved more stable, aloof, hieratic, like the French Symbolism from which it derived; even its experiments now seem olympian. Enacted by such "individual talents" as Valéry, Proust, and Gide, the early Joyce,

Yeats, and Lawrence, Rilke, Mann, and Musil, the early Pound, Eliot, and Faulkner, it commanded high authority, leading Delmore Schwartz to chant in *Shenandoah:* "Let us consider where the great men are / Who will obsess the child when he can read. . . ." But if much of modernism appears hieratic, hypotactical, and formalist, postmodernism strikes us by contrast as playful, paratactical, and deconstructionist. In this it recalls the irreverent spirit of the avant-garde, and so carries sometimes the label of neo-avant-garde. Yet postmodernism remains "cooler," in McLuhan's sense, than older vanguards—cooler, less cliquish, and far less aversive to the pop, electronic society of which it is a part, and so hospitable to kitsch.

Can we distinguish postmodernism further? Perhaps certain schematic differences from modernism will provide a start:

↕	↔
Modernism	Postmodernism
Romanticism/Symbolism	'Pataphysics/Dadaism
Form (conjunctive, closed)	Antiform (disjunctive, open)
Purpose	Play
Design	Chance
Hierarchy	Anarchy
Mastery/Logos	Exhaustion/Silence
Art Object/Finished Work	Process/Performance/Happening
Distance	Participation
Creation/Totalization	Decreation/Deconstruction
Synthesis	Antithesis
Presence	Absence
Centering	Dispersal
Genre/Boundary	Text/Intertext
Semantics	Rhetoric
Paradigm	Syntagm
Hypotaxis	Parataxis
Metaphor	Metonymy
Selection	Combination
Root/Depth	Rhizome/Surface
Interpretation/Reading	Against Interpretation/Misreading
Signified	Signifier
Lisible (Readerly)	*Scriptible* (Writerly)
Narrative/*Grande Histoire*	Anti-narrative/*Petite Histoire*
Master Code	Idiolect
Symptom	Desire
Type	Mutant
Genital/Phallic	Polymorphous/Androgynous

Paranoia	Schizophrenia
Origin/Cause	Difference-Differance/Trace
God the Father	The Holy Ghost
Metaphysics	Irony
Determinacy	Indeterminacy
Transcendence	Immanence

The preceding table draws on ideas in many fields—rhetoric, linguistics, literary theory, philosophy, anthropology, psychoanalysis, political science, even theology—and draws on many authors—European and American—aligned with diverse movements, groups, and views. Yet the dichotomies this table represents remain insecure, equivocal. For differences shift, defer, even collapse; concepts in any one vertical column are not all equivalent; and inversions and exceptions, in both modernism and postmodernism, abound. Still, I would submit that rubrics in the right column point to the postmodern tendency, the tendency of indetermanence, and so may bring us closer to its historical and theoretical definition.

The time has come, however, to explain a little that neologism: "indetermanence." I have used that term to designate two central, constitutive tendencies in postmodernism: one of indeterminacy, the other of immanence. The two tendencies are not dialectical; for they are not exactly antithetical; nor do they lead to a synthesis. Each contains its own contradictions, and alludes to elements of the other. Their interplay suggests the action of a "polylectic," pervading postmodernism. Since I have discussed this topic at some length earlier, I can advert to it here briefly.[15]

By indeterminacy, or better still, *indeterminacies,* I mean a complex referent that these diverse concepts help to delineate: ambiguity, discontinuity, heterodoxy, pluralism, randomness, revolt, perversion, deformation. The latter alone subsumes a dozen current terms of unmaking: decreation, disintegration, deconstruction, decenterment, displacement, difference, discontinuity, disjunction, disappearance, decomposition, de-definition, demystification, detotalization, delegitimization—let alone more technical terms referring to the rhetoric of irony, rupture, silence. Through all these signs moves a vast will to unmaking, affecting the body politic, the body cognitive, the erotic body, the individual psyche—the entire realm of discourse in the West. In literature alone our ideas of author, audience, reading, writing, book, genre, critical theory, and of literature itself, have all suddenly become questionable. And in criticism? Roland Barthes speaks of literature as "loss," "perversion," "dissolution"; Wolfgang Iser formulates a theory of reading based on textual "blanks"; Paul de Man conceives rhetoric—that is, literature—as a force that "radically suspends logic and opens up vertiginous possibilities of referential aberration"; and Geoffrey Hartman affirms that "contemporary criticism aims at the hermeneutics of indeterminacy."[16]

Such uncertain diffractions make for vast dispersals. Thus I call the second major tendency of postmodernism *immanences,* a term that I employ without religious echo to designate the capacity of mind to generalize iself in symbols, intervene more and more into nature, act upon itself through its own abstractions and so become, increasingly, im-mediately, its own environment. This noetic tendency may be evoked further by such sundry concepts as diffusion, dissemination, pulsion, interplay, communication, interdependence, which all derive from the emergence of human beings as language animals, *homo pictor* or *homo significans,* gnostic creatures constituting themselves, and determinedly their universe, by symbols of their own making. Is "this not the sign that the whole of this configuration is about to topple, and that man is in the process of perishing as the being of language continues to shine ever brighter upon our horizon?" Foucault famously asks.[17] Meanwhile, the public world dissolves as fact and fiction blend, history becomes derealized by media into a happening, science takes its own models as the only accessible reality, cybernetics confronts us with the enigma of artificial intelligence, and technologies project our perceptions to the edge of the receding universe or into the ghostly interstices of matter.[18] Everywhere—even deep in Lacan's "lettered unconscious," more dense than a black hole in space—everywhere we encounter that immanence called Language, with all its literary ambiguities, epistemic conundrums, and political distractions.[19]

No doubt these tendencies may seem less rife in England, say, than in America or France where the term postmodernism, reversing the recent direction of poststructuralist flow, has now come into use.[20] But the fact in most developed societies remains: as an artistic, philosophical, and social phenomenon, postmodernism veers toward open, playful, optative, provisional (open in time as well as in structure or space), disjunctive, or indeterminate forms, a discourse of ironies and fragments, a "white ideology" of absences and fractures, a desire of diffractions, an invocation of complex, articulate silences. Postmodernism veers towards all these yet implies a different, if not antithetical, movement toward pervasive procedures, ubiquitous interactions, immanent codes, media, languages. Thus our earth seems caught in the process of planetization, transhumanization, even as it breaks up into sects, tribes, factions of every kind. Thus, too, terrorism and totalitarianism, schism and ecumenism, summon one another, and authorities decreate themselves even as societies search for new grounds of authority. One may well wonder: is some decisive historical mutation—involving art and science, high and low culture, the male and female principles, parts and wholes, involving the One and the Many as pre-Socratics used to say—active in our midst? Or does the dismemberment of Orpheus prove no more than the mind's need to make but one more construction of life's mutabilities and human mortality?

And what construction lies beyond, behind, within, that construction?

1. For the best history of the term *postmodernism* see Michael Köhler, " 'Postmodernismus': Ein begriffsgeschichtlicher Überblick," *Amerikastudien,* vol. 22, no. 1 (1977). That same issue contains other excellent discussions and bibliographies on the term; see particularly Gerhard Hoffmann, Alfred Hornung, and Rüdiger Kunow, " 'Modern,' 'Postmodern,' and 'Contemporary' as Criteria for the Analysis of 20th Century Literature."

2. Irving Howe, "Mass Society and Postmodern Fiction," *Partisan Review,* vol. 26, no. 3 (Summer 1959), reprinted in his *Decline of the New* (New York, 1970), 190–207; and Harry Levin, "What Was Modernism?", *Massachusetts Review,* vol. 1, no. 4 (August 1960), reprinted in *Refractions* (New York, 1966), 271–295.

3. Leslie Fiedler, "The New Mutants," *Partisan Review,* vol. 32, no. 4 (Fall 1965), reprinted in his *Collected Essays,* vol. 2 (New York, 1971), 379–400; and Ihab Hassan, "Frontiers of Criticism: Metaphors of Silence," *Virginia Quarterly,* vol. 46, no. 1 (Winter 1970). In earlier essays I had also used the term "anti-literature" and "the literature of silence" in a proximate sense; see, for instance, Ihab Hassan, "The Literature of Silence," *Encounter,* vol. 28, no. 1 (January 1967), and pp. 3–22 above.

4. Daniel Bell, *The Coming of Post-Industrial Society* (New York, 1973), 53.

5. See pp. 46–83 above.

6. Matei Calinescu, for instance, tends to assimilate "postmodern" to "neo-avant-garde" and sometimes to "avant-garde," in *Faces of Modernity: Avant-Garde, Decadence, Kitsch* (Bloomington, 1977), though later he discriminates be-

tween these terms thoughtfully, in "Avant-Garde, Neo-Avant-Garde, and Postmodernism," unpublished manuscript. Miklos Szabolcsi would identify "modern" with "avant-garde" and call "postmodern" the "neo-avant-garde," in "Avant-Garde, Neo-Avant-Garde, Modernism: Questions and Suggestions," *New Literary History,* vol. 3, no. 1 (Autumn 1971); while Paul de Man would call "modern" the innovative element, the perpetual "moment of crisis" in the literature of every period, in "Literary History and Literary Modernity," in *Blindness and Insight* (New York, 1971), chapter 8; in a similar vein, William V. Spanos employs the term "postmodernism" to indicate "not fundamentally a chronological event, but rather a permanent mode of human understanding," in "De-Struction and the Question of Postmodern Literature: Towards a Definition," *Par Rapport,* vol. 2, no. 2 (Summer 1979), 107. And even John Barth, as inward as any writer with postmodernism, now argues that postmodernism is a synthesis yet to come, and what we had assumed to be postmodernism all along was only late modernism, in "The Literature of Replenishment: Postmodernist Fiction," *Atlantic Monthly* 245, no. 1 (January 1980).

7. In my own earlier and later essays on the subject I can discern such a slight shift. See "POSTmodernISM," pp. 25–45 above, "Joyce, Beckett, and the Postmodern Imagination," *TriQuarterly* 34 (Fall 1975), and "Culture, Indeterminacy, and Immanence," pp. 46–83 above.

8. Though some critics have argued that postmodernism is primarily "temporal" and others that it is mainly "spatial," it is in the particular relation between these single categories that postmodernism probably reveals itself. See the two seemingly contradictory views of William V. Spanos, "The Detective at the Boundary," in *Existentialism* 2, ed. William V. Spanos (New York, 1976), 163–89; and Jürgen Peper, "Postmodernismus: Unitary Sensibility," *Amerikastudien,* vol. 22, no. 1 (1977).

9. Susan Sontag, "One Culture and the New Sensibility," in *Against Interpretation* (New York, 1967), 293–304; Leslie Fiedler, "Cross the Border—Close the Gap," in *Collected Essays,* vol. 2 (New York, 1971), 461–85; and Ihab Hassan, "The New Gnosticism," *Paracriticisms: Seven Speculations of the Times* (Urbana, 1975), chapter 6.

10. For some views of this, see Ihab Hassan and Sally Hassan, eds., *Innovation/Renovation: Recent Trends and Reconceptions in Western Culture* (Madison, Wis., 1983).

11. At stake here is the idea of literary periodicity, challenged by current French thought. For other views of literary and historical change, including "hierarchic organization" of time, see Leonard Meyer, *Music, the Arts, and Ideas* (Chicago, 1967), 93, 102; Calinescu, *Faces of Modernity,* 147ff; Ralph Cohen, "Innovation and Variation: Literary Change and Georgic Poetry," in Ralph Cohen and Murray Krieger, *Literature and History* (Los Angeles, 1974); and my *Paracriticisms,* chapter 7. A harder question is one Geoffrey Hartman asks: "With so much historical knowledge, how can we avoid historicism, or the staging of history as a drama in which epiphanic raptures are replaced by epistemic ruptures?" Or, again, how can we "formulate a theory of reading that would be historical rather than historicist"? *Saving the Text: Literature/Derrida/Philosophy* (Baltimore, 1981), xx.

12. Writers as different as Marshall McLuhan and Leslie Fiedler have explored the media and pop aspects of postmodernism for two decades, though their ef-

forts are now out of fashion in some critical circles. The difference between postmodernism, as a contemporary artistic tendency, and postmodernity, as a cultural phenomenon, perhaps even an era of history, is discussed by Richard E. Palmer in "Postmodernity and Hermeneutics," *Boundary* 2, vol. 5, no. 2 (Winter 1977).

13. Charles Altieri, "Postmodernism: A Question of Definition," *Par Rapport,* vol. 2, no. 2 (Summer 1979), 90. This leads Altieri to conclude: "The best one can do who believes himself post-modern . . . is to articulate spaces of mind in which the confusions can not paralyze because one enjoys the energies and glimpses of our condition which they produce," p. 99.

14. Harold Rosenberg, *The Tradition of the New* (New York, 1961), 9.

15. See pp. 65–72 above. Also, my "Innovation/Renovation: Toward a Cultural Theory of Change," *Innovation/Renovation,* chapter 1.

16. See, for instance, Roland Barthes and Maurice Nadeau, *Sur la littérature* (Paris, 1980), 7, 16, 19f., 41; Wolfgang Iser, *The Act of Reading* (Baltimore, 1978), *passim;* Paul de Man, *Allegories of Reading* (New Haven, Conn., 1979), 10; and Geoffrey H. Hartman, *Criticism in the Wilderness* (New Haven, 1980), 41.

17. Michel Foucault, *The Order of Things* (New York, 1970), 386.

18. "Just as Pascal sought to throw dice with God . . . so do the decisions theorists, and the new intellectual technology, seek their own *tableau entier*—the compass of rationality itself," Daniel Bell remarks in "Technology, Nature, and Society," in *Technology and the Frontiers of Knowledge* (Garden City, 1975), 53. See also the more acute analysis of *"l'informatique"* by Jean-François Lyotard, *La Condition postmoderne* (Paris, 1979), *passim.*

19. This tendency also makes for the abstract, conceptual, and irrealist character of so much postmodern art. See Suzi Gablik, *Progress in Art* (New York, 1977), whose argument was prefigured by Ortega y Gasset, *The Dehumanization of Art* (Princeton, 1968). Note also that Ortega presaged the gnostic or noetic tendency to which I refer here in 1925: "Man humanizes the world, injects it, impregnates it with his own ideal substance and is finally entitled to imagine that one day or another, in the far depths of time, this terrible outer world will become so saturated with man that our descendants will be able to travel through it as today we mentally travel through our own inmost selves—he finally imagines that the world, without ceasing to be like the world, will one day be changed into something like a materialized soul, and, as in Shakespeare's *Tempest,* the winds will blow at the bidding of Ariel, the spirit of ideas," p. 184.

20. Though postmodernism and poststructuralism can not be identified, they clearly reveal many affinities. Thus in the course of one brief essay, Julia Kristeva comments on both immanence and indeterminacy in terms of her own: "postmodernism is that literature which writes itself with the more or less conscious intention of expanding the signifiable, and thus human, realm"; and again: "At this degree of singularity, we are faced with idiolects, proliferating uncontrollably." Julia Kristeva, "Postmodernism?" in *Romanticism, Modernism, Postmodernism,* ed. Harry R. Garvin (Lewisburg, Pa., 1980), 137, 141.

Part III Postmodern Literature and Criticism

5 (   ): *Finnegans Wake* and the Postmodern Imagination

Preamble

I have no title, only a phrase held together by an ambitious conjunction. The phrase is an invitation to place this most outrageous of books, this parodic myth of all myths, this endless sound of language and its echolalias—I mean *Finnegans Wake*—help place it in the field of our consciousness.

The invitation is collective, which gives me leave to wander and license to digress within the limits of my time and everyone's patience. There are several questions that I hope to raise, and several, no doubt, that will arise, unbidden, troublesome, spontaneous. But all my own questions finally come to one:

> How does *Finnegans Wake* accord
> with, how does it make itself avail-
> able to, the postmodern imagination?

Obviously, to argue the question is not to prove influences but rather to speculate on concordances.

I confess it from the start: I am no deep reader of that book. I lack the cryptogrammatic sensibility that rejoices in "The keys to. Given" (628.15). I have little to say that will illumine its puns and patterns, its susurrus and sources. Yet I am convinced that the work stands as a monstrous prophecy that we have begun to discover (thanks to many deep readers) but have not yet decided how to heed.

Admittedly, Joyce was a man of many superstitions; repeatedly, he told Stuart Gilbert that the *Wake* included "premonitions of incidents that subsequently took place." But Joyce was not only superstitious; he was also increasingly vatic. He was Stephen and he was Dedalus; he became both Bloom and Ulysses; and his Penelope remained Nora as well as Flaubert. Yet in the end, in *Finnegans Wake*, Joyce glimpsed the great mystery beyond the Pillars of Hercules. Once again, the question returns: what is there for us to see in that Joycean vision beyond the seas?

Let me now end this preamble with a brief note on method. I want to present seven perspectives of the central question. Against these thematic perspectives, I will permit myself a counterpoint made of postmodern rumors and random reflections, through which the mind may pause or run. Fittingly, I close with a personal postamble.

COUNTERPOINT

In my notes I have found these admonitions to myself: "Avoid puns and portmanteaus; leave Joyce to his imitative forms. Resist the temptation to quote from your 1969 Dublin Scenario; the 'Missisliffi' flows backwards only by moonlight. Quote, however, all the Joyceans present in the 1973 symposium—if possible." But these are only intentions. True gaiety in form surprises itself.

Perspective I: A Death Book and Book of Life

The book is more determinedly cyclical than Vico and the very seasons of the unforgetting earth: "The seim anew" (215.22). This sometimes obscures for us the depth of its deathly hue. The *Wake* is not only Joyce's "funferall," designed "for that ideal reader suffering from an ideal insomnia"; it is itself a presentiment of ends. "*Finnegans Wake* will be my last book," Joyce said. "There is nothing left for me to do but die." Coincidentally, this book of night appears in 1939, when night descends on the world.

For humanist readers, for children of reason and history and a bourgeois social order, that is, for most of us, the unspoken intimation of this novel must be death of the self, death of the old reader himself. I must return to this topic later; here I only wish to signal the secret threat of the *Wake.* Make no mistake: this book of universals avers our mortality. Oliver Gogarty, who was so often and so interestingly wrong about Joyce—because he was in some perverse way right—says about the *Wake*: "To me it is like a shattered cathedral through the ruins of which, buried deep and muted under the debris, the organ still sounds with all its stops pulled out at once." Only Père Ubu, I suppose, went further: one must also destroy the ruins, he cried.

For the reader who happens also to be a writer, *Finnegans Wake* offers the aspect of a labyrinth with all its ends seemingly dead. We know the resistance that the book encountered. It was not only Alfred Noyes, Arnold Bennett, H. G. Wells, G. B. Shaw, Desmond McCarthy, Sean O'Faolain, and Oliver Gogarty who expressed their grave discomforts with the work; it was also, and more viciously, such modernists as Gertrude Stein and Wyndham Lewis. Even supporters balked. Mary Colum thought that *Finnegans Wake* would remain "outside literature," and Harriet Weaver grumbled about the "Wholesale Safety Pun Factory," and like a good English governess, scolded Joyce: "It seems to me you are wasting your genius."

Is *Finnegans Wake* outside of literature? Or is it pointing the way for literature to go beyond itself? Or, again, is it a prophecy of the end of literature as we have come to know it? These three questions are really the same question I have asked from the start. And I would answer all three: YES. That is why I call *Finnegans Wake* not only a death book but also a book of life, not simply an end but a progress as well.

COUNTERPOINT

A progress toward what? A new vision of universal consciousness?

How express my distaste, my desperation, my strange allegiance—all provoked by this book? Once, scholars and savants—Ernst Robert Curtius and Carl Gustav Jung, for example—understood Joyce little and liked him less. And now, without understanding Finnegans Wake *a great deal more, men turn to the book like sunflowers to a secret sun.*

Take Norman O. Brown or Marshall McLuhan or Michel Butor—or take Theodore Roszak and William Irwin Thompson, more pert and trendy still—all have something to say about the Wake. *Here is Brown: "Darkness at noon. A progressive darkening of the everyday world of common sense.* Finnegans Wake. *Second sight is the dark night."[1] Here is McLuhan: "*Finnegans Wake *. . . is a verbal universe in which press, movie, radio, TV merge with the languages of the world to form a Feenichts Playhouse or metamorphoses." And Butor?*

He calls the Wake *the greatest single effort to transcend language by means of itself.*

Whether we think with modernist Northrop Frye that the work is the "chief ironic epic of our time" or think with various post-modernists—Butor, McLuhan, Brown—this or that, the work still stands, like a word ziggurat, teasing our sense of human possibilities. Yes, more than A la Recherche du temps perdu, The Sound and the Fury, Der Zauberberg, Women in Love, *and even* Das Schloss.

Yet, how many ever read Finnegans Wake? *Ah, Mr. Wilder, though you say some works permeate the culture unread, the question still nags, and nags.*

Perspective II: High Art, Popular Culture, and Beyond

The *Portrait* depicts the Artist alone; *Ulysses* presents the Artist seeking Everyman to be atoned; and *Finnegans Wake* gives "Allmen." That, at least, is a plausible view of the work of James Augustine Joyce. And here is the paradox that gives credence to this view: Joyce was among the most autobiographical of artists and the most impersonal, the most self-obsessed and also the most dramatically universal. There is really no paradox at all: he simply pushed his subjective will so far that it became superfluous to distinguish between subject and object, self and world. Like a Berkeleyan god, he hoped to create the universe in his mind-languages, all but abolishing God's original book. Paul Léon put it another way: "Continuous self-confession, for Joyce, meant continuous creation." There is a willed unity in Joyce's art and life. And it is precisely this willed unity of the outcast mind that compels us to review the categories not only of self and world but also of high art and popular culture as they apply to Joyce.

We all know that none possessed a brow higher than "Sunny Twimjim" (211.07). "The demand that I make of my reader is that he should devote his whole life to reading my works," he said, and though he said it smiling, he repeated it to make a bad joke deadly earnest. Thus the ascetics of high art. Twelve hundred hours spent on the composition of "Anna Livia Plurabelle" justified some mortification on the reader's part. Herbert Read easily concludes: "Mr. Joyce is the high priest of modern literature precisely because literature is a priesthood and has a sanctuary more inaccessible than the monasteries of Thibet." But there is another side to this picture: the face of Joyce on the cover of *Time* magazine. With infinitely more cunning than silence in his exile, Joyce succeeded in making *Finnegans Wake* the most famous of unread books.

Preposterous as it may seem to us, Joyce also believed that the *Wake* could appeal to a wide and varied audience, believed that his "Big Language" could win the common as well as the uncommon reader. And why not? The book, after all, abounds in wit and sentimentality, in folklore, ribaldry, and song; the sounds of music hall, the pub, and the street crackle in its pages. The bizarre, the lowly, the gushy, the factual, the obscene—all crowd into his later work, hodge-podge, mish-mash, hurly-burly, pell-mell, together with the purest poesy. In the end the distance between the sublime and the ridiculous is contracted into a pun and expanded into endless parody. Pop, which Leslie Fiedler identifies with postmodern, is never far from the edge of *Finnegans Wake.*

But the affinity of this book with popular culture is still more complex. When Joyce said to Jolas: "This book is being written by the people I have met or known," he was not suddenly overcome by modesty. The book of "Allmen" needs, in theory at least, a collective author. It requires also a communal reader. What else can a "Joyce industry" produce but such a reader? J. Mitchell Morse puts it more pleasantly: "Reading *Finnegans Wake* is a collective enterprise of no ordinary kind: what takes place is no mere quantitative gathering and mechanical assembling of parts into larger units, but a blending of objective and subjective elements—a kind of communion—in which one person's information calls from another's subconscious an inference that validates the conjecture of a third. Joyce has revived the magical function of the old bards and shamans in what by convention we consider a most unlikely place, the seminar room."

Perhaps the seminar room is as close as most of us come to popular culture; or perhaps the seminar without walls will become itself the culture of a "deschooled society." The point I want to make is simply this: *Finnegans Wake* carries the tendencies of high art and of popular culture to their outer limits, there where all tendencies of mind may meet, there where the epiphany and the dirty joke become one. If this still be elitism, it is elitism of a special kind.

COUNTERPOINT

I wonder if Fendant de Sion will be provided at the banquet for Joyceans. "The Archduchess" at dinner?

I wonder, too, about "dreck." In Snow White *Donald Barthelme says: "We like books that have a lot of dreck in them, matter which presents itself as not wholly relevant (or indeed, at all relevant) but which, carefully attended to, can supply a kind of 'sense' of what is going on." Is* Finnegans Wake *full of magical dreck? Does the refuse of an old consciousness remake itself into bricks of the new?*

There are other matters. Assume for the moment that the Wake *challenges the modernist idea of high art and in some ways prefigures the postmodernist idea of pop culture. Not only because of its mixed tone (after all, "Lil's husband got demobbed" earlier), not only because of its slapstick and obscenity, but also because of its myth of a collective mind in which the author himself must disappear as privileged person.*

No, I am not speaking of "impersonality" as Hulme, Eliot, or Pound spoke of it; I am thinking of the "death of the author" as Roland Barthes thinks of it. Barthes, that cool and canny semiotician, may seem an odd ally of Pop; but let us hear him anyway: "Once the Author is gone, the claim to 'decipher' a text becomes quite useless. To give an Author to a text is to impose upon the text a stop clause, to furnish it with a final signification, to close *the writing." For Barthes, then—and here Morse unwittingly joins him—the true locus of writing is reading. Thus, "a text consists of multiple writings, issuing from several cultures and entering into dialogue with each other, into parody, into contestation; but there is one place where this multiplicity is collected, united, and this place is not the author, as we have hitherto said it was, but the reader. . . ."*

What text could celebrate the "death" of the author and the "birth" of a new reader better than Finnegans Wake? *Ultimately, in another kind of literature perhaps, may not author and reader become true coevals? But for the time being, have we not witnessed the advent of a youthful reader, not Pop but its parody, a lexical player, amorous in* Ada, *agile in* Giles Goat-Boy, *skipping weightlessly in* Gravity's Rainbow?

Perspective III: Dream and Play (and Later Structure)

The disorder of dreams, the purposelessness of play, the cunning of structure seem contradictory; yet it is on that contradiction that *Finnegans Wake* balances itself.

Actually, the balance is less miraculous than managed, a supreme act of prestidigitation. For as a dream book, the *Wake* is an effort of huge wakefulness. The comedy and wit of the work, which remind Arland Ussher of "the delicious absurdities of a Marx Brothers film," are intensely conscious of themselves. Whether Joyce ever dreamt or not, we must recognize that his words constitute a metalanguage, not a dream. Certainly the work obsessed him: "Since 1922," he says, "my book has been a greater reality for me than reality. Everything gives way to it." Obsession makes for hyperconsciousness. "What about the mystery of consciousness?" Joyce asked Budgen. "What do they know of that?" The dream element in *Finnegans Wake,* then, seen from the point of view of its author, is simply his freedom: his freedom to alter language and reality. The dream is literary fantasy. We are "whenabouts in the name of space?" (558.33).

COUNTERPOINT

Michel Butor suggests that Finnegans Wake *is not the description of a dream but a "machine for provoking and helping the reader himself to dream." Or rather, helping the reader to* play. *Play is the vice and joy of postmodernism; play is fatuousness but also fantasy.*

Think of all our fantasists and geomancers: Beckett, Barth, Bernhardt, Burgess, Becker, Barthelme, Butor, Blanchot, Burroughs, Brautigan, Borges, Bichsel, Nabokov. Ronald Sukenick, himself one, speaks of still later writers as dancers of the Bossa Nova: "Needless to say the Bossa Nova has no plot, no story, no character, no chronological sequence, no verisimilitude, no imitation, no allegory, no symbolism, no subject matter, no 'meaning.' "

But that's not Finnegans Wake, *we all want to cry. Yet it is an ablation of the Wake; it is the* Wake *deprived of its paranoiac intentionality; it is the* Wake *without work, the surface as grimace, comedy as absurd and precise play. Whether or not he meant it to be so, when God became the Dreamer, everything became possible.*

Perspective III: Continued

Dream, then, becomes game, an exercise in fantasy and number. Above all, dream and play provide the invisible latticework of comedy. Someday, someone may devise a theory of comedy based entirely on *Finnegans Wake.* She (or he) may refer to the work of Hugh Kenner and Vivian Mercier on this zany subject; consider the goliardic, macaronic, parodic, satiric, and all other comic traditions; consult philosophers of every kind; ponder the statement of Karl Marx about history repeating itself, the first time as tragedy, the second as farce; and perhaps finally pray: "Loud, heap miseries upon us yet entwine our arts with laughters low!" (259.07). For myself, I simply want to note that comedy links dream, game, and structure in the *Wake,* that it objectifies dream and democratizes structure while relieving game from the logic of banality. From the smallest pun to the largest parodic pattern, comedy asserts its power, not only to amuse or even to surprise us, but far more to multiply meanings, to compound complexities. In this book comedy is the tuning fork of language, vibrating in a vacuum, forever.

BRIEF COUNTERPOINT

Vacuum. Exactly!

Some would call the infinite vibrations of comedy nihilism. The parody of a parody of a parody that was once comedy. Eternity as absurd recurrence. No evaluation, no value. Is that what "The Gracehoper . . . always jigging ajog, hoppy on akkant of his joyicity" (414.22) has done to the novel?

Still, what major postmodern fiction is conceived but in the comic mode? And who are its ancestors but Joyce and Kafka? Unless it be that obscure man, Raymond Roussel?

( )

Perspective IV: Structure

What can I possibly add to this subject, except perhaps to suggest that all good structuralists go to *Finnegans Wake* on their way to heaven, and that is perhaps why they are so long in reaching their destination?

We know that the novel is both structurally overdetermined and semantically underdefined. Its structural principles include numbers, symbols, leitmotifs, collages, montages, mythic patterns, simulated dreams, mystic correspondences, musical ratios, multiple and receding perspectives, game theories, parodies, puns, alliterations, and much else in the lexicon of classical rhetoric. Yet *Finnegans Wake* is not only supremely aware of itself as structure; it is also aware of the more obscure need to de-structure itself. "Samuel Beckett has remarked that to Joyce reality was a paradigm, an illustration of a possibly unstatable rule. Yet perhaps the rule can be surmised," Ellmann says. "It is not a perception of order or of love; more humble than either of these, it is the perception of *coincidence* [italics mine]."

Now coincidence as a structural principle means both identity and accident, recurrence and divergence. Coincidence implies the frightening disorder that every fanatic order itself implies. Four legs of a horse, four seasons, four evangelists. Is this the coincidence of secret design or of dementia in reality? To the very end, Joyce seems to have qualified his emergent vision of correspondences by his ineluctable irony. The more mystical he became—or is it merely superstitious?—the more ruthless his self-parody. His great Dedalian labor includes a deep instinct of unmaking.

Thus, on the one hand, *Finnegans Wake* acknowledges the totality of Joyce's artifice and effort. The ending of Book 4, for instance, may be read to include the endings of all his other works; and various passages of the *Wake* recapitulate the design of the whole novel. But the structure of the novel also reflects upon itself, and in so doing heightens its fictitiousness. The shady character of Shem the Penman, the pervasive motif of the Letter, the reflexive references to Joyce, the wry comments on the manuscript of the novel itself, its progress and reception—"Your exagmination round his factification for incamination of a warping process" (496.36)—all these are instances of artifice recognizing its own artificiality. Thus, on the other hand, *Finnegans Wake* accepts the gratuitousness of every creative act. Indeed, as we shall see, Joyce identified creation with original sin, the most necessary and gratuitous of all acts.

COUNTERPOINT

Shem the Penman, "Sniffer of carrion, premature gravedigger, seeker of the nest of evil in the bosom of a good word" (189.28), Shem, Cain, Satan, Nick and Glugg, Ishmael, Set, Taff and Mutt, Iago, Romeo, Bottom and Puck, Stephen Dedalus, James Joyce, "still today insufficiently malestimated notesnatcher" (125.21), "nay, condemned fool, anarch, egoarch, hiresiarch, you have reared your disunited kingdom on the vacuum of your most intensely doubtful soul" (188.15).

Ah, we say, here is a Portrait of the Artist as Nasty Man. But this artist, Shem Joyce, creates peculiarly postmodern forms and here is why:

a. Parodic Reflexiveness. *The novel that parodies and reflects upon its own structure is not new. Gide's* Les Faux-Monnayeurs *(1925) and Gombrowicz'* Ferdydurke *(1937), for instance, antecede the* Wake *in this, as does* Tristram Shandy *(1760–1767). But the genre, with its multiple, fractured, and ambiguous perspectives, becomes current only after the war in such diverse works as Nabokov's* Pale Fire, *Cortazar's* Hopscotch, *Borges'* Ficciones, *Genet's* Journal d'un voleur, *Beckett's* How It Is, *and Barth's* Lost in the Fun House.

b. The Re-creation of Reality. *The conventional ideas of time, place, character, plot are shattered; reality is re-created. In modernist literature this is sometimes achieved by a quasi-cubist breakdown of surfaces, as in the works of Gertrude Stein or Alfred Döblin; at other times it is achieved by dissolving surfaces, absorbing them into an interior language, as in the works of Proust or Faulkner. The first method appears quasi-objective, the second quasi-subjective; yet both remake reality in words. Joyce masters both these methods. In that sense* Finnegans Wake *clears the way for both "neo-realist" and "surrealist" fictions—for Robbe-Grillet's* La Jalousie *and Butor's* Mobile *on the one hand, and Hawkes's* The Cannibal *and Wurlitzer's* Nog *on the other. In either case the re-creation of reality requires us to abandon the distinction between objective and subjective catego-*

ries within the pervasive fantasy of the work. Fact and fiction acquire the same aspect. This, too, is postmodern: Capote's "non-fiction novel," In Cold Blood; *Styron's "meditation on history,"* The Confessions of Nat Turner; *Mailer's "history as a novel, the novel as history,"* Armies of the Night; *even the New Journalism in America—all these perceive, however partially, that from a certain vantage, fact and fiction must blur. The enormous volume of the World is matched by even greater expansions of language until reality becomes a declaration of the Word.*

c. Nonlinear Form. *Circular, simultaneous, coincident—a mesh or mosaic or montage or Moebius time strip of motifs—that, too, is* Finnegans Wake. *We think of myth, music, the kabala, and electrical systems as prototypes of the nonlinear structure of the book, creating a perception that exists outside of conventional time and space. It is not only that time is spatialized as Joseph Frank has argued about the modern novel; in this work both time and space are fantasticated. By rejecting linear or discursive logic, by simulating dream, the* Wake *maintains itself in the "pressant" time and unlimited space of mind. Speaking of Marc Saporta's so-called "shuffle novel,"* Composition No. 1, *Sharon Spencer makes this pertinent point: "Saporta's narrative procedure takes from the dream a rationale for dissolving the conventional distinctions between memory (the past), desire (implying the future), and fantasy (suggesting present being) and for substituting a timeless and preeminently visual mode of organization." Though it appears idiosyncratic, Saporta's work shares with most postmodern fiction the assumption of nonlinear form, which is always visual and inevitably auditory but, above all, seeks to engage the mind directly.*

d. The Problematics of the Book. *Technologies have altered the nature of the book. From Marshall McLuhan to Michel Butor, writers have reflected upon this question; and in* The Stoic Comedians, *Kenner has specifically noted the uses that Joyce made of movable type. It is plain for everyone to see:* Finnegans Wake *employs footnotes, marginalia, lists, sketches, and a variety of types, and it defies sequential reading from cover to cover. More than other works, it is a mixed medium, both discontinuous and whole, visual and auditory, poetic and narrative. Some features of its format may recall the figures of Döblin's* Alexanderplatz Berlin, *the captions of Dos Passos'* U.S.A., *the blanks of Mallarmé's* Un Coup de dés*—may even recall* Gargantua et Pantagruel *or* The Book of Kells. *The same typographic features preview the experiments of John Cage, Ronald Sukenick, Donald Barthelme, Raymond Federman, and Eugene Wildman, to mention only some American postmodernists. But typography is not the real issue; the old concept of the book is at stake. "Throughout* Finnegans Wake,*" McLuhan says, "Joyce plays some of his major variation on this theme of 'abcedmindedness'. . . . His 'verbivocovisual' presentation of an 'all nights newsery reel' is the first dramatization of the very media of communication as both form and vehicle of the flux of human cultures." One cannot help but wonder: what will the next verbisensual process of communication in our culture be?*

Perspective V: Eroticism

The eroticism of *Finnegans Wake* is inclusive as its life, varied as its language; yet it remains peculiarly Joycean. Margaret Solomon perceives sex as "Joyce's cosmic joke": "Taking upon himself the role of a God engrossed in sex—and using all the religious myths and symbols of creation to perpetuate his joke—was one way of using his jesuitical training in an act of defiance." But the *Wake* also goes beyond defiance, and the permutations of sex in it are, unlike Beckett's, both sacred and satiric.

The novel offers a non-Euclidean geometry of sex, as Ms. Solomon shows. People stand for genitals, and diagrams stand for people. Creativity is associated with both waste and generation. There are many entries and exits in nature, and many sensuous sides to every question. As above, so below; as in the beginning, so in the end. But as Fritz Senn notes: "The ups and downs and ins and outs are as erotic as they are political" in Joyce's night-book. The book contains everything Eros and Ellis and Kraft-Ebbing ever dreamed: romantic love, narcissism, coprophilia, incest, sodomy, onanism, lesbianism, voyeurism, exhibitionism, sadomasochism, impotence, every so-called perversion—not to mention the *osculum ad anum diaboli* of the Black Mass—as well as the fruitful love of HCE and ALP: "The galleonman jovial on his bucky brown nightmare. Bigrob dignagging his lylyputana. One to one bore one!" (583.08).

That is the mystery of love in the novel: the one coming from the many, the many becoming one again. The final point is not perversion but at-one-ment. Thus the composite sexuality of various characters, their male and female "bisectualism," which permits even Mohammed, Shakespeare, and Napoleon to invert their sex. Thus, too, the composite unity of the Earwicker family, which identifies father with sons, mother with daughter, and all with their incestuous counterparts. The sexual fall of Humpty Dumpty signals the eternal metamorphosis of word and flesh, seeking wholeness. Yet Darcy O'Brien says that affection and sensuality are rarely united in Joyce's life or work. Can it be so because final unity is always and wholly impersonal?

COUNTERPOINT

Eroticism in the postmodern age—there are plenty of dirty books now, dirty movies and dirty pictures—imagine Judge Woolsey at a screening of "Deep Throat."

But let us do our age justice.

Consider Norman O. Brown and Norman Mailer—Esalen Institute and Kinsey Institute—Grove Press and Oympia Press—Women's Lib and Gay Liberation—the Pill, Playboy, Penthouse, *Portnoy, Pornotopia, and Pornopolitics—all express the dim desire to connect—express the desire and its failure—orgasm as program and sex as solipsism or ideology—yet a new erotic will persists in seeking larger configurations of itself—the death of the family (David Cooper) and the search for androgyny (Carolyn Heilbrun)—a new tribalism, a new polymorphousness and perversity—isn't* Finnegans Wake *relevant?*

Certainly, but with a difference—it, too, affirms larger configurations of love—a love, however, closer to myth and mutability than to will and ideology—a love closer still to language—sex as the language of fantasy—"Psing a Psalm of psexpeans, apocryphul of rhyme" (242.30)—the sex speech of postmodern fiction?

Perspective VI: The Language of Babel

"Although it uses the syntax of other languages," Strother Purdy says of *Finnegan's Wake,* "it cannot be considered to be written in . . . the speech of any group." One wonders: Did Joyce seek to recover the unity of human speech before God said, looking down on the Tower of Babel: "Go to, let us go down, and there confound their language, that they may not understand one another's speech"? Frank Budgen remembers that Joyce once claimed to have discovered the secret of Babel; but Budgen never asked and we shall never know.

We can guess. Joyce senses that if reality can be identified with language, language can be identified with itself. This is not to deny his decreative fury in the *Wake,* his will to silence natural speech, tear asunder the mother's tongue. But Joyce's fury seeks "words" that can become im-mediately pure meaning. Harrowing 29 (?) of the world's languages, he also creates a metalanguage from the chaos of the world's phonemes, fusing the Viconian modes of hieroglyph, metaphor, and abstraction.

Joyce, we know, also employs puns, stutters, riddles, seemingly to arrest the mind in discontinuities. But his puns become metonymies; the stutters stress recurrence; and even riddles conceal a unity at the incestuous heart of the universe. However much he owed to the Jabberwocky of Lewis Carroll, Joyce's own language is less often analytic than synthetic. His "sentence" is a word in which syntax gives way to phonemic cluster. From the clear sentences of the earliest drafts to the packed, layered interpolations of the last, the process of Joyce's composition reveals a vast effort of syncretism in which all the elements of *Finnegans Wake* take part. When Biddy the Hen pecked out the Letter from the midden heap of time, she may have discovered the original language of Babel on a soiled palimpsest. "Lead, kindly fowl!" (112.09).

COUNTERPOINT

There is another way of putting it. Finnegans Wake *is "a kind of Logos of the Einsteinian vision of the universe," William Troy wrote in the review that Joyce liked best. But the novel is also "associated with scriptures and sacred books, and treats life in terms of the fall and awakening of the human soul and the creation and apocalypse of nature," Northrop Frye has said. Can we then conclude that in the language of this work the old gnostic and the new technological dream meet, the dream of unifying mind and nature, science and myth, into a single truth—beyond matter?*

I cannot answer. But I am aware that the postmodern endeavor in literature acknowledges that words have severed themselves from things, that language now can only refer to language. And what book, or rather what language, calls attention to itself as language, as ineluctably verbal and quite finally so, more than Finnegans Wake? *John Fletcher understands the influence of Joyce even on the most secretive stylist: "What Beckett really learnt from Joyce was the importance of words and how to make them perform in exercises irrelevant to their superficial meaning but faithful to their essence."*

The word has become essence indeed, essence or energy, subject to continuous change, yet indestructible and compact like that single book in Borges' "The Library of Babel" which contains all books, past, present, and future, in its infinitesimally thin pages.

Perspective VII: Toward Universal Consciousness

As I draw to a close, my theme becomes more obvious: *Finnegans Wake* aspires to the conditions of a universal consciousness. Consider its design.

Item: Vico says: "Individuality is the concretion of universality, and every individual action is at the same time superindividual"; so it is for Joyce, for whom no character is bound by this time or that place.

Item: Characters are subject to a constant process of recurrence, metempsychosis, and superimposition; and opposites—Shem and Shaun, HCE and ALP—become the other.

Item: The actual and the possible, the historical and the fabulous, have equal validity in eternity; in this gnostic view, Joyce follows Bruno; fact and fiction fuse.

Item: In a world of simultaneity, cause and effect coincide; eternity and the instant merge in the Perpetual Now, as in mystic doctrines; sequence becomes synchronicity.

Item: Joyce chose the night world; as death is the great equalizer so is sister sleep; and in our dreams we exchange all the symbols of the race, without miserliness or shame.

Item: Whoever the Dreamer or Narrator may be, he is All; yet Bernard Benstock is also right: "On the creative level it is Joyce himself giving form to what he has experienced and learned and understood (in the same way in which the Demiurge, creating the universe, dreams away its cycles of evolution)."

Item: The creative process, like the Holy Ghost, invades and unifies all media; television and telepathy, the famous Letter and spirit writing, film and shadows in Plato's cave, copulation and language, become one.

Item: The book wants to include everything; it is not an encyclopedia but a true universe; and through its correspondences of microcosm with macrocosm, it wants to become *the* universe.

The strategies of unification in the novel are as numerous as they have grown familiar. Yet I think many of us have allowed Joyce's demon, called Parody, to obscure this possibility: that the language of *Finnegans Wake* strains toward a gnostic truth. There is a sense in which the totality of the book, its effort toward a universal consciousness, fails to parody or subvert itself, fails to ironicize itself.

James S. Atherton: "Joyce does not deny the existence of sensible material objects. . . . But Berkeley's view of Laws of Nature which he describes in *Siris* as being: 'applied and determined by an Infinite Mind in the macrocosm of universe, with unlimited power and according to stated rules—as it is in the microcosm with limited power and skill by the human mind,' seems to me to be a possible source for the entire structure of the *Wake.*"

William Troy: "Humanity is impressive not in its actuality but in its immanence. And this becomes something comparable to the conception of the Divine Idea of the medieval theologians—that which is capable of taking on matter but is itself infinite in time and space."

COUNTERPOINT

"Be that as it may, but for that light phantastic of his gnose's glow as it slid lucifericiously within an inch of its page . . ." (182.04), the postmodern writer might have been like others who have preceded him.

The germ of the new gnosticism invades the word-flesh of literature. It is not only William Burroughs who sees the word as a "virus" attacking our damaged "central nervous system," preventing us from enjoying "non-body experience." Less extreme in their utterances, perhaps, other postmodern authors, both of science and unscientific fiction, want to dissolve the given world, absorb its intractable and conditioned elements, into a vision, dream, or afflatus that may render even language redundant. Whether they are minimalists like Beckett and Borges or maximalists like Nabokov and Pynchon, one feels that they strain toward a region of articulate silence, of intelligent noise, fantasy-filled. This region, which I have too often attempted to explore, rings, as Susan Sontag says, with "an energetic secular blasphemy, the wish to attain the unfettered, unselective, total consciousness of 'God.' "

Is that not the cry of Finnegans Wake?

Postamble

"Traduced into jinglish janglage" (275.n6), *Finnegans Wake,* I repeat, stands as a monstrous prophecy of our postmodernity. In so many particular ways this seems to me so. But is that prophecy not ultimately hollow? The query leads to others, and that may be the way to end.

All my questions about Joyce, all my qualms really, seem to revert to his peculiar sense of Creation—I mean the creation of life, of people and stars and flowers. God created the world, and that, Joyce believed, was the original sin; for the creative act is always crooked. This flaw is in all generation, in sex as well as artifice. Thus Joyce could never see sex without the hidden taint and excitement of error. And suddenly I find myself wondering: did the lapsarian irony of this sensualist sometimes turn into final despair and thus turn into a kind of malice? In fact, how much malice lies in the mocking multiplicity of *Finnegans Wake,* and how much delight in the fullness of being? Adaline Glasheen refers to the "good-tempered nihilism" of the novel. Does the epithet also apply to the Joyce who wrote: "And from time to time I lie back and listen to my hair growing white . . ."?

Above all, why could Joyce never leave Dublin behind? Never, never, never, never, never. Whence this obsessive Imagination of Repetition? "mememormee," "mememormee" is the wail on the last page of "Finn, again!" Did Joyce really ever conceive a difference between birth and rebirth, occurrence and recurrence? And is not creation flawed precisely insofar as memory hovers over our copulation and lies in wait for the child as its *given* name?

These questions are perhaps too personal, and may seem too harshly put. Criticism, I know, has its own brand of malice, which I am not eager to display. Nor do I wish to disparage Joyce, who scarcely needs to be praised as a great novelist, among the very greatest to this day. The pilgrimages we all make to these symposia—Joyceans, crypto-Joyceans, meta-Joyceans, and para-Joyceans like myself—are often made in search of learning, sodality, and romance. Still, are they not all begun and concluded in his name?

Yet having emphasized the prophetic sense of Joyce's master riddle, part of me cries (yes, it is the cry of some exorbitant hope akin to pride): Human destiny may be larger than this vast, retrograde, and reversible riddle implies.

Movingly, Hélène Cixous writes: "After Bloom, the deluge, but Joyce had already prepared *Finnegans Wake* as an ark to contain all human myths and types; the world, in its blind lust to seek its own destruction, could wipe itself out, for *Finnegans Wake* had saved its symbols, its notations, and its cultural patterns."

Is this enough for the largest effort of the imagination in our time? Unabashedly, I would ask not only to save the heavy ark, nor only to seek the rainbow sign in the sky, but even to become the very matter of which all rainbows are made. Or perhaps more: NEW LIGHT. . . .

1. Brown's *Closing Time* (1973) appeared after the writing of this essay.

6 The Critic as Innovator: A Paracritical Strip in X Frames

Frame One

We have already begun. Invisible frames form our transactions as we read or think or dream in the verbal space of these pages. In *Frame Analysis* Erving Goffman concerns himself with "realms of being," "codes of behavior," "constitutive rules," "worlds of make-believe"; he attends minutely to various "figures within frames" as these frames slip or shift or break:

> I start with the fact that from an individual's point of view, while one thing may momentarily appear to be what is going on, in fact what is actually happening is plainly a joke, or a dream, or an accident, or a mistake, or a misunderstanding, or a deception, or a theatrical performance, and so forth.

"What is really happening," then, is itself a function of frames, which are a kind of fiction. As Goffman concludes: "Life may not be an imitation of art, but ordinary conduct . . . is an imitation of the properties, a gesture at the exemplary forms, and the primal realization of these ideals belongs more to make-believe than to reality."

Our situation "in this time and place" thus is framed; the subject, criticism, is itself framed; and so is my own discourse, which will proceed in a series of frames broken by montages. These montages are superimpositions, or perhaps merely impositions, and they tend to be digressive, questioning, and rather ill-humored. But as my verbal strip moves, it slips, revealing interframes. I call these embarrassing flashes *slippage.*

Frame and Montage and Slippage: three modes of this strip, three tracks in a carping tape. It is all done in the hope of bringing inadmissible evidence into partial evidence.

Here comes the first Slippage.

SLIPPAGE

He recalls an exhibit of Renaissance picture frames at the Alte Pinakothek in Munich. The frames were empty, hung against white walls; elsewhere in the museum, the masterpieces of Altdorfer, Grünewald, and Dürer, of Breughel and Rembrandt, hung in their plenitude. He sensed that the museum had now become the frame of frames. And the frame of the museum? Finally, of course, the Universe.

But the Universe was an unspeakable fiction—a "thing" turned into fiction precisely in order to be spoken. Did framing and its opposite, deconstruction, then turn everything into fiction?

He refuses the thought. Desire and Death, he needs to assume, are "literal." Else the Universe is but a trope on the Void. This goes against something in him.

Frame Two

In his celebrated work, *The Structure of Scientific Revolutions,* Thomas S. Kuhn argues that scientists tend to operate within a "consensus of research," which he calls a paradigm. Paradigms are not impervious to private or public influences: "An apparently arbitrary element, compounded of personal and historical accident, is always a formative ingredient of the beliefs espoused by a given scientific community at a given time," Kuhn admits. Nonetheless, scientific paradigms do take hold, organizing both theory and experiment, until an intolerable crisis in both compels scientists—or at least the most alert and inventive among them—to discard one paradigm for another. Paradigms are thus enabling structures. But these enabling structures also constrain; their enemies are anomalies, "*unexpected* novelty," genuine surprise.

Kuhn's argument is rather more complex; he was later to distinguish between *kinds* of paradigms and to call the most comprehensive a "disciplinary matrix." Still, even a naïve outline can underscore certain differences between the organization and development of knowledge in the sciences and in the humanities. For in the latter, the equivalent of a scientific paradigm seems to be a *school.* Now competing schools do sometimes exist in the sciences, but only in "pre-paradigmatic" periods, before a paradigm reigns. In the humanities schools are less the exception than the rule. "If we doubt, as many do," Kuhn says, "that nonscientific fields make progress . . . it must be because there are always competing schools, *each of which constantly questions the very foundations of the others.* The man who argues that philosophy, for example, has made no progress emphasizes that there are still Aristotelians, not that Aristotelianism has failed to progress" (my italics). This is but another way of saying that scientists and humanists adopt very different views of their past. "Scientific education," Kuhn continues, "makes use of no equivalent for the art museum or library of classics, and the result is sometimes a drastic distortion in the scientist's perception of his discipline's past."

Applied to the humanities, Kuhn's ideas probably need a rest. But there are others, more sensitive to our enterprise, who also doubt the authority of paradigms in our indisciplines. Here is Victor Turner speaking very much to the point in *Dramas, Fields, and Metaphors:*

> The result of confrontation between monolithic, power-supported programs and their many subversive alternatives is a socio-cultural "field" in which many options are provided. . . . As my colleague Harold Rosenberg . . . has often argued, the culture of any society at any moment is more like the debris, or "fall-out," of past ideological systems, than it is itself a system, a coherent whole. Coherent wholes may exist . . . but human social groups tend to find their openness to the future in the variety of their metaphors for what may be the good life and in the contest of their paradigms.

To exchange "paradigms" for "schools" or "fields," then, is to exchange a *largely* epistemological view of a discipline for another that more freely admits history and desire. Indeed, the latter may have more to do with the principles and prejudices of Criticism than we ever confess.

Three points follow from this discourse so far:

a. Acceptability in criticism depends on our conscious or semi-conscious, hyperconscious or unconscious, loyalty to a critical school, including the Eclectic School. There are no dominant paradigms in the humanities; there are only some vague areas of "tacit knowledge" (Polanyi), which are becoming vaguer and fewer. Consequently, nothing I say here can possibly "invalidate" or render "obsolete" other critical persuasions. (Historical Scholars, Formalists, Marxists, Freudians, Jungians, Structuralists, Semioticians, Speech Actors—please relax.)

b. Fields, schools, and frames in the humanities lack military and, alas, economic power to back them, and so share a certain insecurity. Thus they pretend to ignore what disconfirms them. In truth, we work (read, write, teach) among breaking and intersecting frames. Thus we are all open to each other's discomforts—not to say animadversions.

c. More specifically, the absence of a sovereign paradigm in criticism makes innovation easier and more doubtful than in the sciences. For us, there are fewer constraints; there are also fewer enabling structures. We enjoy a certain "weightlessness"—and suffer from it. Such is the burden of our Freedom in this postmodern moment of unmakings.

Montage

Some animadversions on the literary situation:

1. American foundations have been generous to the Humanities. But what is their long-range impact on the American mind? Do they inhibit innovation or encourage it? Dedicated all to "excellence," do they not tend to define it in traditional terms, and so reward conventional work? These and more searching questions may be particularly pertinent to the National Endowment for the Humanities, which dispenses large governmental grants.

2. American universities often seem more open, their society more fluid, than their European counterparts. Why, then, do avant-garde trends in criticism originate in Europe rather than in America? And why do avant-garde critics meet with less suspicion there than in our universities?

3. Why does the reviewer of the year's work in literary criticism, writing in The New Republic *of 25 September 1975, mention an article by a Yale colleague—it* was *an important article—yet overlook a major work by George Steiner,* After Babel, *which is of distinct relevance to the literary culture? Yet do plasma physicists, say, pretending to honor scientific paradigms, really behave differently?*

4. Certain magazines are very much in the critical news today. For instance, New Literary History, Critical Inquiry, Yale French Studies, Diacritics, Glyph, Salmagundi, *etc. They also happen to be quite fine. Yet do such congregations of talent contribute not only to the intensity but also to the constriction of critical discourse, and seduce critics into mannerisms of language and thought? For a small example: in certain quarters,* aufhebung *is now translated as "elation." For a larger instance: critical discourse now centers obsessively on a few names—Marx, French Nietzsche, French Freud, Heidegger, Derrida. Is there some benefit in decentering the circles of our intellectual reference? What about, say, Emerson or William James?*

Frame Three

The preponderance of schools in the humanities is an awkward condition of critical innovation. But there are others: for instance, the coincidence of critical and poetic talent in the same person. The classics of criticism, as the truism goes, were most often composed by poets: Sidney, Dryden, Pope, Wordsworth, Coleridge, Shelley, Poe, Eliot, to mention only those writing in English. Yet rarely have these authors illumined the relation between analysis and poesis in a manner that satisfies our modern sense of the creative process. Coleridge and Valéry, perhaps, remain among the exceptions to this cavil. Eliot in *The Sacred Wood,* however, only adds to our perplexity when he says about Swinburne, "This gives us an intimation why the artist is—each within his own limitations—oftenest to be depended upon as a critic; his criticism will be criticism, and not the satisfaction of a suppressed creative wish—which, in most persons, is apt to interfere fatally"—and then proceeds to demolish Swinburne, in his following essay, as too imperfect a critic.

I suspect that the issue of the poet as critic will remain problematic until we know more about the physiology of the human brain and the phenomenology of the creative process. The question, however, becomes more manageable if we formulate it thus: to what degree, and precisely in what epistemological sense, is all criticism a fiction? Far from shocking us, this formulation has a historic claim on our attention.

The claim was most cleverly advanced by Oscar Wilde at the turn of the century. Surprisingly, Wilde has been rehabilitated. Richard Ellmann has edited his essays, in *The Artist as Critic;* Lionel Trilling has referred to his ideas, in *Sincerity and Authenticity;* and current critics brightly associate him with an even more fashionable figure: Nietzsche, not the philosopher of Becoming but the darling and deconstructing dandy of poststructuralist thought. All this does not obscure Wilde's faults. His coyness distracts; his oxymorons can become tedious; his aphorisms sometimes pall. But the man had satiric genius, and perhaps even a darker, deeper genius within his gaiety.

Frame within Frame

With America's Bicentennial still in mind, I offer this Wilde passage:

> "The crude commercialism of America, its materialising spirit, its indifference to the poetical side of things, and its lack of imagination and of high unattainable ideals, are entirely due to that country having adopted for its national hero a man, who according to his own confession, was incapable of telling a lie, and it is not too much to say that the story of George Washington and the cherry-tree has done more harm, and in a shorter space of time, than any other moral tale in the whole of literature."

The passage is from "The Decay of Lying," first published in 1889. Wilde could not have known about Cambodia, Watergate, and the grisly antics of the CIA. Would the renascence of lying in America have cheered him? I think not. Wilde believed that true lying is imagination, a faculty wholly beyond the powers of politicians, who can only misrepresent. Yet more than most nations, America manufactures dreams, nightmares, *and* profound critiques of both.

For our purpose Wilde's most pertinent essay is "The Critic as Artist." Matthew Arnold, we recall, enjoined critics (in 1864 in "The Function of Criticism at the Present Time") "to see the object as in itself it really is." This precept soon began to shift toward a more subjective focus in the criticism of Ruskin and Pater. But it remained for Wilde to stand Arnold on his head, and scandalously to suggest that the aim of the critic is to see the object as it really is not. There is method in Wilde's scandal, however, and we do well to allow him to speak for himself through the infamous Gilbert:

> The antithesis between them [the creative and the critical faculties] is entirely arbitrary. Without the critical faculty, there is no artistic creation at all.
>
> But, surely, Criticism is itself an art. . . . Why should it not be? It works with materials, and puts them into a form that is at once new and delightful. What more can one say of poetry? Indeed, I would call criticism a creation within a creation. For just as the great artists, from Homer and Aeschylus, down to Shakespeare and Keats, did not go directly to life for their subject-matter, but sought for it in myth, legend and ancient tale, so the critic deals with materials that others have, as it were, purified for him, and to which imaginative form and colour have been already added. Nay, more, I would say that the highest Criticism, being the purest form of personal impression, is in its way more creative than creation, as it has least reference to any standard external to itself, and is, in fact, its own reason for existing, and, as the Greeks would put it, in itself, and to itself, an end.
>
> The artistic critic, like the mystic, is an antinomian always.

Scandal, sacrilege, and high camp—all of us who have been trained in Positivist Scholarship or the New Criticism want to cry! (Indeed, I shudder to think of the ruin of Graduate English Departments, should everyone suddenly take after Wilde; fortunately, graduate students are much too sensible thus to jeopardize their future tenures by committing premature academic suicide.) Yet frivolous, perverse, or extreme as Wilde's statements may seem, his position in some sense anticipates that of many other critics, including W. K. Wimsatt on the "intentional fallacy," Harold Bloom on "poetic misprision," Wolfgang Iser on the "implied reader," and Roland Barthes on the illicit "pleasures of the text." For the basic impulse of Wilde—no matter how mauve or *fin de siècle* his manner may appear—is to deny the author a privileged view of his text, deny the text itself any ultimate concreteness or unity. The critic, Wilde insists, should not be fair, sincere, or rational. "There are two ways of disliking art. . . . One is to dislike it. The other is to like it rationally," he has Gilbert quip; and again: "What people call insincerity is simply a method by which we can multiply our personalities." Here Wilde approaches that notion of the "empty" or indefinite "subject" so crucial to later structuralists, who believe with Nietzsche that what we call a self is at best a rendezvous of several people.

For Wilde's "critic as artist," then, the act of reading is constitutive; it is an act of creation. The text (or object) is multiple and "shifting," a word dear to Wilde; so is the self (or subject). Indeed, subject and object sometimes shift or exchange their places. And transgression (stepping across), in life as in criticism or art, "is an essential element of progress." Here are all the elements of the critic's epistemological Freedom—and all the unresolved problems too.

Montage

But why think of the critic only? Isn't his/her activity as constitutive awareness or creative agonism a political fact as well? Wilde brings to mind Karl Marx. Here is Marx, in his letter of 22 July 1861, to Ferdinand Lassalle, on political "misprision":

> Otherwise it might be said that every achievement of an older period, which is adopted in later times, is part of the *old misunderstood.* . . . Thus, too, all modern constitutions rest in great part on the *misunderstood* English constitution. . . . The misunderstood form is precisely the general form, applicable for general use at a definite stage of social development.

History as "misunderstanding"? Criticism as the politics of literary misunderstanding?

And who, precisely, tends to become a critic, instead of a doctor, computer technician, or diplomat? Are there innumerable types, or are there certain identifiable, certain recurrent types? Should we pursue such dismaying queries? Or should we rather assume that Criticism is best defined abstractly, without reference to Person, defined in terms of such institutions as Literature or the University?

The questions are perhaps worth mooting: the politics of criticism (more of this later) is not altogether alien to the personae of critics.

SLIPPAGE

He thinks of Hegel's primal beast called Recognition.

Having waited decades to meet it, he chose then to seek it out in the world, its lair. Vain quest. Once, sitting in his study alone, he felt behind him some immense breath, raw, ontic, older than time. Turning slowly, he saw . . . nothing. A small heap of ashes on the carpet may have dropped from his cigar.

He continues to seek the Beast, as a formality, suspecting all the time that it is tracking him to his grave.

Frame Four

Oscar Wilde was not the only writer to bruit the case for the critic as artist. His French contemporary, Rémy de Gourmont, did quite as much and possibly with greater consequence. Half a century later, a man who had little in common with either Wilde or Gourmont made an even stronger case for the liberty of the critic as everyman. I mean Jean-Paul Sartre. In *What Is Literature?*, Sartre scathingly portrays the traditional critic:

> The critic lives badly; his wife does not appreciate him as she ought to; his children are ungrateful; the first of the month is hard on him. But it is always possible for him to enter his library, take down a book from the shelf, and open it. It gives off a slight odor of the cellar, and a strange operation begins which he has decided to call reading.

It is this operation, this activity we call reading (which has become even more problematic in our day), that Sartre wants to redefine, to revitalize. Sartre's dialectical bias is already clear.

> But the operation of writing implies that of reading as its dialectical correlative and these two connected acts necessitate two distinct agents. It is the conjoint effort of author and reader which brings upon the scene that concrete and imaginary object which is the work of the mind. There is no art except for and by others.

This leads Sartre to conclude what now seems to us so obvious: that reading is a "synthesis of perception and creation." True, in this synthesis the great Existential Marxist does not give to language the primacy that both Structuralists and the New Critics were to accord it. Yet in his conception of the literary work, created by the reader's freedom, and of literature itself, as the subjectivity of a society in permanent revolution, he offers a moral and historical basis for the act of critical innovation. For its philosophical basis, Sartre demands that we surpass even Kant in declaring the work of art without finality or end, a work constituted by each glance of the beholder, responding to each appeal, "a pure exigence to exist."

Those other neo-Kantians, our own old New Critics, took an antithetical view of the matter. Yet even during their reign, there were some who kept the possibility of the critic as innovator alive. Thus, for instance, in the *Kenyon Review* Symposium of 1950–51, entitled "My Credo," Leslie Fiedler argues for an "amateur criticism," and Herbert Read movingly speaks of the "critic as a man of feeling." Even that collage of New Critical ideas, R. W. Stallman's *The Critic's Notebook* (1950), has for an epigraph these lines from Martin Turnell: "The critic possesses a dual personality. He is at once an 'artist' and a 'thinker,' the 'man of feeling' and the 'intellectual'. . . . He is an artist, *but a special kind of artist*" (italics mine).

This formulation may strike us as philosophically naïve. Consider, however, a later writer: Paul de Man, surely one of the most subtle critics, steeped in the European tradition, inward with current thought. De Man knows that the relation of "authentic criticism" to literary studies is at best problematic; he does not want to force criticism upon a propadeutic endeavor to which it might be alien. In *Blindness and Insight,* he candidly notes:

> Whether authentic criticism is a liability or an asset to literary studies as a whole remains an open question. One thing, however, is certain; namely, that literary studies cannot possibly refuse to take cognizance of its existence. It would be as if historians refused to acknowledge the existence of wars because they threaten to interfere with the serenity that is indispensable to an orderly pursuit of their discipline.

Furthermore, de Man realizes that "all true criticism occurs in the mode of crisis"; for him, a crisis in criticism is in some measure redundant since crisis makes for genuine insight, for critical authenticity. He also notes that genres are no longer as pure as we once liked to believe. "The gap between the manifestoes and the learned articles," he says, "has narrowed to the point where some manifestoes are quite learned and some articles—though by no means all—are quite provocative." Thus criticism, in becoming cousin to the manifesto, proclaims its right to newness.

More significantly, perhaps, de Man clearly perceives the implications of Heidegger's "hermeneutic circle" to the art of critical interpretation: the latter becomes endless. No totality of meaning or closure of form can suffice. "The hermeneutic understanding is always, by its very nature, lagging behind: to understand something is to realize that one had always known it, but, at the same time, to face the mystery of this hidden knowledge." And again, speaking now of Derrida, de Man observes: "Not only does the critic say something that the work does not say, but he even says something that he himself does not mean to say. The semantics of interpretation have no epistemological consistency and can therefore not be scientific." Thus the "authentic" critic begins his job by accepting the inevitable discrepancy between the original text and his critical discourse. On this point de Man is emphatic:

> The necessary immanence of the [critic's] reading in relation to the text is a burden from which there can be no escape. It is bound to stand out as the irreducible philosophical problem raised by all forms of literary criticism, however pragmatic they may seem or want to be. We encounter it here in the form of a constitutive discrepancy, in critical discourse, between the blindness of the statement and the insight of the meaning.

It is precisely this "constitutive discrepancy" in critical discourse, recognized intuitively by Wilde as by later critics, that makes for the initial condition of innovation in criticism—again, its Freedom. But is it also a *sufficient* condition? I think not.

Frame Five

The critic's Freedom is anxious and fractious; it is initiative, responsive, and reflexive all at the same time. But it can provide only the ground for innovation. A critic needs more, needs an erotic sense of Style and an intuition of the New.

An original style neither seeks nor evades "difficulty," though a degree of "defamiliarization" (*ostranenie,* The Russian formalists called it) may be an aspect of it. True, critical languages, as we all know, now suffer from jargon, neologism, and abstraction; they have become technical and idiolectic at the same time. (God guard us against the transumptions, metalepses, paronomasias, catabases, and apotropies that afflict our eristic discourse.) Yet we also sense that the style of a Blackmur or a Barthes, uncouth as it may seem to limpid minds, expresses a curious energy—a kind of love?

Blackmur now is half forgotten. Yet in such essays as "A Critic's Job of Work," "A Burden for Critics," and "The Enabling Act of Criticism," Blackmur, despite his inclination to dense technical analysis, maintains the stance of an artist or lover, both disciplined and freed by what he loves. "Criticism, I take it, is the formal discourse of an amateur," he writes in *Language as Gesture.* "When there is enough love and enough knowledge represented in the discourse it is a self-sufficient but by no means an isolated art. It witnesses constantly in its own life its interdependence with the other arts." But it is Blackmur's style, more than anything else, that betrays the artist in him; dark, original, poetic, the style is forever at the point of re-creating everything that it touches. It is itself touched by that perversity of the critical genius, that quiddity of the artistic temperament, which evokes two other wholly different critics: Marxist Walter Benjamin and Structuralist/Poststructuralist Roland Barthes.

About Benjamin I will have nothing to say here except that he must be counted with Barthes among the rare critical geniuses of our century. As for the latter, protean structuralist, cunning semiotician, oblique amateur (lover) of language, he has from the start averred the privileges of the critic as a "special kind of artist." Thus in *Critique et vérité,* Barthes desires both "criticism and works always to say: *I am literature,*" since the critic can only "continue the metaphors of the work, never reduce them" to any intelligibility. In his later works, Barthes is even more explicit and paradoxical about the role of criticism. Here he is in *Critical Essays:*

> It is by acknowledging itself as no more than a language (or more precisely, a metalanguage) that criticism can be—paradoxically but authentically—both objective and subjective, historical and existential, totalitarian and liberal. . . . Thus begins, at the heart of the critical work, the dialogue of two histories and two subjectivities, the author's and the critic's. But this dialogue is egoistically shifted toward the present: criticism is not an "homage" to the truth of the past or to the truth of "others"—it is a construction of the intelligibility of our time.

This paradoxical conception need not paralyze criticism, though it does betray the structuralist tendency to oscillate between the poles of logic and fantasy, science and solipsism. For Barthes, such oscillations are checked by a complex commitment to *pleasure.* "The pleasure of the text," as Barthes says in a book by that name, is perverse and polymorphous; it is erotic, constituted by the intermittences not only of the heart but more of the body. "The text is a fetishistic object and that fetish desires me," he confides. Criticism—or more precisely, critical style—becomes the fumbling response to that requited desire. Far from obeying the imperatives of logic as Barthes had earlier suggested, critical style embraces the text, only to discover its own muteness, discover, that is, its inability to say anything except: "this is it for me! This 'for me' is neither subjective, nor existential, but Nietzschean. . . ." But critical muteness now recovers speech under another imperative: neither the imperative of Logic nor simply of erotic Style but of *Novelty.* Here is the crucial passage in *The Pleasure of the Text,* which finally defines for Barthes the function of the critic as innovator:

> The New is not a fashion, it is a value, upon which is founded all criticism: our valuation of the world no longer depends, at least directly, as in Nietzsche, upon the opposition between the *noble* and the base, but rather upon the opposition between the Old and the New. . . . To escape from the alienation of present society, there is only one way: *escape forward:* all old languages are immediately compromised, and all languages become old as soon as they are respected.

Barthes's insight into the role of the critic as innovator is difficult—some would say crepuscular or impenetrable. It is an insight based, as Susan Sontag had hoped, upon an erotics rather than a hermeneutics of texts, an erotics *and* politics of the New. And the secret agent of that insight is for Barthes, as it was for Blackmur and Benjamin, critical Style!

Style may be the secret agent; but in structuralist circles, of which there are many, the public demand is to abolish familiar distinctions between "criticism" and "literature." Thus Eugenio Donato summarizes this assumption in *The Languages of Criticism and the Sciences of Man:*

> Derrida's enterprise also reveals within our modern context the impossibility of drawing an essential line between literature and criticism. Literature can only be a denunciation of literature and is not therefore different in essence from criticism. Criticism, in as much as it is a denunciation of literature, is, itself, nothing but literature.

The name of Derrida, magus of grammatology, has been uttered. Soon, I must speak of his and others' unmakings; for therein lies another aspect of critical innovation. But a montage once again clouds my frame.

Montage

Do I quote from others too much? Very well, then, I quote too much, and I must need quote some more. But what does it mean "to quote"?

We rarely quote nowadays to appeal to authority—Leonardo: "Whoever refers to authorities in disputing ideas, works with his memory rather than his reason"—though we quote sometimes to display our sapience and erudition. Some authors we quote against. Some we quote not at all, offering them our scrupulous avoidance, and so make them part of our "white mythology." Other authors we constantly invoke, canting their names in cerebral rituals of propitiation or ancestor worship. Others still, we quote for the pleasure or prestige of their company. (It is a little like being seen in public with Raquel Welch or, in another time, with the Duke of Windsor.) And there are authors, finally, whom we quote in the spirit of elective sympathy.

Do will, vanity, and desire (Blackmur's Moha?*), then, always insinuate themselves in our quotation marks? I can not answer without quoting further. This exposes another problem.*

In a statement on "the critic as innovator," quotations seem a bizarre aporia or contradiction. Yet aporias may have uses that reason refuses. By playing texts against texts, voices against voices, do I permit language to open a new space, begin an intertextual discourse

(Kristeva) that may "say" what I cannot say? And is this still another aspect of the critic's Freedom?

I leave the "dear reader" to decide. But as a pacifier to that reader's conscience and mine, I must recapitulate my argument. Here is a quick flashback of my five frames:

1. *Frames or fields shape our actions and utterances, including critical discourse; frames are really a kind of fiction.*

2. *Schools (in America, this often means Graduate Schools) rather than paradigms prevail in criticism; schools render critical innovation both easier and more ambiguous within shifting frames. For they are open to history and desire.*

3. *Criticism is a constitutive discourse, like literature itself; thus the critic as a frame-worker, a "special kind of artist," enjoys some epistemological Freedom.*

4. *The critic as a "special kind of artist" reveals him/herself in Style, and in a complex, erotic attitude toward the New.*

5. *All this, as we shall see, leads into politics, the critic's multiple Concern, and into the bounds and circumference of imagination.*

Frame Six

All my comments so far evade the peculiar provocations of our postmodern thought. It is an antinomian moment that assumes a vast unmaking in the Western mind—what Michel Foucault might call a postmodern *épistémè*. I say "unmaking" though other terms are now *de rigeur*: from deconstruction to dispersal to a variety of virtual "deaths." Such terms express an ontological rejection of the traditional full subject, the *cogito* of Western philosophy. They express, too, an epistemological obsession with fragments or fractures, and a corresponding ideological commitment to minorities in politics, sex, and language. To think well, to feel well, to act well, to read well, according to this *épistémè* of unmaking, is to refuse the tyranny of wholes; totalization in any human endeavor is potentially totalitarian.

Two recent examples may impart some sense of this postmodern will to unmaking. They are, in their intellectual styles, strikingly divergent. Yet both clearly share certain assumptions about our moment.

In *La Révolution sans modèle,* three men—François Châtelet, Gilles Lapouge, and Olivier Revault d'Allonnes—discuss informally the possibilities of radical yet unmediated change. The paradox seems inescapable: all human effort is in time, and time decomposes as well as consolidates. Thus innovation becomes inheritance. Furthermore, all human effort is in language. (Indeed, the word revolution itself may signify an obsolete concept of change; that is why Jean-François Lyotard likes to speak of volution instead of revolution.) And language imposes all its patterns on our thoughts and actions. How then escape the structures of discourse? Model, antimodel, without-model?

The authors circle and circle around. Is a model-in-the-making still a model? Can a model convert, subvert, or pervert its own versions, and so keep itself incomplete? What if various models were set against one another, without dominance of a single model? How does an under-determined model (anarchic) suddenly become overdetermined (totalitarian or utopian)? Or is every model of "perfection" really an image of the void?

They quote Julio Cortazar: "One cannot change man without changing his instruments of knowledge, language itself." They quote Roland Barthes: "Today, there is an area of language exterior to bourgeois ideology: our language comes from it, returns to it, remains locked within it. The only possible answer is neither confrontation nor destruction but only theft: to fragment the old texts of culture, of science, of literature, and to disseminate and disguise the fragments in the same way that we diguise stolen merchandise."

The authors finally wonder: is the concept of a revolution without a model not a model itself? Or is a revolution without a model a pleonasm, since all "true" revolutions are indeed without a model, the model coming afterwards? Or again, should the model of every revolution be designed only for one purpose, to engender a revolutionary *movement?* These and other queries suggest how the will to unmaking declares itself in an exoteric work, a work of intellectual journalism at its liveliest.

In contrast *L'Anti-Oedipe* by Gilles Deleuze and Félix Guattari seems esoteric, formidably learned and speculative. Subtitled *"Capitalisme et schizophrénie,"* the book envisions history as the coding and uncoding of an erotic flux, the flux of a *"machine désirante,"* which controls all human effort. The desiring machine has defined three stages of history: *"Sauvages"* (primitive, tribal, prehistoric societies), *"Barbares"* (ancient, despotic states), and *"Civilisés"* (modern, immanent capitalism); these correspond to the "full body," "paranoia," and "schizophrenia." The authors describe themselves as "schizoanalysts," and relentlessly attack the Oedipus complex, which they perceive as a rank misunderstanding of the forms of desire in history.

But what, specifically, is their theory of unmaking? In a complex and technical argument, which considers the material as well as the epistemological basis of capitalism, Deleuze and Guattari conclude that the latter represents a new creativity of "schizoid time." "Civilization," they say, "defines itself by the uncoding and deterritorialization of [erotic] fluxes in capitalist productions." There is thus an "affinity" between capitalist and schizophrenic fluxes, but no exact identity. On the contrary, as schizophrenia represents the *limit* toward which capitalism tends, so does it also represent the destruction against which capitalism must struggle. (Capitalism attempts to save itself from ultimate schizophrenia by coding and "axiomatizing" with one hand what it constantly uncodes with the other.)

Schizophrenia, in short, heralds and hastens the end of capitalism. Thus Deleuze and Guattari designate schizophrenia, not schizophrenics, as the essential revolutionary condition, and paranoia as the essential despotic or fascist state. Schizophrenia fragments, unmakes; it refuses totalization, as in Antonin Artaud, William Burroughs, R. D. Laing, John Cage, as in nearly all postmodern arts. "We no longer believe," the authors say, "in an original totality nor in a totality of destination." For Deleuze and Guattari, then, schizophrenia has become the historical agent of the liberation of desire, which is the source of all production. Unmaking is the human project *par excellence.*

These two works, quixotic in their contrast, are part of a larger frame of deconstruction that must include the work of Derrida, Foucault, Barthes, Kristeva, and Sollers, among others. And that larger frame, is it not a historical development of that still vaster configuration we call modernism in the arts?

In the arts, we know, the will to unmaking began to manifest itself earlier, around the turn of the century. Yet from the ready-mades of Marcel Duchamp and the collages of Hans Arp to the auto-destructive machines of Jean Tinguely and conceptual works of Bruce Nauman, a certain impulse has persisted, turning art against itself in order to remake itself. Sometimes, the artist has turned not only against his art but even against his flesh. Thus Vito Hannibal Acconci, a "body artist," bites himself in public; Chris Burden arranges a party to have himself shot in the arm; and the Viennese, Rudolph Schwartzkogler, slowly amputates his penis before a moving camera. The artist's body has become his medium, and the dismembered medium his message. In this, literary authors lag only a short distance behind.

But the main point is this: art, in process of "de-definition" as Harold Rosenberg says, is becoming, like the personality of the artist, an occurrence without clear boundaries: at worst a kind of social hallucination, at best an opening or inauguration. That is why Jean-François Lyotard enjoins readers "to abandon the safe harbour offered to the mind by the category of 'works of art' or of signs in general, and to recognize as truly artistic nothing but *initiatives* or events, in whatever domain they may occur."

Art as "initiative," as "event"; texts that are, in the words of Barthes, *"scriptible"* rather than *"lisible"*; a postmodern *épistémè* of unmaking. What imperatives of innovation do these impose upon the critic? What new rigors and exigencies? And what omissions or remissions?

Montage

Working with Frames and Montages, how do I select or exclude? Tendentiously, of course, as any maker must. Tendentiously, yes—but also, like The Three Princes of Serendip, *with some happy accidents and fortunate pratfalls? It may be comforting to think so. Yet given the interdebtedness of language and mind, each to itself and each to each, how can anything finally be excluded? Even a catch phrase, "the critic as innovator," creates the very contexts from which it is absent, clusters of thought to which it wants to return. How imply these contexts of absence? In a bibliography of silences?*

Here, for instance, are some omissions in my treatment of the critic as innovator:

1. Criticism and language games. See Ludwig Wittgenstein, Philosophical Investigations, The Blue and the Brown Books, *and* Zettel.

2. The problem of "subjective," "objective," and "transactive" paradigms in literary interpretation. See the essays by David Bleich and Norman N. Holland in New Literary History, *no. 2 (1976).*

3. The role of literary tropes and fictions in historical narratives, including literary history. See Hayden White, Metahistory; *Louis Mink, "History and Fiction as Modes of Comprehension,"* New Literary History *1, no. 3 (1970); and Paul Hernadi, "Clio's Cousins: Historiography as Translation, Fiction, and Criticism,"* New Literary History *7, no. 2 (1976). Some essays of "The Bellagio Symposium,"* New Literary History *7, no. 1 (1975), are also relevant, as is Ralph Cohen and Murray Krieger's* Literature and History.

4. The limits of "objectivity" in American criticism, endless debate. See essays by Murray Krieger, Northrop Frye, and E. D. Hirsch, in L. S. Dembo, ed., Criticisms; *as well as the essays by M. H. Abrams and E. D. Hirsch, in Morton W. Bloomfield, ed.,* In Search of Literary Theory.

5. The phenomenology of the reading process, in its innumerable versions. See, for instance, Georges Poulet, "Phenomenology of Reading," New Literary History *1, no. 1 (1969); Gaston Bachelard,* The Poetics of Reverie; *and Wolfgang Iser,* The Implied Reader.

6. The question of innovation or initiation in language generally. See Edward Said's Beginnings; *for instance, this passage: "Or, in radical criticism, it is the deep anterior claim of the writing, sometimes willfully forgotten, sometimes deliberately attenuated, but always haunting the critic whose reading abuts the mountains and the cav-*

erns of another's, an author's, mind at work: such critics write critical poems imitating the behavior of the mind."

Yet why, in rectifying some of my "omissions," do I include in my "bibliography" articles from only a single journal? And how does such a bibliography, arbitrary still in its own omissions, clarify the imperatives of innovation?

Frame Seven

Inevitably, the imperatives of innovation lead us, through politics, to the critic's Concern. The politics are triple: politics of the page, of academic criticism, and of language and society in general.

Consider the periodical *College English.* Revitalized in the last decade by left/liberal editorial policies, it has set out to change the profession from within. Yet its arguments appear invariably in serried, double columns of an unvarying typeface. They appear, more significantly, in a format that challenges none of the social or technical or sensuous conventions of its own medium: editorial policies, printing rules, subscription forms, advertising practices, etc. Thus, whatever reform *College English* attempts, it does so on the level of abstract rational discourse; that is, on only one level of human discourse in culture. Yet had it attempted more, would it not have lost its credibility for many of us? Our passion may sometimes be our task, but the slogan of our "critical inquiry" remains linear "reasoned discourse"—reasoned, alas, ironically or blandly, aggressively or fearfully, but seldom reasoned to express the full measure of human awareness.

This is not the place to develop a rationale for the Mallarméan project of breaking up the type, the line, the page, the language. Still, any cursory look at certain works by Michel Butor, Philippe Sollers, Maurice Roche, Ernst Jandl, Eugen Gömringer, Helmut Heissenbüttel, Christine Brooke-Rose, Raymond Federman, Ronald Sukenick, Donald Barthelme, Walter Abish, Dick Higgins, Eugene Wildman, Campbell Tatham, or John Cage, among many others, can convey, through expanding eyes, intimations of that project.

Who then will carry this project to criticism and how?

Frames within a Frame

Essaying collections recommended
by Richard Kostelanetz

Bann, Stephen, ed. *The Tradition of Constructivism.* New York: Viking, 1974.

Brockman, John. *Afterwords.* Garden City: Doubleday Anchor, 1973.

Burnham, Jack. *Great Western Salt Works.* New York: Braziller, 1974.

Cage, John. *M.* Middleton, Conn.: Wesleyan University Press, 1973.

Depew, Wally. *Nine Essays on Concrete Poems.* Alamo, Calif.:Holmganger Press, 1974.

Ferguson, Gerald. *The Standard Corpus of Present Day English Usage.* Halifax: Nova Scotia College of Art and Design, 1973.

Gillespie, Abraham Lincoln. *Collected Works.* Edited by Hugh Fox. Forthcoming.

Hassan, Ihab. *Paracriticisms.* Urbana: University of Illinois Press, 1975.

Kostelanetz, Richard. *Recyclings: A Literary Autobiography.* Volume One: 1959–67. New York: Assembling Press, 1974.

LeWitt, Sol. *Arcs, Circles & Grids.* New York: Paul Bianchini, 1972.

Lippard, Lucy R. *Six Years.* New York: Praeger, 1973.

Olson, Charles. *Additional Prose.* Bolinas, Calif.: Four Seasons, 1974.

Queeney, Shiva & Michael Goodenough. *The Be-Cause Look Book.* New York: Links, 1973.

Themerson, Stefan. *Logics Labels and Flesh.* London: Gabberbocchus, 1974.

To which we can add:

Barthes, Roland. *Roland Barthes par Roland Barthes.* Paris: Editions du Seuil, 1975.

Calvino, Italo. *La cittá invisibile.* Milano: Giulio Einaudi, 1972.

Derrida, Jacques. *Glas.* Paris: Galilée, 1974.

Kostelanetz, Richard, ed. *Essaying Essays: Alternative Forms of Exposition.* New York: Out of London Press, 1976.

The politics of the page, no less than its erotics or stylistics, intrudes upon us precisely because, as Barthes said, "all old languages are immediately compromised, and all languages become old as soon as they are respected." And the languages of criticism?

SLIPPAGE

Be serious, he thinks; think of power, of politics.

He fancies that he has accepted his death, or at least lived with it on terms of intimate forgetfulness, ever since that morning in the Alps, an adolescent still, he saw a black hearse wind its way *upwards* through snow and blue ice. Or was it only an imaginary scene, painted by Caspar David Friedrich?

He fancies that he has accepted his death, and so become an amateur of change, mediating between Time and Value. Why, then, should he heed politics?

Politics: a repetition compulsion, oppression or revenge made licit, the actor always exluding much of him/herself from the act in order to act. But also politics: feeding the hungry mouth, stopping the torturer's red hand, giving human Hope its patient due.

He recalls a line from Mao to Chou En-lai: "Our mission, unfinished, may take a thousand years." Perhaps more. But the struggle, he thinks, must always be double: to struggle and *at the same time* struggle to empty all struggle.

Frame Eight

The politics of the page may be part of the inhibiting politics of criticism as an academic institution. The critical article and the scholarly book now reign; they mediate our imagination and knowledge. But why not *also* the essay, the ideal essay rooted etymologically in risk, trial, examination, balance, rooted in *both* risk and balance? "The essay—" someone always asks, "but is it criticism?" Perhaps it is not. But perhaps also what criticism now requires is a text that puts itself in jeopardy with other texts.

Criticism, like Literature, is a historical institution; it is neither a Platonic triangle nor a stone pyramid enduring Time under a yellow sun. Our ideas both of Criticism and of Literature are changing, have changed. Even Northrop Frye, more given to heroic schemata than most of us, understood in his *Anatomy of Criticism* a point we tend to miss: "The total Logos of criticism by itself can never become an object of faith or an ontological personality"; and again: "The presence of incommunicable experience in the center of criticism will always keep criticism an art, as long as the critic recognizes that criticism comes out of it but cannot be built on it."

Yet for some critics—or let us simply say, for some writers of texts—the age demands less building than *bricolage* (Lévi-Strauss), than forage or rummage. This demand may wrench the writer out of the university's noetic frame, perhaps out of literature itself, out and back in again. Edmund Wilson, Edmund Wilson, Edmund Wilson: we intone his single name forever, as if to prove that the man of letters is but recently defunct in America. In France, however, the names of great and eccentric essayists roll easily off the tongue: Bachelard on fire, Caillois on the octopus, Leiris on tauromachy, Bataille on eroticism, Blanchot on absence, Butor on nearly everything—not to mention Sartre or Camus!

The temptation, of course, it to conclude that the natural enemy of the free essay is the university: that society of specialized knowledge and power that has become the main custodian of the critical mind since literature began to be studied in the vernacular (see Walter J. Ong's *The Barbarian Within*). Yet the university itself may be more symptom than cause of intellectual enervation in America. Behind the page, behind the essay, behind the humanities, vaster dispositions of culture loom into view. These are recognized by Serge Doubrovsky in *The New Criticism in France:*

> Criticism is an inoffensive and distant activity only on the surface. In reality, it is the machinery of censorship, the ultimate policing force that a society produces as a means of keeping strict watch on the expression of thought within it and ensuring the preservation of its values.

The emphasis here is perhaps too heavy. But it serves to elicit the ultimate implication of the topic: namely, that innovation in criticism finally aspires not only to epistemological, existential, or aesthetic freedom but also to basic political change. This statement, of course, cries anxiously for qualification. Yet it underscores the present need to move beyond the Arnoldian position, as restated by Northrop Frye in *The Well-Tempered Critic:*

> But it seems clear that Arnold was on solid ground when he made "culture," a total imaginative vision of life with literature at its center, the regulating and normalizing element in social life, the human source, at least, of spiritual authority. Culture in Arnold's sense is the exact opposite of an elite's game preserve; it is, in its totality, a vision or model of what humanity is capable of achieving, the matrix of all Utopias and social ideas.

Culture may be the "matrix" of all human possibilities; yet the societies in which we act still remain at a bitter distance from those "imaginative visions" that culture constantly generates. Can the critic as innovator help to close the Gap of Hope? Can we all begin to understand the disposition of power, avoiding both the etherealizations of the avant-garde ("the consciousness industry," Enzensberger called it) and the reifications of troglodytic Marxism? How would a genuine post-Marxist theory both articulate and change reality? And admit imagination?

Montage

The Gap of Hope. It will certainly not be closed simply by typographic experiment or paracritical play. But neither will it be closed by a criticism that ignores its potential as performance, a performance affecting our societies, our institutions, our languages, and indeed our very senses. *A Promethean performance?*

Why is it, I wonder (ungraciously? unjustly?), that so many American critics, despite their intellectual brilliance, lack prescience about culture, lack also in the power of enabling moral ideas? (There are of course some exceptions—how many?) Is it because so few critics are willing to step out of their academic frame, out of the scholarly book or critical essay? Or is it because, as Frank Kermode pretends, critics are not expected to make sense of our lives as other writers are expected to do? (Has any truly great critic ever held that view?) And why not? Why must criticism invariably *be so discrete, so technical, so exclusive an activity of mind, denying mind so large a part of itself?*

I realize the dangers of making inordinate claims for criticism: bad religion, bad politics, bad prose. (I have sometimes come close to all three myself.) But no danger, I feel, should now inhibit our search for a new liveliness, a new capaciousness, a new potency in criticism. Can humanists otherwise hope to enter the future, release imagination, subvert power with a more equivocal (and so hopeful) power?

The Gap of Hope grows.

Frame Nine

The question persists: what, beyond the critic's Freedom, Style, and intuition of the New, defines Concern, and so empowers the critic's language to enter history? In his *Theory of the Avant-Garde,* we recall, Renato Poggioli thought the judgments of great critics to be posthumous or prophetic: "Great criticism starts with the *Zeitgeist* but tends to anticipate posterity," he wrote. Through such anticipations of concern, the critic's Freedom returns as Responsibility, taking hold of history.

Concern, however, is often a shadowy and shifting thing. From Lukács to Eliot, critics have filled the ideological spectrum with doctrines and myths of concern. My own view of the matter is neither doctrinal nor mythic. The critic's concern is a double wager: one with history, the other with eternity. It determines both his/her politics and moral life. No critic, I suspect, can enlarge the possibilities of a sullen craft without exceptional force and generosity of concern, though no concern alone, however fierce, could make a critic artful. Most obviously, critical concern expresses itself in formative subjects, arch themes. The point is recognized by conservative no less than by radical critics.

In an obscure essay, titled "Experiment in Criticism" and published in *The Bookman* in 1929, T. S. Eliot affirmed: "The various attempts to find the fundamental axioms behind both good literature and good life are among the most interesting 'experiments' of criticism in our time"; such attempts, he thought, showed "that the modern literary critic must be an 'experimenter' outside of what you might at first consider his own province." Eliot had in mind the New Humanism of Babbit and More, and its French equivalent, the Christian Humanism of Ramon Fernandez. We, of course, now have very different matters in mind; indeed, some of us may feel that we may soon enter an altogether posthumanist phase. Yet the conjunctions Eliot made half a century ago between intellectual scope, moral significance, and critical experiment still hold; only their focus and our concerns have changed.

Our concerns: what formative subjects do they now provide criticism? Here I can only wager or guess in rubric form:

a. Theories of the Imagination: a general theory of fictions, including criticism, which can take into account current neurological, psychological, philosophic, and linguistic research.

b. The Politics of the Imagination: how imagination takes power and when it fails to do so, and the nature of the power that imagination *can* take.

c. The Future: prophetic or utopian fictions—models of desire, dream, and hope—that become agents of transformation, become concretions of the future.

d. Mythology and Technology, Mysticism and Science: convergences between their structures in the deeper structures of postmodern culture, and the implications thereof.

e. The One and the Many: the emergent role of mind, extended by technology, in mediating between unity and diversity, organization and chaos, the ecumenical will and the will to secession on earth—toward a new vision, not of sameness but of wholeness.

Stark and huge as some of these Promethean subjects seem, they are of profound practical and theoretical interest to our literary business. Yet in the end, I would not wish simply to identify innovative with self-conscious criticism. It is not merely that "the owl of Minerva takes its flight only when the shades of night are gathering" (Hegel); it is also that the best criticism, like the best art, finds its source in a region unavailable to either theory or action. This is a region that tempts us into both language and silence.

SLIPPAGE

Silence, he thinks, is itself the slippage. But what peeps through, as poor Pip saw, is not I but the Cosmos.

No life wholly fulfilled in literature can bring to it the highest vision. No life entirely satisfied in criticism can bring to literature the deepest insight. Slippage or silence: where biographies begin and very quickly end. Something else begins to happen. . . .

He wonders: "what language of childhood can I call my own?" Having reinvented himself in a "foreign" tongue, has he lost all sense of "foreignness"? Having escaped his "first" language, has he also escaped the primal censor or authority?

Thus, silence or slippage becomes the eternal text of Imagination.

Frame Ten

It is time to clip this paracritical strip. The Imagination, elsewhere I have maintained, may be the teleological force in human evolution; language and metaphor create time continually, and may finally redeem it in a "silence" we can not yet imagine. To what does the road from Babel lead? We do not know. In *After Babel* George Steiner offers these apposite meditations:

> We need a word which will designate the power, the compulsion of language to posit "otherness." That power, as Oscar Wilde was one of the few to recognize, is inherently in every act of form, in art, in music, in the contrarieties which our body sets against gravity and repose. But it is preeminent in language.
>
> The dialectic of "alternity," the genius of language for planned counter-factuality, are overwhelmingly positive and creative. . . . Language is centrally fictive because the enemy is "reality," because unlike the Houyhnhnm man is not prepared to abide with "the Thing which is."

Insofar as Criticism is made both of language and silence, strip and slippage, it participates in the "dialectic of alternity" in ways we have yet to discover. This gives it the ineluctable aspect of arbitrariness, to which history also contributes. Our concept of Literature—like our concept of the Child, the Madman, the Criminal, or the Professor—is no more than two centuries old. "The view that there is an art of literature," René Wellek says, "which includes both poetry and prose in so far as it is imaginative fiction, and excludes information or even rhetorical persuasion, didactic argumentation or historical narration, emerged only slowly in the 18th century." There is no reason to assume that this exclusion will remain permanent, or that it is central to our verbal projects now or in years to come. All change, if innovative, seems at first gratuitous.

The fear of arbitrariness in criticism qualifies our very hopes for it. For criticism may be the Unnecessary Angel who can still cry: "in my sight, you see the earth again."

Alas, the trouble with all angels is their transparence.

7 Parabiography: The Varieties of Critical Experience

The varieties of critical experience are endless. I shall speak only of three: desiring, reading, acting (which here includes making). These are all fragments of an autobiography, itself but a sentient reed in the universe.

Autobiography has become rife, running both in high and low repute: it enjoys the sublime attention of literary theory, suffers the base association with cultural narcissism. More to the point: it has become the form that the contemporary imagination seeks to recover, as recent works of Saul Bellow, William Styron, John Barth, Bernard Malamud, Elizabeth Hardwick, and Michael Herr variously intimate. Yet autobiography remains an impossible—and deadly—form.

Impossible: how can a life come alive to itself without winding in the infinite folds of its own hermeneutic circle? How can self apprehend itself in the very act of its flight from death? But deadly too in this sense: autobiography is abject unless, in the words of Michel Leiris, it exposes itself to the "bull's horn." For writing about ourselves we risk cowardice and mendacity; and more, we risk changing ourselves by that writing into whatever an autobiographer pretends to be.

Grazing the bull's horn, we become, Leiris says, tangents to ourselves and the universe. I have no access to such grace. My defense against the peril of autobiography consists only in naming the peril. I name it in several voices, rendering, perhaps, less a discourse than a human cacophony of the critical spheres. Attend, perpend, what voice you please.

I

The little boy—almond eyed, hair parted and combed smoothly to each side—stands in velvet bolero and black toreador pants. His uncle frowns down upon him from an ogre's height.

"And what will you be when you grow up?"

"A warrior. Greater than Hannibal or Caesar."

"A general?"

"And also a saint."

Faint smiles. Later, something, neither shame nor pride, scalds his eyes.

We know that Freud, a grown man, admired Hannibal inordinately, and thought himself more conqueror than man of science. In thinking so, Freud tacitly admits that thought itself, even in its most reflexive mode, is founded on power and desire. But what kind of desire, and of which desiring self? I call upon four thinkers—Hegel, Nietzsche, William James, and Freud himself—to set the question before us.

Hegel first: in *The Phenomenology of Mind,* desire radically constitutes consciousness. What we call self is but active desire for the recognition of another, which the self sublates—at once negates and maintains—and so affirms its being, *for* itself. The struggle for recognition ends when one, risking death, becomes Master, the other, preserving his life, becomes Slave. Thus history comes into dialectical existence. We need not pursue further the profound paradoxes of the Hegelian dialectic, in which the Master wins an empty victory—since he has won recognition only from a Slave; in which the labor of Slaves, not of Masters, transforms nature into history; in which, finally, freedom comes to the Slave who "overcomes" his bondage rather than the Master who perpetuates his desire. For our purpose we need only recall that death and desire are complicit in the formation of language and mind from the start. For language not only mediates between self and other; it also becomes "the form in which spirit finds existence," as Hegel puts it, "Self-consciousness which as such is there immediately present, and which in its individuality is universal."

Nietzsche, too, perceives language as the supreme problematic of thought, making rhetoric—Paul de Man notes—"ground for the furthest-reaching dialectical speculations." Outside the "prison-house of language," we may vaguely imagine, but never speak, any "thing." No less than Hegel, Nietzsche assumes ontological desire, which he calls "will to power," and from which he derives, without benefit of Hegel's World Spirit, all things human. Virtues are but "refined passions," interpretations but affects of power; and the very "ought" at the heart of language, arising from the ineluctable gap between desire and world, seeks to overcome that world. Thus desire derives from its own insufficiency more power, its aim never simply to be but always to be *more!* The Nietzschean self may be a "fiction," an empty space where various personages come to mingle, squabble, and depart; yet it remains a "fiction" more dense in its desires—including self-annihilation—than any neutron star. This is the burden of Nietzsche's great posthumous work, *The Will to Power.*

He asks his son: "Why do you 'sky gods' like to sky dive?" Long pause, uncertain reply: "Every time you jump, you save your life."

The father thinks to himself: But what if someday the diver decides otherwise? Who knows the circumference of the self? Even Lucifer—in the unimaginable density of pride he cried: "I myself am hell"—even Lucifer evokes the rarity of light.

Whatever the self may be, its earthly form reveals a fierce intricacy of asseveration that no human endeavor escapes. Hegel and Nietzsche define a horizon of that being; in *The Varieties of Religious Experience,* William James defines another. James knows that "civilization is founded on the shambles, and every individual existence goes out in a lonely spasm of helpless agony." The insight is as stark as any Freud gave. Yet James knows as well the need of the self to risk itself at the edge of the ineffable. What he calls "the ontological imagination" realizes "unpicturable being" with a sensuous intensity exceeding a lover's ectasy. Such a faculty overflows the self's finitude, and touches the moral and intellectual center of mystical experience. Thus the mystic or saint accedes to a higher type than the warrior or hero precisely because the former is more adapted to "the highest society conceivable." Ethereal as James's speculations may seem to self-devoted realists, his major hypothesis stands solidly enough: mystics connect to something which, whatever it may be on its *farther* side, "is on its *hither* side the subconscious continuation of our conscious life." This is not far from Freud.

An adolescent still, he sought the desert, walking away from the feculent city, the river, red-brown in his native October, the soft impedients of family. He aspired to fire; his element was air; the desert offered a sterile compromise. He walked day and part of the night, past the tracks of caravans, to burn a palm leaf in the desert.

Freud, we know, holds mysticism in suspicion; his "Nirvana principle" or "oceanic feeling" owes more to the dubious death instinct than to any numinous vision. Yet his theory, more than any other, shapes the modern languages of desire. The theory shifts, changes, as Jean Laplanche shows in his *Life and Death in Psychoanalysis.* The binary terms "ego" and "sexual instincts" become "ego" and "object instincts," become finally "life" and "death." But great Eros, the binding force of life, holds no sway over Thanatos, or death; their titanic struggles, Freud dismally concludes in *Civilization and Its Discontents,* compose the infant's cry to heaven. For instincts demand only their pleasure; Ananke, or scarcity, forbids; the harried ego in the service of reality withers. How, then, resolve this tragic conflict? Perhaps, as always, through another tragedy; that is, through life perceived under new terms of its exigencies.

Freud perceives these exigencies in an earlier work, *Beyond the Pleasure Principle,* which first posits the death wish. Since no ruse of substitution or sublimation can really appease the instincts, the self never maintains itself in balance. Yet death, terminus of the organic project, also proves to have fathered the first instinct: "the instinct to return to the inanimate state." As Laplanche concludes for Freud: "Absent from every unconscious, death is perhaps rediscovered in the unconscious as the the most radical—but also the most sterile—principle of its logic. But it is life which crystallizes the first objects to which desire attaches itself, before even thought can cling to them."

There are, of course, many other views of the matter, notably René Girard's theory of "mimetic desire"—"the subject desires the object because the rival desires it"—advanced forcefully, even obsessively, in his *Violence and the Sacred.* Yet all views press upon us images of being in its most complex ferocity. That ferocity, from Hegel to Freud, seems instinct with varieties of death or violence; and even Girard, who dissents with both thinkers in his ontology, insists that "violence is always mingled with desire." The point is epistemological no less than metaphysical. Thus Michel Foucault remarks in his "Theatrum Philosophicum": "We should not restrict meaning to the cognitive core that lies at the heart of a knowable object; rather, we should allow it to reestablish its flux at the limit of words and things. . . . Death supplies the best example, being both the event of events and meaning in its purest state."

Death, then, is more than our ultimate reunion: it is immanent in our desires as in our knowledge or speech. But how can all this affect a critic's "job of work"? Only thus: no critical gesture—in reading or writing, in praxis or poesis—that fails to confess even as it questions the intricacies of violence and desire—desire for love or death, for being or power—can come near to wisdom, which may itself be our most "refined passion."

The principle is hardly novel; it animates the psychoanalytic movement from the old masters—Freud, Jung, Adler—to the visionary epigones—Marcuse, Brown, Laing. Yet it is in France, of course, that the discourse of desire has recently reached full philosophical loquacity—and opacity. I have in mind the utterances of Jacques Lacan, Roland Barthes, Michel Foucault, Gilles Deleuze, Jean-Francois Lyotard, of whom only the first is a professional analyst. I can do no justice here, or even injustice, to the clouded brilliance and high casuistry of that movement; nor should I dwell on strictures and tergiversations of various sophists and schoolmen on the critical scene. I hope simply to disengage from the current debate certain ideas that the critical self may find seductive.

> *He suffers from a certain logophobia. Once, in another country, he declined to speak for two months, in spite of words. Occasionally, he still feels his brain barely bobbing on a sea of silence. He loses always at Scrabble. From time to time, he thinks of Charlie Starkweather who shot some dozen people in a tavern because "there was too much talk." Unlike those far ancestors, their brains still bicameral, he hears no voices in the head; his readiest intuitions are mute. What, then did mad Hölderlin hear* "wenn die Stille kehrt"?

Like his predecessors, Lacan also locates desire in the interplay between self and other. The interplay, beginning with the infant's "mirror stage," is specular; it constitutes a reflexive alienation from which all subsequent identifications derive. For Lacan, then, desire is still *for the desire* of the other, "not so much because the other holds the key to the object desired, as because the first object of desire is to be recognized by the other." This admits Hegel's "recognition" and Freud's "primal cognition"—on the bodies of our mothers we first learn to construe—and admits as well Nietzsche's insatiable "will," perceived here as the perpetual demand of language, a language never commensurate to self and other. Lacan's genius informs his attention to the question of language, which his own paludal style both reveals and conceals. For not only is the unconscious ("the discourse of the Other") structured as a language; what we call the self is but itself an instance of the "symbolic order." Thus the philosophical status of the subject, from Descartes to the present, remains wholly contingent on the duplicities of discourse.

In his seminal essay, "The Function of Language in Psychoanalysis" (originally delivered in 1953 as the *Discours de Rome*), Lacan says: "In order to liberate the subject's Word, we introduce him into the Language of his desire, that is, into the *primary Language* in which, beyond what he tells us of himself, he is already talking to us unbeknownst to him, and in the symbols of the symptom in the first place." Yet language, we know, implies negation, the absence of the thing signified; this symbolic "murder" or death, Lacan insists, "constitutes in the subject the eternalization of his desire." What follows is Lacan at his outrageous best: "Therefore, when we wish to attain in the subject what was before the serial articulations of the Word, and what is primordial to the birth of symbols, we find it in death, from which his existence takes on all the meaning it has. It is in effect as a desire for death that he affirms himself for others; if he identifies himself with the other, it is by fixing him solidly in the metamorphosis of his essential image, and no being is ever evoked by him except among the shadows of death." Thus, again we see death (or *béance*), language, and desire coterminous in the self, a self articulated by signifiers—the most "privileged" being the phallus—that are the body's own displaced speech.

He has never seen anyone dead. His father and mother, long exiled, were nearly dead to him when they died very old. He was himself more than half a century old when a death finally touched him. He remembered her dying face, as she tried to speak, to recognize his presence, in words, in vain. She died—he was not there—without speaking again. Later, he dreamed of her as a little girl, dressed in white, weightless, whom he carried away from some harm no one could see or name.

II

The human universe is made of lack: such is Lacan's gravamen, and that of his poststructuralist claques. This is because, for them, the human universe is made of language. Thus the language of desire leads to the aesthetics of absence—note the currency of such terms as *degree zero, silence, chiasmus, tear, fissure, crack, rupture, fragment,* and *lapse* in the discourse of, say, Roland Barthes. Though I believe the *human* universe to be neither Full nor Empty, neither Deed nor Word, but rather what we choose continually to make of it, I now turn to the work of Barthes, which joins for us the issues of desire and reading, the first two terms in my triad.

Barthes's later work seems as much a meditation on the reading self as an amatory ritual or verbal caress—no doubt polymorphous—of certain texts, or perhaps of textuality itself This does not inhibit the author from proposing several moot distinctions in *The Pleasure of the Text.* The arch distinction refers to the experiences of pleasure (*plaisir*) and of bliss (*jouissance*) in reading—the first expressible, the latter unutterable (*in-dicible, inter-dit*). The text of pleasure fills, "grants euphoria," even as it enters the purview of culture and history; that of bliss, asocial, permits no "recuperation," especially of the self in bliss. Yet even pleasure is "atopic," and so evades ideological "prattle" and praxis. Pleasure does serve, however, to link "the reading neurosis to the hallucinated form of the text," thus revealing the true individuality of the subject. Based on that conjunction between personal neurosis and imagined text, Barthes further distinguishes four kinds of readers: "the fetishist," haunted by parts and division of the text; "the obsessive," including philologists, semioticians, metalinguists; "the paranoiac," argumentative, ideological, egotistic; and "the hysteric," immersed in the text, surrendering to it in near bliss. (Armine Kotin gives an excellent reading of these four types of readers in the first issue of *The Journal of Practical Structuralism* [July 1979].) Yet Barthes quickly confesses that such distinctions waver—"I stumble, I err," he slyly cries—and so provide no solid ground for a science of reading. In any case the text is gossamer; the critic's business is *hyphology* (from *hyphos,* the spider's web); and the reader, in near bliss, "unmakes himself, like a spider dissolving in the constructive secretions of its web." Talismanic, full of subtle subversion rather than theory, this slim work ends by reviving, with infinite delicacy, the Nietzschean dualism of Apollonian and Dionysian as modes of reading.

Fragments of a Lover's Discourse affords us a more febrile experience; for pain and solitude here attend the subject more than pleasure, as do jealousy and spite. Simulating discreetly a lover's speech, rendering it in broken "figures," such as a modern dancer may perform, the book also presents us with an "encyclopedia of affective culture," ordered by no principle other than the alphabet of desire. Yet the spirit of the Erinyes pervades its pages; and the text to which it always returns, without ever leaving, is that incontinent book of love, death, and madness, *The Sorrows of Young Werther,* which so many in Europe read and, reading, learned to sigh and die. Thus both love and suicide become textual mimesis: the question is still one of reading. Barthes suggests that this book should be ideally dedicated to lovers and readers united. But united in what? In the sense of death? In the inadequacies of love? Certainly in the immanence of a language that continually creates and betrays, speaks and silences, desire itself. Here the contradictions of readers and writers, lunatics and lovers, seem in the dis-ease of language compact.

These contradictions converge on the erotic self whose very words we read. For if Barthes writes to simulate a lover's plaintive or morbid discourse (the lover is never a "*sujet saint*"), he offers us also a counterfeit autobiography, cunning in its confessions, artful in its masks. This is not merely because Barthes is wily, or that his lovers are condemned to stealth by their love; it is also because language and desire meet at the limits of their mutual destructions in the subject of love. There is really no possibility of explication, of hermeneutics, in this forlorn confession. Indeed, for Barthes, true knowledge depends on the "unmaking of the *I*, superb organ of miscognition [*méconnaissance*]." This "unmaking of the I" is a political, a utopian, project, affecting reading and writing, self and society. In the book of Barthes, the erotic undoing of the articulate self comes finally to this: "I want to change systems: no longer to unmask, no longer to interpret, but to make of consciousness itself a drug, and thus to accede to a vision of irreducible reality, to the great dream of clarity, to prophetic love." Suddenly, Barthes calls us closer to Boehme than Quintillian.

Venus influenced his house in the zodiac. Yet for many years in his life, he suffered the tug of two obsessions: women and work. (He can almost recall all the "perfect legs" he has seen, climbing out of cabs, crossed in restaurants, clicking on the streets of cities; and see, in the glaucous mirror of desire, those golden-thighed women of the north, with their lupine eyes.) Women and work: how can intellect choose perfection of desire or the spirit? No tantrist, he ages, locked a little in the banality of fantasy and time.

Yet Venus, at last, who influenced his birth, sent an emissary to his house.

The stance of Roland Barthes toward the text is radical anarchic—he would prefer to say ideolectic. Yet the political terms are apposite; for a textual theory assumes a theory of society as well as of desire, and reading is an act we perform in the name of tacit cultural constraints. Such constraints do not preclude for Barthes the possibility of innovation. A political revolution and a mutation in desire share the same *telos,* which is "the absolute New." Similarly, in reading, by choosing the Lover against the Interpreter or Priest, Barthes chooses the uncodified, the enchanted, the "*intraitable,*" and so invokes the New. Yet the New, as we all sadly know, never remains novel. Thus Barthes espouses the sexual and textual politics of permanent revolution.

In George Steiner, however, we meet a critic of nearly antithetical persuasion. His censures of pornography, too famous to reiterate here, express his acute discomfort with a discourse that at once corrupts and coerces human polity. In the recent collection, *On Difficulty,* Steiner confronts the wider question of literacy. Recognizing the manifold nexus of literature and sexuality throughout history, he still deplores the devaluation of erotic as of religious language in our world. "The two devaluations . . .," Steiner argues, "are obviously related. Together they amount to an almost programmatic 'thinning out' of the interior medium." Such loss of "internality," such incursions on the privacy of love or worship, strike him as a baleful aspect of our modernity. To this process, even psychoanalysis has lent its prestige; for its voluble therapies help to erode "the autonomous energies of inward diction and plenitude." As the balance of "internal speech" shifts toward "public verbalization," toward publicity in its largest sense, the self risks its own "voidance"; "less lodged in ourselves," we become less adequate to the very stresses we generate. (Characteristically, Steiner cannot resist to add: "the American house is, or was until very recently, open to all comers.")

It is the economy of the speaking and reading and writing self, then, that vitally concerns George Steiner, and his concern puts to challenge the "empty subject" of Nietzsche, Derrida, and Barthes. Nor does Steiner favor democratic or idiosyncratic readings of texts, which help to undermine informed authority. The extroversion of the self, the prepotence of technology, the dispersal of judgment in mass society—who knows what serves as cause here and what as effect?—have instituted a new kind of illiteracy, hostile to reading as to thought. For right reading is a stringent and solitary act, requiring disciplined attention and remembrance, honed skills of language, a tensed will. It requires, too, a cultural tradition or central syllabus, assuring that density of allusion and range of reference, that interactive power of sympathies, we now call "intertextuality." "The 'text' flourishes in a context of authority," Steiner starkly asserts. The "humanities," in their classic sense, entail no "ready equivalence," no "unforced co-existence with 'humanism' in a mass-liberal or socialist scheme of values." Now that affluence seems on the wane in the West, the latent incongruence of culture and democracy may break out. Steiner stoically views the dismal prospect, and calls for "houses of reading," where a few can still be taught to read again with rigor and delight, "proudly, *con amore,*" so that the text may remain for us "the vital circumstance, the informing 'context' of our being."

I may have lent the argument more austerity or asperity than Steiner intended. Certainly, he recognizes that "texts are inexhaustible to our needs," and that a degree of "disinterested irresponsibility"—one thinks of deconstruction—may enhance our quickness to literature. Moreover, in a recent essay entitled " 'Critic'/'Reader' " (*New Literary History* [Spring 1979]), Steiner seeks to discriminate between literary experiences in a more optative mood. Nor is the distance between Barthes and Steiner absolute; between them, various theorists—for instance, Geoffrey Hartman, Wolfgang Iser, Norman Holland, David Bleich—mediate the reading act. Still, the issue becomes clearest when we maintain contrastive space between the two critics. For their advocacies remain antithetical; and Steiner's catholic priesthood of reading, reverting to Péguy and Benda, would find no welcome in the heteroclite culture of desire of Barthes.

Such varied dispositions toward text, self, and society lead us again to wonder: can the act of reading ever acquire consensual definition? My own contention, throughout, has been that no epistemology of literature can usefully answer the question, though an ontology of desire may help us to start. As an aspect of the primal will, reading consists of a complex *fiat* of our being in Language—which is to say, in relation to the Other, be it mother, rival, history, death, or the unconscious. Hence "reading" is always party to a continually broken, perpetually revised "social contract." Inescapably, we ask: who reads? But, imperatively, we must also know: to what end does that reader construe the text and in what historical context?

As if by accident, he comes upon a text, vaguely autobiographical, published more than a quarter of a century ago. He reads from that text, written between him and birth, interposed between him and death, thinking wryly that every reading gives life to the dead, even if the latter prove to be only himself, in another country. He reads these words in a text that may be this text's context:

> . . . schoolboys of all classes jostled their prejudices and bandied their enmities with characteristic ferocity in the drab classrooms of governmental schools. At the black, iron-grilled gates, which shut at five minutes past eight with frightening finality, and opened only at five minutes to three, the parental Mercedes, Rolls, or Packard may have been waiting for the fortunate students. But once inside, these abandoned all hope, and shifted for themselves as best they could, relying on wit and fist (some fought also with their unbreakable skulls), to absolve themselves bloodily of cowardice, effeminacy, and good breeding. One played at soccer between classes, with a makeshift ball of old socks—the rest was work. . . . It was not unusual for students who failed their final examinations—the lists were there, tacked to peeling walls—to attempt suicide.

He thinks of another scene, decades later, a graduate student, subsisting mainly on apples and Hershey bars, earning his doctorate in a foreign tongue. The department chairman—renowned, a former president of his professional association—stares at him through fishbowl glasses and gently rasps:

"We've given you scholarships and fellowships. But we can't give you a teaching assistantship now: you have elements in your speech that are not standard."

Quite true, he thinks. But then, there were "nonstandard elements" even when he spoke his "mother tongue."

III

In desiring, in reading, in making, the critic acts out his autobiography, compounded of many selves. Such enactments, though personal, refer us also to history. Thus Hans-Georg Gadamer—who clearly sees that prejudices constitute our being far more than judgments—avers in his *Philosophical Hermeneutics:* "It is not really we ourselves who understand: it is always a past that allows us to say, 'I have understood.' " This active pastness of the self, this vital historicity of understanding—so different from the *passéisme* of genteel academics—projects itself into the future and so engages the critic's praxis.

This is plain in Foucault's "archaeology of knowledge," which bares encoded patterns of power and so brings me to the last term in my triad. Of Foucault's many archaeologies—of words and madness, of penal and medical systems—that of sexuality is the most proximate to my theme. In an early work, *The Order of Things,* Foucault had noted that Death, Language (or Law), and Desire delimit the foundations of human society, the edge of the "unthought" (*l'impensé*). In his recent *History of Sexuality* (the first volume), he goes farther to assay the various languages of desire. These, he strikingly maintains, far from being repressive, richly articulate given powers. But what does Foucault mean by power? This: an immanence of effective discourse, an interplay of relations, a field of dispersed forces; in short, power "is the name one lends to a complex strategic situation in a particular society." This view, anathema to Marxists, perceives sexuality as the seam between the human body and the body politic, the suture between personal freedom and social control. By making sexuality sexy and desire desirable, by privileging eroticism as a signifier, the discourse of power further creates a manageable identity for each of us—whether homosexual or heterosexual—and so perpetuates itself. The ancient right of tyrants to kill their subjects now yields to the right of states to enforce a particular life on their citizens; the old "*symbolique du sang*" gives way to the new "*analytique de la sexualité.*" Thus, for Foucault, true freedom invokes not the idea of "*le sexe-désire*" but "bodies in their pleasure."

We may challenge this peculiar concept of power, as Jean Baudrillard does in *Oublier Foucault.* (Power for Baudrillard, incidentally, is not an immanent field or grid, but a seduction, a provocation, a *leurre.*) But we cannot refuse Foucault's grand insight: that all discourse implicates itself deeply in the structures of power. For him, the very idea of epistemic continuity shields society from break, crisis, and change—hence the aversion of families, churches, states, to discontinuities of every kind. Similarly, the creed of Humanism reinforces social organization by prohibiting shifts both in the shape and intent of power. At the center of the Humanist creed lies the concept of the Western self, which Foucault wants to attack doubly: "either by a 'desubjectification' of the will to power (that is, through political struggle . . .) or by the destruction of the subject as a pseudosovereign (that is, through an attack on 'culture' . . .)," he writes in *Language, Counter-Memory, Practice.* In brief, the critic acts not only by demystifying the languages of desire but also by assaulting both the epistemic and political structures of society; or, in Foucault's words, by the "simultaneous agitation of consciousness and institutions. . . ."

Yet the critic's praxis—here Michel Foucault and Gilles Deleuze agree—cannot mesh completely with theory; for there are always *blockages,* disruptions, that neither can nor should be eliminated by "totalization." This last, of course, appears to poststructuralists as the ultimate abomination. Hence their justified equivocations about Freud or Marx. Can Freudian biological instinct desire against itself? Can Marxist class interest overrule desire? Deleuze would answer: interest gives no final answer to the riddle of power, since "there are investments of desire that function in a more profound and diffuse manner than our interests dictate"; to which Foucault would add: "the relationships between desire, power, and interest are more complex than we ordinarily think, and it is not necessarily those who exercise power who have an interest in its execution; nor is it always possible for those with vested interests to exercise power."

This politics of dispersal or displacement renders praxis ambiguous if not anarchic. Deleuze—and also Lyotard as we shall see—happily avow this tendency. Deleuze's major work, *L'Anti-Oedipe,* coauthored with Félix Gauttari, carries the telling subtitle: "*Capitalisme et Schizophrénie.*" Declaring itself against both the Marxist thesis of social production and the Freudian principle of Oedipal repression, the book dazzlingly propounds the immanent "flux" of desire, which various systems, conjunctive or disjunctive, regulate. Men and women thus appear as "desiring machines," the latter being the authors' term for any system of breaks (*coupures*) which "schizo-analysis" aspires to liberate. This summary, though grossly simplified, may still educe the stubborn tendency of the book: to disrupt the structures of power and desire, and disrupt even more our understanding of these structures.

The disruptive, dispersive tendency extends to that slim antitract, *Rhizome.* Here Deleuze and Guattari coyly choose the figure of the rhizome—a living, amorphous plant stem—to convey their sense of emergent things: a diffuse self, fugitive forms, a culture open to syntagma and parataxis instead of hierarchic or generative models of organization. In their view the rhizome, unlike the root, shows no direction or center, only circumference, growing by variation, a jumble of self-modifying systems. The authors end breezily by enjoining us: "Faites rhizome et pas racine, ne plantez jamais! Ne semez pas, piquez! Ne soyez pas un ni multiple, soyez des multiplicités! Faites la ligne et jamais le point!" ("Make rhizome, not root; never plant! Do not sow, puncture! Be neither one nor many, be multiplicities! Make the line, and never the period!")

Deleuze clarifies the politics of this rhizomology in another brief work, *Dialogues,* with Claire Parnet. History, he believes, consists of various lines of motion or flight, "fluxes of deterritorialization," fluid like the wandering of the Jews or Vandals or Tartars, or like the Long March of Mao. Society itself follows certain lines of flight, which direct change at the deepest level. The true revolutionary perceives these lines and poses the practical question: what covert organization of energies, refusing the State, refusing its binary models of power, can still summon a new state? Deleuze concludes with a query of his own: instead of presaging the impossibility of revolution or the advent of world totalitarianism, why not concede that a *new kind* of change may already be in progress, and that various mutant and living "machines" may now conspire to subvert the known forms of World and State? The question, Deleuze insists, is neither utopian nor improvisational: it simply assumes another perspective on desire, knowledge, and power.

Possessed by a certain idea of America, he ended his first book with these words:

A country without prehistory, it has suddenly entered history with the intention to rape and redeem time in its heart. A country of illimitable spaces, it has confronted men with nature in the raw, inducing in them permanent and atavistic solitude, and it has been turned by them into the most profoundly denatured spectacle on record. Conceived as a dream, it has shown that dreamers may also awake in the cold sweat of a nightmare, and sleep to dream again. . . . The curse of Columbus is still with us: everyone must rediscover America—alone!

Foreign born, he still recalls that nothing terrified him more than the prospect of forced repatriation. He opened every letter from the Immigration and Naturalization Service with dry mouth, leaden hand. But now his impatience with America grows. For there is a crank in him, organ-grinding Jeremiah, ill-tempered, unreasonable, uncouth—a creature twisted of dream and hope. This is how the organ-grinder rasps:

"What's wrong with us now? A 'crisis of confidence'? You wouldn't know it, the way America rides on roller skates. But in the parks, the future walks with transistors instead of ears. The dollar's up and down, the dollar bills themselves torn and dirty. Everywhere, gas-guzzlers, gouged hulks, rust-cankered. The streets cracked, the lawns alitter; subways, whole cities, reeking harm in the night. We do love funk and horror; so, like Mom and Dad, Television and the Mafia give us what we need. For the rest, flabbiness like ocean to ocean carpeting, up to the knees.

"We have become a nation of first names. Oleaginous egos, spread thinly, like a smile or stain. Occlusions of desire, seeking in violence release. Perhaps this is what the poet had in mind when he wailed:

'For the error bred in the bone
Of each woman and each man
Craves what it cannot have,
Not universal love
But to be loved alone.' "

The crank now pauses, then turns political on his hurdy-gurdy:

"Fractious Factions everywhere, claiming Justice. But Justice—fragile, frangible, fugacious—soon yields to Vengeance, her darker sister. No hope in political Parties: the Right acts on fear, the Left on spite, except when fear and spite exchange their places. The Right, cramped in crotch, lies against time's infractions. The Left, infantile, remains fixed in futile abstractions. And the Middle, soft as always, whispers: 'death happens to other people, we're not responsible for their actions'."

The crank in him ceases cranking. Now the accuser stands accused. He thinks of his own life, full of losses and lapses. How make of personal slippage a veridical politics?

Truth, the idea of Truth itself, must be placed in doubt: so maintains Jean-Francois Lyotard, pushing the politics of desire to its limit. In *Économie libidinale,* a work energized by a Nietzschean poetics of intransigence, Lyotard conceives human reality as *"la grande pellicule éphémère,"* a libidinal membrane on which history inscribes itself, much as it did in the work of Deleuze. Ubiquitous, Möbius-like, without "depth," this great pellicule acts, however, more as a pulse than a strip. In its "figural space," desire "connives" to "transgress" textual organization and the habitual order of signifiers. Thus poetry, ally of desire, instigates change more than the alienated discourse of politics; and Marx himself emerges as *"le désir nommé Marx,"* an author of liberating lunacies rather than stodgy theories. Zanily, wittily, Lyotard invites us to stroke Marx's beard as a "complex libidinal volume," without contempt, without devotion, simply as an affective gesture, a conflation of passions. Indeed, the "Old Man" contains an erotic and subversive creature, "little Miss Marx" (*la petite Marx*), whom Lyotard compares to Madame Edwarda, George Bataille's notorious prostitute.

Scandalous as all this may seem, Lyotard knows no cynicism in his effort to release the Human Abstract from systemic bondage. In this effort Marxist discourse—endless chatter, perpetual revision—seems to him nugatory. The pulses of intensity, the exchanges of power, prove life to be a secret currency, running through all domains, sacred and profane, practical and theoretical. A libidinal economy *is* a political economy. Lyotard ends with this appeal: *"Nul besoin de déclarations, de manifestes, d'organisations, de provocations, nul besoin même d'actions exemplaires. Faites jouer la dissimilation en faveur des intensités. Complot invulnérable. . . . Nous n'inventons rien, ça y est, oui, oui, oui, oui"* ("No need for declarations, manifestoes, organizations, provocations, no need even for *exemplary actions.* Put in play dissimilarities in favor of intensities. Invulnerable conspiracy. . . . We invent nothing, it is already here, yes, yes, yes, yes.")

Lyotard's politics may appear, as Matei Calinescu has noted ("Marxism as a Work of Art," *Stanford French Review* [Spring 1979]), fundamentally aesthetic, their spirit tropic or figural. Yet his politics are also humorously pragmatic, enacted by a terrorist, a marginal, and a trickster all in one. Two short works, *Instructions païennes* and *Rudiments païens*, speak playfully to the point. In the first Lyotard invokes both justice and impiety, or rather justice *in* impiety, to create a "pragmatic narrative"—made up of anecdotes, riddles, conversations, fragments—meant to undermmine the Great Signifier of society. This tactic requires "riposte" rather than "reaction"—requires, that is, a constant and exultant shift of perspectives on the enemy. In the second work, Lyotard resorts to the English word "patchwork"—instead of Lévi-Strauss's "*bricolage*"—to designate the tactics of displacement. Aggravate nihilism, he cries; hasten the crisis of values; become enterprising in decadence! At the same time, permit no class to control the discourse—specifically the metalanguage—of all society. And though conflict and violence may ensue, as the American example has rabidly shown, promote the cause of minorities in a "heterogeneous space." This "new perspective," Lyotard claims, resists Unity, Finality, Truth (all in capitals), following the "logic of sophists," not of "master logicians," the "time of opportunity," not of "world history." Like the pagan gods, politic, protean, unveridical, and so often cruel, Lyotard would free praxis at the expense of all human pieties—except some vehement, some joyful idea of justice that even the gods lack.

Taut at its limits, Lyotard's thought helps us to refine, if not define, our own. In so far as it sentimentalizes terrorism, it seems blind to an arrogance that it calls justice, and so strikes us as rebarbative. Yet in its audacious vision, it confronts us with the Gorgon-stare of the age. The challenge to a critic's praxis comes finally to this: how act *in extremis*, and in whose name, without making a monster of oneself, turning self into stone:

He jogs, pumping blood and adrenaline, and conducts imaginary conversations.

A Marxist colleague accuses him: "You put truth before praxis. This is bourgeois, decadent." He answers, feet pounding: "Separate truth from action, and you end with terrorism or its bigger brother, totalitarianism. I choose neither: both serve themselves while claiming to serve others."

A friend admonishes him often: "We must make distinctions, we must make sharp distinctions." Panting, he retorts: "Indeed we must, and must distinguish between distinctions: some inert, habitual, others creative, mindbracing."

A colleague twits him: "That's just macho." He thinks: "Machismo can be puerile and can be deadly. But its thrust got us out from the back of the cave into this dubious light. Besides, Hemingway and Mishima, Malraux and Mailer, are more emotionally literate than most men and women I meet."

Another junior colleague boasts to him: "I am becoming more conservative every day." Sweating now, as another jogger is about to overtake him, he mutters, "So am I, if conservative means exacting. Otherwise, never! Let a thousand risks bloom."

Laced with small aggressions, his mute conversations are less imaginary than ontological, a running critique of being in the world, as he runs to delay his dying.

In-Conclusion

Finally, no one knows of what the self is made, though luck, genes, and achievement help us to gain some working sense of it. That self is certainly a construct, an interpretation, to various degrees effective or ineffectual, yet never so capable—despite the Grandees of Neurosis—as when least anxious in its skin. The construct, however, remains unfinished, as Ortega said long ago, "a personage . . . never completely realized, a stimulating Utopia, a secret legend, which each of us guards in the bottom of his heart." It is this legend that I have tried to elicit from the critical self in three continuous movements: desiring, reading, acting. In the process, elicitation became solicitation as I called on certain authors to provide both a cultural and theoretical context for the argument. Calling on various authors, did I then betray my self?

Betrayal is always double: it discloses even as it deceives. The texts I have chosen speak a tendency in myself no less than in the culture of which we are all a part (apart). The tendency is radical in that, searching for the roots of knowledge and being, it risks itself in strenuous gestures of discontinuity, bellicose illusions of newness. Gestures and illusions rarely alter reality; yet they may vex both reality and ourselves into a larger, stronger, quicker apprehension of things. How many of us walk like somnambulists through existence, harkening to ancestral voices that are but the sound of our own fearful breath?

Half of the authors I have discussed are French. This is not adventitious. England offers nothing bracing in criticism now; Germany in reaction to its past may have locked its mind, with some rare exceptions, in academic Marxisms; and America, excepting a handful of critics, has become a virtuoso of sullen scholarship or gallic parody. Nor is French thought itself impeccable. I have elsewhere registered my impatience with its fanatic unmakings and Gongoresque styles. Yet no other thought, I think, has opened for us so many perspectives of theory as of praxis, sharpened our sense of the verbal self, and so enriched the critic's life. Moreover, no other thought, despite its cant, has moved us closer to that perception of our contemporaneity that constitutes the postmodern *epistémè*.

The nature of our contemporaneity merits some attention, though it defies clarity. For we live in an interstitial moment, one both of barbarism and decadence, a time both of violence and timidity in the West, which now includes the Russian Empire. What beast slouches toward Bethlehem then? I suppose it to be the dream or specter of planetization, transhumanization. For the "decline of the West" will not yield the Earth to another rising civilization, as it has so often yielded in the past; it will cede it, rather, to peaceable or savage planetization, one world yet ever so various, the North/South axis collapsing convulsively into the East/West. We may wonder: what role can the critic play when history shakes? Perhaps only a modest but dual role: one of subversion, the other of making.

We require versatile subversion to free the mind from that deadening, *and* deadly, discourse that both Right and Left impose. (An anti-ideology may constitute a kind of ideology, yet it remains one of very different kind.) For once, Lacan speaks lucidly: "It is the irony of revolutions that they engender a power all the more absolute in its actions, not because it is more anonymous, as people say, but because it is more reduced to the words which signify it." We need "subtle subversion," by which Barthes means: "What is not directly concerned with destruction, evades the paradigm, and seeks some *other* term: a third term, which is not, however, a synthesizing term but an eccentric, extraordinary term." Precisely, what I have called side-stepping, slippage, the politics of displacement, the praxis of self-surprise.

As for the critic's making—which I have expounded elsewhere—I need claim for it here only what we would claim for any act of the plenary intelligence: both imaginative freedom and moral force. I insist on the imaginative relation in the critic's life because I sense that without it, without *poesis,* the critical relation becomes a form of Nietzschean *ressentiment,* a consummation of the ironic self, a spite of mind. For beyond irony, subversion, or deconstruction—here I part decisively with Derrida—our presence and absence, like warp and woof in the loom of the universe, call us to an asseveration that few critics have been willing to make. This asseveration, perhaps fiercer than those I have earlier remarked, finds its voice not in any pale grammatology or white semiology but in the tradition of Goethe, Blake, and Emerson—a "visionary company," as Harold Bloom knows, lacking in neither a dialectical awareness nor political acumen.

The strongest self is least self-absorbed; it opens and imperils itself continually. Its best achievement, both mystics and nonmystics say, may consist in self-overcoming. Yet for all that, it is neither single nor insubstantial. "What else am I who laughed or wept yesterday," Emerson asks in "History," "who slept last night like a corpse, and this morning stood and ran? And what see I on any side but the transmigrations of Proteus?"

He tries to imagine precisely the unimaginable: his own death. He succeeds only in making it literary. Unlike Ivan Karamazov, he does not prize Justice over Reality, and so will not "return his ticket" to God. He would rather drown in Reality:

> "Not drowned entirely, though. Rather carried down alive to wondrous depths, where strange shapes of the unwarped primal world glided to and fro before his passive eyes; and the miser-merman, Wisdom, revealed his hoarded heaps, and among the joyous, heartless, ever-juvenile eternities, Pip saw the multitudinous, God-omni-present, coral insects, that out of the firmament of waters heaved the colossal orbs. He saw God's foot upon the treadle of the loom, and spoke it. . . ."

Drown in Reality. But then, grasping at a straw, he thinks: not yet, not yet.

8 Pluralism in Postmodern Perspective

I

Postmodernism once more—that breach has begun to yawn! I return to it by way of pluralism, which itself has become the irritable condition of postmodern discourse, consuming many pages of both critical and uncritical inquiry. Why? Why pluralism now? This question recalls another that Kant raised two centuries ago—"*Was heisst Aufklärung?*"—meaning, "Who are we now?" The answer was a signal meditation on historical presence, as Michel Foucault saw.[1] But to meditate on that topic today—and *this* is my central claim—is really to inquire "*Was heisst Postmodernismus?*"

Pluralism in our time finds (if not founds) itself in the social, aesthetic, and intellectual assumptions of postmodernism—finds its ordeal, its rightness, there. I submit, further, that the critical intentions of diverse American pluralists—M. H. Abrams, Wayne Booth, Kenneth Burke, Matei Calinescu, R. S. Crane, Nelson Goodman, Richard McKeon, Stephen Pepper, not to mention countless other artists and thinkers of our moment—engage that overweening query, "What is postmodernism?" engage and even answer it tacitly. In short, like a latter-day M. Jourdain, they have been speaking postmodernism all their lives without knowing it.

But what *is* postmodernism? I can still propose no rigorous definition of it, any more than I could define modernism itself. The time to theorize it, though, to historicize it, is nearly at hand, without muting its errancies, vexations. These bear on problems of cultural modeling, literary periodization, cultural change—the problems of critical discourse itself in an antinomian phase.[2] Still, the exhaustions of modernism, or at least its self-revisions, have prompted incongruous thinkers to moot its supervention. Thus Daniel Bell, a "conservative" sociologist, testifies to "the end of the creative impulse and ideological sway of modernism, which, as a cultural movement, has dominated all the arts, and shaped our symbolic expressions, for the past 125 years."[3] And thus, too, a "radical" philosopher, Jürgen Habermas, tries to distinguish—vainly, as I see it—between the "premodernism of old conservatives," the "antimodernism of the young conservatives," and the "postmodernism of the neoconservatives."[4]

All "superventions" aside, let me offer a catena of postmodern features, a paratactic list, staking out a cultural field. My examples will be selective; my traits may overlap, conflict, or antecede themselves. Still, together they limn a region of postmodern "indetermanences" (indeterminacy lodged in immanence) in which critical pluralism takes shape.[5]

II

Here, then, is my catena:

1. *Indeterminacy*, or rather, indeterminacies. These include all manner of ambiguities, ruptures, and displacements affecting knowledge and society. We think of Werner Karl Heisenberg's principle of uncertainty, Kurt Gödel's proof of incompleteness, Thomas Kuhn's paradigms, and Paul Feyerabend's dadaism of science. Or we may think of Harold Rosenberg's anxious art objects, de-defined. And in literary theory? From Mikhail Bakhtin's dialogic imagination, Roland Barthes' *textes scriptibles*, Wolfgang Iser's literary *Unbestimmtheiten*, Harold Bloom's misprisions, Paul de Man's allegorical readings, Stanley Fish's affective stylistics, Norman Holland's transactive analysis, and David Bleich's subjective criticism, to the last fashionable *aporia* of unrecorded time, we undecide, relativize. Indeterminacies pervade our actions, ideas, interpretations; they constitute our world.

2. *Fragmentation.* Indeterminacy often follows from fragmentation. The postmodernist only disconnects; fragments are all he pretends to trust. His ultimate opprobrium is "totalization"—any synthesis whatever, social, epistemic, even poetic. Hence his preference for montage, collage, the found or cut-up literary object, for paratactic over hypotactic forms, metonymy over metaphor, schizophrenia over paranoia. Hence, too, his recourse to paradox, paralogy, parabasis, paracriticism, the openness of brokenness, unjustified margins. Thus Jean-François Lyotard

exhorts, "Let us wage a war on totality; let us be witnesses to the unpresentable; let us activate the differences and save the honor of the name."[6] The age demands differences, shifting signifiers, and even atoms dissolve into elusive subparticles, a mere mathematical whisper.

3. *Decanonization.* In the largest sense, this applies to all canons, all conventions of authority. We are witnessing, Lyotard argues again, a massive "delegitimation" of the mastercodes in society, a desuetude of the metanarratives, favoring instead *"les petites histoires,"* which preserve the heterogeneity of language games.[7] Thus, from the "death of god" to the "death of the author" and "death of the father," from the derision of authority to revision of the curriculum, we decanonize culture, demystify knowledge, deconstruct the languages of power, desire, deceit. Derision and revision are versions of subversion, of which the most baleful example is the rampant terrorism of our time. But "subversion" may take other, more benevolent, forms such as minority movements or the feminization of culture, which also require decanonization.

4. *Self-less-ness, Depth-less-ness.* Postmodernism vacates the traditional self, simulating self-effacement—a fake flatness, without inside/outside—or its opposite, self-multiplication, self-reflection. Critics have noted the "loss of self" in modern literature, but it was originally Nietzsche who declared the "subject" "only a fiction": "the ego of which one speaks when one censures egoism does not exist at all."[8] Thus postmodernism suppresses or disperses and sometimes tries to recover the "deep" romantic ego, which remains under dire suspicion in poststructuralist circles as a "totalizing principle." Losing itself in the play of language, in the differences from which reality is plurally made, the self impersonates its absence even as death stalks its games. It diffuses itself in depthless styles, refusing, eluding, interpretation.[9]

5. *The Unpresentable, Unrepresentable.* Like its predecessor, postmodern art is irrealist, aniconic. Even its "magic realism" dissolves in ethereal states; its hard, flat surfaces repel mimesis. Postmodern literature, particularly, often seeks its limits, entertains its "exhaustion," subverts itself in forms of articulate "silence." It becomes liminary, contesting the modes of its own representation. Like the Kantian Sublime, which thrives on the formlessness, the emptiness, of the Absolute—

"Thou shalt not make graven images"—"the postmodern would be," in Lyotard's audacious analogue, "that which, in the modern, puts forward the unpresentable in presentation itself."[10] But the challenge to representation may also lead a writer to other liminal states: the Abject, for instance, rather than the Sublime, or Death itself—more precisely, "the exchange between signs and death," as Julia Kristeva put it. "What is unrepresentability?" Kristeva asks. "That which, through language, is part of no particular language. . . . That which, through meaning, is intolerable, unthinkable: the horrible, the abject."[11]

Here, I think we reach a peripety of negations. For with my next "definien," Irony, we begin to move from the deconstructive to the coexisting reconstructive tendency of postmodernism.

6. *Irony.* This could also be called, after Kenneth Burke, perspectivism. In absence of a cardinal principle or paradigm, we turn to play, interplay, dialogue, polylogue, allegory, self-reflection—in short, to irony. This irony assumes indeterminacy, multivalence; it aspires to clarity, the clarity of demystification, the pure light of absence. We meet variants of it in Bakhtin, Burke, de Man, Jacques Derrida, and Hayden White. And in Alan Wilde we see an effort to discriminate its modes: "mediate irony," "disjunctive irony," and "postmodern" or "suspensive irony" "with its yet more radical vision of multiplicity, randomness, contingency, and even absurdity."[12] Irony, perspectivism, reflexiveness: these express the ineluctable recreations of mind in search of a truth that continually eludes it, leaving it with only an ironic access or excess of self-consciousness.

7. *Hybridization,* or the mutant replication of genres, including parody, travesty, pastiche. The "de-definition," deformation, of cultural genres engenders equivocal modes: "paracriticism," "fictual discourse," the "new journalism," the "nonfiction novel," and a promiscuous category of "para-literature" or "threshold literature," at once young and very old.[13] Cliché and plagiarism ("playgiarism," Raymond Federman punned), parody and pastiche, pop and kitsch enrich *re*-presentation. In this view image or replica may be as valid as its model (the *Quixote* of Borges' Pierre Menard), may even bring an "*augment d'être.*" This makes for a different concept of tradition, one in which continuity and discontinuity, high and low culture, mingle not to imi-

tate but to expand the past in the present. In that plural present, all styles are dialectically available in an interplay between the Now and the Not Now, the Same and the Other. Thus, in postmodernism, Heidegger's concept of "equitemporality" becomes really a dialectic of equitemporality, an intertemporality, a new relation between historical elements, without any suppression of the past in favor of the present—a point that Fredric Jameson misses when he criticizes postmodern literature, film, and architecture for their ahistorical character, their "presentifications."[14]

8. *Carnivalization.* The term, of course, is Bakhtin's, and it riotously embraces indeterminacy, fragmentation, decanonization, selflessness, irony, hybridization, all of which I have already adduced. But the term also conveys the comic or absurdist ethos of postmodernism, anticipated in the "heteroglossia" of Rabelais and Sterne, jocose prepostmodernists. Carnivalization further means "polyphony," the centrifugal power of language, the "gay relativity" of things, perspectivism and performance, participation in the wild disorder of life, the immanence of laughter.[15] Indeed, what Bakhtin calls novel or carnival—that is, antisystem—might stand for postmodernism itself, or at least for its ludic and subversive elements that promise renewal. For in carnival "the true feast of time, the feast of becoming, change, and renewal," human beings, then as now, discover "the peculiar logic of the 'inside out' (*à l'envers*), of the 'turnabout,' . . . of numerous parodies and travesties, humiliations, profanations, comic crownings and uncrownings. A second life."[16]

9. *Performance, Participation.* Indeterminacy elicits participation; gaps must be filled. The postmodern text, verbal or nonverbal, invites performance: it wants to be written, revised, answered, acted out. Indeed, so much of postmodern art calls itself performance, as it transgresses genres. As performance, art (or theory for that matter) declares its vulnerability to time, to death, to audience, to the Other.[17] "Theatre" becomes—to the edge of terrorism—the active principle of a paratactic society, decanonized if not really carnivalized. At its best, as Richard Poirier contends, the performing self expresses "an energy in motion, an energy with its own shape"; yet in its "self-discovering, self-

watching, finally self-pleasuring response to . . . pressures and difficulties," that self may also veer toward solipsism, lapse into narcissism.[18]

10. *Constructionism.* Since postmodernism is radically tropic, figurative, irrealist—"what can be thought of must certainly be a fiction," Nietzsche thought[19]—it "constructs" reality in post-Kantian, indeed post-Nietzschean, "fictions."[20] Scientists seem now more at ease with heuristic fictions than many humanists, last realists of the West. (Some literary critics even kick language, thinking thus to stub their toes on a stone.) Such effective fictions suggest the growing intervention of mind in nature and culture, an aspect of what I have called the "new gnosticism" evident in science and art, in social relations and high technologies.[21] But constructionism appears also in Burke's "dramatistic criticism," Pepper's "world hypothesis," Goodman's "ways of worldmaking," White's "prefigurative moves," not to mention current hermeneutic or poststructuralist theory. Thus postmodernism sustains the movement "from unique truth and a world fixed and found," as Goodman remarked, "to a diversity of right and even conflicting versions or worlds in the making."[22]

11. *Immanence.* This refers, without religious echo, to the growing capacity of mind to generalize itself through symbols. Everywhere now we witness problematic diffusions, dispersals, dissemination; we experience the extension of our senses, as Marshall McLuhan crankily presaged, through new media and technologies. Languages, apt or mendacious, reconstitute the universe—from quasars to quarks and back, from the lettered unconscious to black holes in space—reconstitute it into signs of their own making, turning nature into culture, and culture into an immanent semiotic system. The language animal has emerged, his/her measure the intertextuality of all life. A patina of thought, of signifiers, of "connections," now lies on everything the mind touches in its gnostic (noö)sphere, which physicists, biologists, and semioticians, no less than mystic theologians like Teilhard de Chardin, explore. The pervasive irony of their explorations is also the reflexive irony of mind meeting itself at every dark turn.[23] Yet in a consuming society such immanences can become more vacuous than fatidic. They become, as Jean Baudrillard says, pervasively "ob-scene," a "collective vertigo of

neutralization, a forward escape into the obscenity of pure and empty form."[24]

These eleven "definiens" add up to a surd, perhaps absurd. I should be much surprised if they amounted to a definition of postmodernism, which remains, at best, an equivocal concept, a disjunctive category, doubly modified by the impetus of the phenomenon itself and by the shifting perceptions of its critics. (At worst, postmodernism appears to be a mysterious, if ubiquitous, ingredient—like raspberry vinegar, which instantly turns any recipe into *nouvelle cuisine.*)

Nor do I believe that my eleven "definiens" serve to distinguish postmodernism from modernism; for the latter itself abides as a fierce evasion in our literary histories.[25] But I do suggest that the foregoing points—elliptic, cryptic, partial, provisional—argue twin conclusions: (*a*) *critical pluralism is deeply implicated in the cultural field of postmodernism;* and (*b*) *a limited critical pluralism is in some measure a reaction against the radical relativism, the ironic indetermanences, of the postmodern condition; it is an attempt to contain them.*

III

So far, my argument has been prelusive. I must now attend to those efforts that seek to limit—quite rightly, I believe—the potential anarchy of our postmodern condition with cognitive, political, or affective constraints. That is, I must briefly consider criticism as genre, power, and desire—as Kenneth Burke did, long ago, in his vast synoptics of motives.

Is criticism a genre? Critical pluralists often suppose that it may be so.[26] Yet even that most understanding of pluralists, Wayne Booth, is forced finally to admit that a full "methodological pluralism," which must aspire to a perspective on perspectives, only "seems to duplicate the problem with which we began"; so he concludes, "I cannot promise a finally satisfactory encounter with these staggering questions, produced by my simple effort to be a good citizen in the republic of criticism."[27] Booth's conclusion is modest but also alert. He knows that the epistemic foundations of critical pluralism themselves rest on moral, if not spiritual, grounds. "Methodological perspectivism" (as he sometimes calls his version of pluralism) depends on "shared tenancies" which in turn depend on a constitutive act of rational, just, and vitally sympathetic understanding. In the end Booth stands on a kind of Kantian—or is it Christian?—categorical imperative of criticism, with all that it must ethically and metaphysically imply.

Could it have been otherwise? Throughout history, critics have disagreed, pretending to make systems out of their discord and epistemic structures out of their beliefs. The shared tenancies of literary theory may make for hermeneutical communities of provisional trust, enclaves of genial critical authority. But can any of these define criticism both as a historical and cognitive genre? That may depend on what we intend by genre. Traditionally, genre assumed recognizable features within a context of both persistence and change; it was a useful assumption of identity upon which critics (somewhat like Stanley and Livingstone) often presumed. But that assumption, in our heteroclitic age, seems ever harder to maintain. Even genre theorists invite us, nowadays, to go beyond genre—"the finest generic classifications of our time," Paul Hernadi says, "make us look beyond their immediate concern and focus on the *order of literature,* not on *borders between literary genres.*"[28] Yet the "order of literature" itself has become moot.

In boundary genres particularly—and certain kinds of criticism may have become precisely that—the ambiguities attain new heights of febrile intensity. For as Gary Saul Morson notes, "it is not meanings but appropriate procedures for discovering meaning" that become disputable—"not particular readings, but how to read."[29] Since genres find their definition, *when* they find any, not only in their formal features but also in labile interpretive conventions, they seldom offer a stable, epistemic norm. This makes for certain paradoxes in the "law of genre," as Derrida lays it, a "mad law," though even madness fails to define it. As one might expect from the magus of our deconstructions, Derrida insists on undoing genre, undoing its gender, nature, and potency, on exposing the enigma of its "exemplarity." The mad "law of genre" yields only to the "law of the law of genre"—"a principle of contamination, a law of impurity, a parasitical economy."[30]

One is inclined to believe that even without the de-creations of certain kinds of writing, like my own paracriticism, the configurations we call literature, literary theory, criticism, have now become (quite like postmodernism itself) "essentially contested concepts," horizons of eristic discourse.[31] Thus, for instance, the latest disconfirmation of critical theory, the latest "revisionary madness" is Steven Knapp and Walter

Benn Michaels's statement against theory.[32] Drawing on the pragmatism of Richard Rorty and the stylistics of Stanley Fish, the authors brilliantly, berserkly contend that "true belief" and "knowledge" are epistemologically identical, that critical theory has no methodological consequences whatever. "If our arguments are true, they can have only one consequence . . . ; theory should stop," the authors conclude.[33] In fact it is their own conclusion that will have little consequence, as Knapp and Michaels themselves admit. So much, then, for the case of the self-consuming theorist.

My own conclusion about the theory and practice of criticism is securely unoriginal: like all discourse, criticism obeys human imperatives, which continually redefine it. It is a function of language, power, and desire, of history and accident, of purpose and interest, of value. Above all, it is a function of *belief*, which reason articulates and consensus, or authority, both enables and constrains.[34] (This statement itself expresses a reasoned belief.) If, then, as Kuhn claims, "competing schools, *each of which constantly questions the very foundations of the others*" reign in the humanities; if, as Victor Turner thinks, the "culture of any society at any moment is more like the debris, or 'fall out' of past ideological systems, rather than itself a system"; if also, as Jonathan Culler contends, " 'interpretive conventions' . . . should be seen as part of . . . [a] boundless context"; again, if as Jeffrey Stout maintains, "theoretical terms should serve interests and purposes, not the other way around"; and if, as I submit, the principles of literary criticism are historical (that is, at once arbitrary, pragmatic, conventional, and contextual, in any case not axiomatic, apodictic, apophantic), then how can a generic conception of criticism limit critical pluralism or govern the endless deferrals of language, particularly in our indetermanent, our postmodern period?[35]

IV

To exchange a largely cognitive view of our discipline for another that more freely admits politics, desires, beliefs is not necessarily to plunge into Hades or ascend Babel. It is, I think, an act of partial lucidity, responsive to our ideological, our human needs. The act, I stress, remains partial, as I hope will eventually become clear. For the moment, though, I must approach power as a constraint on postmodern relativism and, thus, as a factor in delimiting critical pluralism.

No doubt, the perception that power profoundly engages knowledge reverts to Plato and Aristotle, if not to the *I Ching* and the Egyptian *Book of the Dead.* In the last century, Marx theorized the relation of culture to class; his terms persist in a variety of movements, from totemic Marxism to Marxism with a deconstructionist mask or receptionist face. But it is Foucault, of course, who has given us the most cunning speculations on the topic.[36] The whole burden of his work, since *Folie et déraison* (1961), has been to expose the power of discourse and the discourse of power, to discover the politics of knowledge. More recently, though, his ideology had become antic, to the chagrin of his orthodox critics.

Foucault still maintained that discursive practices "are embodied in technical processes, in institutions, in patterns for general behavior, in forms of transmission and diffusion."[37] But he also accepted the Nietzschean premise that a selfish interest precedes all power and knowledge, shaping them to its own volition, pleasure, excess. Increasingly, Foucault saw power itself as an elusive relation, an immanence of discourse, a conundrum of desire: "It may be that Marx and Freud cannot satisfy our desire for understanding this enigmatic thing which we call power, which is at once visible and invisible, present and hidden, ubiquitous," he remarks.[38] That is why, in his late essay "The Subject and Power," Foucault seemed more concerned with promoting "new kinds of subjectivity" (based on a refusal of those individual identities which states force upon their citizens) than with censuring traditional modes of exploitation.[39]

In a Foucauldian perspective, then, criticism appears as much a discourse of desire as of power, a discourse, anyway, both conative and affective in its personal origins. A neo-Marxist like Jameson, however, would found criticism on collective reality. He would distinguish and "spell out the priority, within the Marxist tradition, of a 'positive hermeneutic' based on social class from those ['negative hermeneutics'] still limited by anarchist categories of the individual subject and individual experience."[40] Again, a leftist critic like Edward Said would insist that the "realities of power and authority . . . are the realities that make texts possible, that deliver them to their readers, that solicit the attention of critics."[41]

Other critics, less partisan and less strenuously political, might concur. Indeed, the "institutional view" of both literature and criticism now prevails among critics as incongruous in their ideologies as Bleich, Booth, Donald Davie, Fish, E. D. Hirsch, Frank Kermode, and Richard Ohmann. Here, bravely, is Bleich:

> Literary theory should contribute to the changing of social and professional institutions such as the public lecture, the convention presentation, the classroom, and the processes of tenure and promotion. Theoretical work ought to show how and why no one class of scholars, and no one subject (including theory) is self-justifying, self-explanatory, and self-sustaining.[42]

The ideological concern declares itself everywhere. A bristling issue of *Critical Inquiry* explores the "politics of interpretation," and the facile correlation of ideology with criticism drives a critic even so disputatious as Gerald Graff to protest the "pseudo-politics of interpretation" in a subsequent number.[43] At the same time, a critic as exquisitely reticent as Geoffrey Hartman acknowledges the intrusions of politics in his recent work.[44] The activities of GRIP (acronym for the Group for Research on the Institutionalization and Professionalization of Literary Study) seem as ubiquitous as those of the KGB or the CIA, though far more benign. And the number of conferences on "Marxism and Criticism," "Feminism and Criticism," "Ethnicity and Criticism," "Technology and Criticism," "Mass Culture and Criticism," keeps American airports snarled and air carriers in the black.

All these, of course, refract the shifts in our "myths of concern" (Northrop Frye's term) since the fifties. But they reflect, too, the changes in our idea of criticism itself, from a Kantian to a Nietzschean, Freudian, or Marxist conception (to name but three), from an ontological to a historical apprehension, from a synchronous or generic discourse to a diachronic or conative activity. The recession of the neo-Kantian idea, which extends through Ernst Cassirer, Suzanne Langer, and the old New Critics, ambiguously to Murray Krieger, implies another loss—that of the imagination as an autochthonous, autotelic, possibly redemptive power of mind. It is also the loss, or at least dilapidation, of the "imaginary library," a total order of art, analogous to André Malraux's *musée imaginaire,* which triumphs over time and brute destiny.[45] That ideal has now vanished; the library itself may end in rubble. Yet in our eagerness to appropriate art to our own circumstances and exercise our will on texts, we risk denying those capacities—not only literary—which have most richly fulfilled our historical existence.

I confess to some distate for ideological rage (the worst are now full of passionate intensity *and* lack all conviction) and for the hectoring of both religious and secular dogmatists.[46] I admit to a certain ambivalence toward politics, which can overcrowd our responses to both art and life. For what is politics? Simply, the right action when ripeness calls. But what is politics again? An excuse to bully or shout in public, vengeance vindicating itself as justice and might pretending to be right, a passion for self-avoidance, immanent mendacity, the rule of habit, the place where history rehearses its nightmares, the *dur désir de durer,* a deadly banality of being. Yet we must all heed politics because it structures our theoretical consents, literary evasions, critical recusancies—shapes our ideas of pluralism even as I write here, now.

V

Politics, we know, becomes tyrannical. It can dominate other modes of discourse, reduce all facts of the human universe—error, epiphany, chance, boredom, pain, dream—to its own terms. Hence the need, as Kristeva says, for a "psychoanalytic intervention . . . a counterweight, an antidote, to political discourse which, without it, is free to become our modern religion: the final explanation."[47] Yet the psychoanalytic explanation can also become as reductive as any other, unless desire itself qualifies its knowledge, its words.

I mean desire in the largest sense—personal and collective, biological and ontological, a force that writers from Hesiod and Homer to Nietzsche, William James, and Freud have reckoned with. It includes the Eros of the Universe that Alfred North Whitehead conceived as "the active entertainment of all ideals, with the urge to their finite realization, each in its due season."[48] But I mean desire also in its more particular sense, which Paul Valéry understood when he wryly confessed that every theory is a fragment of an autobiography. (Lately, the fragments have grown larger, as anyone who follows the oedipal *psychomachia* of critics must agree.) And I mean desire, too, as an aspect of the pleasure principle, that principle so freely invoked and seldom evident in criticism.

Here Barthes comes elegantly to mind. For him, the pleasure of the text is perverse, polymorph, created by intermittences of the body even more than of the heart. Rupture, tear, suture, scission enhance that pleasure; so does erotic displacement. "The text is a fetish object, and *this fetish desires me,*" he confides.[49] Such a text eludes judgment by anterior or exterior norms. In its presence we can only cry, "That's it for me!" This is the Dionysiac cry par excellence—Dionysiac, that is, in that peculiarly Gallic timbre. Thus, for Barthes, the pleasure of the text derives both from the body's freedom to "pursue its own ideas" and from "value shifted to the sumptuous rank of the signifier."[50]

We need not debate here the celebrated, if dubious, distinctions Barthes makes in that talismanic text; we need only note that pleasure becomes a constitutive critical principle in his later work. Thus in *Leçon,* his inaugural lecture at the Collège de France, Barthes insists on the "truth of desire" which discovers itself in the multiplicity of discourse: *"autant de langages qu'il y a de désirs."*[51] The highest role of the professor is to make himself "fantasmic," to renew his body so that it becomes contemporaneous with his students, to unlearn (*désapprendre*). Perhaps then he can realize true *sapientia: "nul pouvoir, un peu de savoir, un peu de sagesse, et le plus saveur possible."*[52] And in *A Lover's Discourse,* which shows a darker side of desire, Barthes excludes the possibility of explication, of hermeneutics; he would rather stroke language in erotic foreplay: *"Je frotte mon langage contre l'autre. C'est comme si j'avais des mots en guise de doigts."*[53]

Other versions of this critical suasion come easily to mind.[54] But my point is not only that critical theory is a function of our desires, nor simply that criticism often takes pleasure or desire as its concern, its theme. My point is rather more fundamental: much current criticism conceives language and literature themselves as organs of desire, to which criticism tries to adhere erotically (*"se coller,"* Barthes says), stylistically, even epistemically. "Desire and the desire to know are not strangers to each other," Kristeva notes; and "interpretation is infinite because Meaning is made infinite by desire."[55] Happily, this last remark leads into my inconclusion.

Let me recover, though, the stark lineaments of my argument. Critical pluralism finds itself implicated in our postmodern condition, in its relativisms and indetermanences, which it attempts to restrain. But cognitive, political, and affective restraints remain only partial. They all finally fail to delimit critical pluralism, to create consensual theory or practice—witness the debates of this conference. Is there anything, in our era, that *can* found a wide consensus of discourse?

VI

Clearly, the imagination of postmodern criticism is a disestablished imagination. Yet clearly, too, it is an intellectual imagination of enormous vibrancy and scope. I share in its excitement, my own excitement mixed with unease. That unease touches more than our critical theories; it engages the nature of authority and belief in the world. It is the old Nietzschean cry of nihilism: "the desert grows!" God, King, Father, Reason, History, Humanism have all come and gone their way, though their power may still flare up in some circles of faith. We have killed our gods—in spite or lucidity, I hardly know—yet we remain ourselves creatures of will, desire, hope, belief. And now we have nothing—nothing that is not partial, provisional, self-created—upon which to found our discourse.

Sometimes I imagine a new Kant, come out of Königsberg, spirited through the Iron Curtain. In his hand he holds the "fourth critique," which he calls *The Critique of Practical Judgment.* It is a masterwork, resolving all the contradictions of theory and praxis, ethics and aesthetics, metaphysical reason and historical life. I reach for the sublime treatise; the illustrious ghost disappears. Sadly, I turn to my bookshelf and pick out William James's *The Will to Believe.*

Here, it seems, is friendly lucidity, and an imagination that keeps reason on the stretch. James speaks crucially to our condition in a "pluralistic universe." I let him speak:

> He who takes for his hypothesis the notion that it [pluralism] is the permanent form of the world is what I call a radical empiricist. For him the crudity of experience remains an eternal element thereof. There is no possible point of view from which the world can appear an absolutely single fact.[56]

This leaves the field open to "willing nature":

> When I say "willing nature," I do not mean only such deliberate volitions as may have set up habits of belief that we cannot now escape from,—I mean all such factors of belief as fear and hope, prejudice and passion, imitation and partisanship, the circumpressure of our caste and set. As a matter of fact we find ourselves believing, we hardly know how or why. [*W*, 9]

This was written nearly a century ago and remains—so I *believe*—impeccable, unimpugnable. It proposes a different kind of "authority" (lower case), pragmatic, empirical, permitting pluralist beliefs. Between these beliefs there can be only continual negotiations of reason and interest, mediations of desire, transactions of power or hope. But all these still rest on, rest in, beliefs, which James knew to be the most interesting, most valuable, part of man. In the end our "passional nature," he says, decides "*an option between propositions, whenever it is a genuine option that cannot by its nature be decided on intellectual grounds*" (*W*, 11). James even suggests that, biologically considered, "our minds are as ready to grind out falsehood as veracity, and he who says, 'Better go without belief forever than believe a lie!' merely shows his own preponderant private horror of becoming a dupe" (*W*, 18).

Contemporary pragmatists, like Rorty, Fish, or Michaels, may not follow James so far. Certainly they would balk, as do most of us now, when James's language turns spiritual:

> Is it not sheer dogmatic folly to say that our inner interests can have no real connection with the forces that the hidden world may contain? . . . And if needs of ours outrun the visible universe, why *may* not that be a sign that an invisible universe is there? . . . God himself, in short, may draw vital strength and increase of very being from our fidelity. [*W*, 55, 56, 61]

I do not quote this passage to press the claims of metaphysics or religion. I do so only to hint that the *ultimate* issues of critical pluralism, in our postmodern epoch, point that way. And why, particularly, in our postmodern epoch? Precisely because of its countervailing forces, its indetermanences. Everywhere now we observe societies riven by the double and coeval process of planetization and retribalization, totalitarianism and terror, fanatic faith and radical disbelief. Everywhere we meet, in mutant or displaced forms, that conjunctive/disjunctive technological rage which affects postmodern discourse.

It may be that some rough beast will slouch again toward Bethlehem, its haunches bloody, its name echoing in our ears with the din of history. It may be that some natural cataclysm, world calamity, or extra terrestrial intelligence will shock the earth into some sane planetary awareness of its destiny. It may be that we shall simply bungle through, muddle through, wandering in the "desert" from oasis to oasis, as we have done for decades, perhaps centuries. I have no prophecy in me, only some slight foreboding, which I express now to remind myself that all the evasions of our knowledge and actions thrive on the absence of consensual beliefs, an absence that also energizes our tempers, our wills. This is our postmodern condition.

As to things nearer at hand, I openly admit: I do not know how to prevent critical pluralism from slipping into monism or relativism, except to call for pragmatic constituencies of knowledge that would share values, traditions, expectancies, goals. I do not know how to make our "desert" a little greener, except to invoke enclaves of genial authority where the central task is to restore civil commitments, tolerant beliefs, critical sympathies.[57] I do not know how to give literature or theory or criticism a new hold on the world, except to remythify the imagination, at least locally, and bring back the reign of wonder into our lives. In this, my own elective affinities remain with Emerson: "Orpheus is no fable: you have only to sing, and the rocks will crystallize; sing, and the plant will organize; sing, and the animal will be born."[58]

But who nowadays believes it?

1. "Maybe the most certain of all philosophical problems is the problem of the present time, of what we are, in this very moment," writes Michel Foucault in "The Subject and Power," reprinted as "Afterword" in *Michel Foucault: Beyond Structuralism and Hermeneutics,* ed. Hubert L. Dreyfus and Paul Rabinow (Chicago, 1982), 210. The essay also appeared in *Critical Inquiry* 8 (Summer 1982): 777–96.

2. I have discussed some of these problems in *The Dismemberment of Orpheus: Toward a Postmodern Literature,* 2d ed. (Madison, Wis., 1982), 262–68. See also Claus Uhlig, "Toward a Chronology of Change," Dominick LaCapra, "Intellectual History and Defining the Present as 'Postmodern,' " and Matei Calinescu, "From the One to the Many: Pluralism in Today's Thought," in *Innovation/Renovation: New Perspectives on the Humanities,* ed. Ihab Hassan and Sally Hassan (Madison, Wis., 1983).

3. Daniel Bell, *The Cultural Contradictions of Capitalism* (New York, 1976), 7.

4. Jürgen Habermas, "Modernity versus Postmodernity," *New German Critique* 22 (Winter 1981): 13.

5. For homologies in scientific culture, see my *The Right Promethean Fire: Imagination, Science, and Cultural Change* (Urbana, Ill., 1980), 139–71.

6. Jean-François Lyotard, "Answering the Question: What is Postmodernism?" trans. Régis Durand, in *Innovation/Renovation,* 341. On the paratactic style in art and society, see also Hayden White, "The Culture of Criticism," in *Liberations: New Essays on the Humanities in Revolution,* ed. Ihab Hassan (Mid-

dletown, Conn., 1971), 66–69; and see William James on the affinities between parataxis and pluralism: "It *may* be that some parts of the world are connected so loosely with some other parts as to be strung along by nothing but the copula *and*. . . . This pluralistic view, of a world of *additive* constitution, is one that pragmatism is unable to rule out from serious consideration" (*"Pragmatism," and Four Essays from "The Meaning of Truth"* [New York, 1955], 112).

7. See Jean-François Lyotard, *La Condition postmoderne: rapport sur le savoir* (Paris, 1979). For other views of decanonization, see *English Literature: Opening Up the Canon*, ed. Leslie Fiedler and Houston A. Baker, Jr., Selected Papers from the English Institute, 1979, n.s. 4 (Baltimore, 1981), and *Critical Inquiry* 10 (September 1983).

8. Friedrich Nietzsche, *The Will to Power*, ed. Walter Kaufmann, trans. Walter Kaufmann and R. J. Hollingdale (New York, 1967), 199; see Wylie Sypher, *Loss of Self in Modern Literature and Art* (New York, 1962); see also the discussion of the postmodern self in Charles Caramello, *Silverless Mirrors: Book, Self, and Postmodern American Fiction* (Tallahassee, Fla., 1983).

9. The refusal of depth is, in the widest sense, a refusal of hermeneutics, the "penetration" of nature or culture. It manifests itself in the white philosophies of post-structuralism as well as in various contemporary arts. See, for instance, Alain Robbe-Grillet, *For a New Novel: Essays on Fiction*, trans. Richard Howard (New York, 1965), 49–76, and Susan Sontag, *Against Interpretation* (New York, 1966), 3–14.

10. Lyotard, "Answering the Question," 340. See also the perceptive discussion of the politics of the sublime by Hayden White, "The Politics of Historical Interpretation: Discipline and De-Sublimation," *Critical Inquiry* 9 (September 1982): 124–28.

11. Julia Kristeva, "Postmodernism?" in *Romanticism, Modernism, Postmodernism*, ed. Harry R. Garvin (Lewisburg, Pa., 1980), 141. See also her *Powers of Horror: An Essay on Abjection*, trans. Leon S. Roudiez (New York, 1982), and her most recent discussion of "the unnameable" in "Psychoanalysis and the Polis," trans. Margaret Waller, *Critical Inquiry* 9 (September 1982): 84–85, 91.

12. Alan Wilde, *Horizons of Assent: Modernism, Postmodernism, and the Ironic Imagination* (Baltimore, 1981), 10. Wayne Booth makes a larger claim for the currency of irony in postmodern times, a "cosmic irony," deflating the claims of man's centrality, and evincing a striking parallel with traditional religious languages. See his "The Empire of Irony," *Georgia Review* 37 (Winter 1983): 719–37.

13. The last term is Gary Saul Morson's. Morson provides an excellent discussion of threshold literature, parody, and hybridization in his *The Boundaries of Genre: Dostoyevsky's "Diary of a Writer" and the Traditions of Literary Utopia* (Austin, Tex., 1981), esp. 48–50, 107–8, and 142–43.

14. See Fredric Jameson, "Postmodernism and Consumer Society," in *The Anti-Aesthetic: Essays on Postmodern Culture*, ed. Hal Foster (Port Townsend, Wash., 1983). For a counterstatement, see Paolo Portoghesi, *After Modern Architecture*, trans. Meg Shore (New York, 1982), p. 11, and Calinescu, "From the One to the Many," 286.

15. See M. M. Bakhtin, *Rabelais and His World*, trans. Helena Iswolsky (Cam-

bridge, Mass., 1968), and *The Dialogic Imagination: Four Essays by M. M. Bakhtin,* ed. Michael Holquist, trans. Caryl Emerson and Michael Holquist, University of Texas Press Slavic Series, no. 1 (Austin, Tex., 1981). See also the forum on Bakhtin, *Critical Inquiry* 10 (December 1983).

16. Bakhtin, *Rabelais,* 10–11.

17. See Régis Durand's defense, against Michael Fried, of the performing principle in postmodern art ("Theatre/SIGNS/Performance: On Some Transformations of the Theatrical and the Theoretical," in *Innovation/Renovation,* 213–17). See also Richard Schechner, "News, Sex, and Performance Theory," *Innovation/Renovation,* 189–210.

18. Richard Poirier, *The Performing Self: Compositions and Decompositions in the Languages of Contemporary Life* (New York, 1971), xv, xiii. See also Christopher Lasch, *The Culture of Narcissism: American Life in an Age of Diminishing Expectations* (New York, 1978).

19. Nietzsche, *The Will to Power,* 291.

20. James understood this when he said: "You can't weed out the human contribution . . . altho the stubborn fact remains that there *is* a sensible flux, what is *true of it* seems from first to last to be largely a matter of our own creation" (*Pragmatism,* 166).

21. See Ihab Hassan, *Paracriticisms: Seven Speculations of the Times* (Urbana, Ill., 1975), 121–50; and Hassan, *The Right Promethean Fire,* 139–72. It was José Ortega y Gasset, however, who made a prescient, gnostic statement (see p. 96, above). And before Ortega, James wrote: "The world is One just so far as its parts hang together by any definite connexion. It is many just so far as any definite connexion fails to obtain. And finally it is growing more and more unified by those systems of connexion at least which human energy keeps framing as time goes on" (*Pragmatism,* 105). But see also Jean Baudrillard's version of a senseless immanence, "The Ecstacy of Communication," in *The Anti-Aesthetic,* 126–34.

22. Nelson Goodman, *Ways of Worldmaking* (Indianapolis, 1978), x.

23. Active, creative, self-reflexive patterns seem also essential to advanced theories of artifical intelligence. See the article on Douglas R. Hofstadter's latest work by James Gleick, "Exploring the Labyrinth of the Mind," *The New York Times Magazine,* 21 August 1983:23–100.

24. Jean Baudrillard, "What Are You Doing After the Orgy?" *Artforum* (October 1983):43.

25. See, for instance, Paul de Man, "Literary History and Literary Modernity," *Blindness and Insight: Essays in the Rhetoric of Contemporary Criticism* (New York, 1971), and Octavio Paz, *Children of the Mire: Modern Poetry from Romanticism to the Avant-Garde* (Cambridge, Mass., 1974).

26. See, for instance, the persuasive article of Ralph Cohen, "Literary Theory as Genre," *Centrum* 3 (Spring 1975): 45–64. Cohen also sees literary change itself as a genre. See his essay, "A Propadeutic for Literary Change," and the responses of White and Michael Riffaterre to it, in *Critical Exchange* 13. (Spring 1983):1–17, 18–26, and 27–38.

27. Wayne Booth, *Critical Understanding: The Powers and Limits of Pluralism* (Chicago, 1979), 33–34.

28. Paul Hernadi, *Beyond Genres: New Directions in Literary Classification* (Ithaca, N.Y., 1972), 184. See, further, the two issues on convention and genre of *New Literary History* 13 (Autumn 1981) and 14 (Winter 1983).

29. Morson, *The Boundaries of Genre,* 49.

30. Jacques Derrida, "La Loi du genre/The Law of Genre," *Glyph* 7 (1980): 206. This entire issue concerns genre.

31. The term "essentially contested concept" is developed by W.B. Gallie in his *Philosophy and the Historical Understanding* (New York, 1968). See also Booth's lucid discussion of it, *Critical Understanding,* 211–15 and 366.

32. See Steven Knapp and Walter Benn Michaels, "Against Theory," *Critical Inquiry* 8 (Summer 1982): 723–42, and the subsequent responses in *Critical Inquiry* 9 (June 1983). "Revisionary Madness: The Prospects of American Literary Theory at the Present Time" is the title of Daniel T. O'Hara's response (pp. 726–42).

33. Steven Knapp and Walter Benn Michaels, "A Reply to Our Critics," *Critical Inquiry* 9 (June 1983): 800.

34. The relevance of belief to knowledge in general and conventions in particular is acknowledged by thinkers of different persuasions, even when they disagree on the nature of truth, realism, and genre. Thus, for instance, Nelson Goodman and Menachem Brinker agree that belief is "an accepted version" of the world; and E. D. Hirsch concurs with both. See Goodman, "Realism, Relativism, and Reality," Brinker, "On Realism's Relativism: A Reply to Nelson Goodman," and Hirsch, "Beyond Convention?" All appear in *New Literary History* 14 (Winter 1983).

35. Thomas S. Kuhn, *The Structure of Scientific Revolutions,* 2d ed. (Chicago, 1970), 163, my emphasis; Victor Turner, *Dramas, Fields, and Metaphors: Symbolic Action in Human Society* (Ithaca, N.Y., 1974), 14; Jonathan Culler, "Convention and Meaning: Derrida and Austin," *New Literary History* 13 (Autumn 1981): 30; Jeffrey Stout, "What Is the Meaning of a Text?" *New Literary History* 14 (Autumn 1982): 5. I am aware that other thinkers distinguish between "variety" and "subjectivity" of understanding in an effort to limit radical perspectivism; see, for instance, Stephen C. Pepper, *World Hypotheses: A Study in Evidence* (Berkeley and Los Angeles, 1942); Stephen Toulmin, *Human Understanding: The Collective Use and Evolution of Concepts* (Princeton, N.J., 1972); and George Bealer, *Quality and Concept* (Oxford, 1982). But I wonder why their arguments have failed to eliminate, or at least reduce, their differences with relativists; or why, again, Richard Rorty and Hirsch find it possible to disagree about the "question of objectivity," which became the theme of a *conference* at the University of Virginia in April 1984.

36. Jürgen Habermas, in *Knowledge and Human Interests,* trans. Jeremy J. Shapiro (Boston, 1971), and *Technik und Wissenschaft als "Ideologie"* (Frankfurt am Main, 1968), also offers vigorous neo-Marxist critiques of knowledge and society. Kenneth Burke, in *A Grammar of Motives* (New York, 1945), preceded both Foucault and Habermas in this large political and logological enterprise.

37. Michel Foucault, *Language, Counter-Memory, Practice: Selected Essays and Interviews,* ed. Donald F. Bouchard, trans. Bouchard and Sherry Simon (Ithaca, N.Y., 1977), 200.

38. Ibid., 213

39. See *Michel Foucault: Beyond Structuralism,* 216–20.

40. Fredric Jameson, *The Political Unconscious: Narrative as a Socially Symbolic Act* (Ithaca, N.Y., 1981), 286.

41. Edward Said, *The World, the Text, and the Critic* (Cambridge, Mass., 1983), 5.

42. David Bleich, "Literary Theory in the University: A Survey," *New Literary History* 14 (Winter 1983): 411. See also *What Is Literature?* ed. Hernadi (Bloomington, Ind., 1978), 49–112.

43. See *Critical Inquiry* 9 (September 1982); and see Gerald Graff, "The Pseudo-Politics of Interpretation," *Critical Inquiry* 9 (March 1983): 597–610.

44. See Geoffrey Hartman, "The New Wilderness: Critics as Connoisseurs of Chaos," in *Innovation/Renovation,* 87–110.

45. "If social circumstances . . . contradict too powerfully the [Romantic] world-view of literature, then the Imaginary Library, first its enabling beliefs and eventually its institutional manifestations, can no longer exist," remarks Alvin B. Kernan, *The Imaginary Library: An Essay on Literature and Society* (Princeton, N.J., 1982), 166.

46. Though "everything is ideological," as we nowadays like to say, we need still to distinguish between ideologies—fascism, feminism, monetarism, vegetarianism, etc.—between their overt claims, their hidden exactions. Even postmodernism, as a political ideology, requires discriminations. Lyotard, for instance, believes that "the postmodern condition is a stranger to disenchantment as to the blind positivity of delegitimation" (*La Condition postmoderne,* 8; my translation); while Foster claims a "postmodernism of resistance," a "counterpractice not only to the official culture of modernism but also to the 'false normativity' of a reactionary postmodernism" (*The Anti-Aesthetic,* xii). Interestingly enough, French thinkers of the Left—Foucault, Lyotard, Baudrillard, Gilles Deleuze—seem more subtle in their ideas of "resistance" than their American counterparts. This is curious, perhaps paradoxical, since the procedures of "mass," "consumer," or "postindustrial" society are more advanced in America than in France. But see also, as a counterstatement, Said's critique of Foucault, "Travelling Theory," *Raritan* 1 (Winter 1982): 41–67.

47. Kristeva, "Psychoanalysis and the Polis," 78. In our therapeutic culture, the language of politics and the discourse of desire constantly seek one another, as if the utopian marriage of Marx and Freud could find consummation, at last, in our words. Hence the political use of such erotic or analytic concepts as "libidinal economy" (Jean-François Lyotard, *Economie libidinale* [Paris, 1974]), "seduction" (Jean Baudrillard, *De la séduction* [Paris, 1979]), "delirium" or "abjection" (Julia Kristeva, *Powers of Horror*) "anti-Oedipus" (Gilles Deleuze and Félix Guattari, *Anti-Oedipus: Capitalism and Schizophrenia,* trans. Robert Hurley, Mark Seem, and Helen R. Lane [New York, 1977]), "bliss" (Roland Barthes, *The Pleasure of the Text,* trans. Richard Miller [New York, 1975]), and "the political unconscious" (Jameson, *The Political Unconscious*). See also Ihab Hassan, "Desire and Dissent in the Postmodern Age," *Kenyon Review,* n.s. 5 (Winter 1983):1–18.

48. Alfred North Whitehead, *Adventures of Ideas* (New York, 1955), 276.

49. Barthes, *The Pleasure of the Text,* 27.

50. Ibid., 17, 65.

51. Roland Barthes, *Leçon inaugurale faite le vendredi 7 janvier 1977* (Paris, 1978), 25.

52. Ibid, 46.

53. Roland Barthes, *Fragments d'un discours amoureux* (Paris, 1977), 87. A few sentences in the paragraph which this sentence concludes have appeared in my earlier essay, "Parabiography: The Varieties of Critical Experience," *Georgia Review* 34 (Fall 1980):600.

54. In America, the work of Leo Bersani has addressed such questions as "Can a psychology of fragmentary and *dis*continuous desires be reinstated? What are the strategies by which the self might be once again theatricalized? How might desire recover its original capacity for projecting nonstructurable *scenes?*" And it answers them by suggesting that *the* "desiring self might even disappear as we learn to multiply our discontinuous and partial desiring selves" in language. See *A Future for Astyanax: Character and Desire in Literature* (Boston, 1976), 6–7.

55. Kristeva, "Psychoanalysis and the Polis," 82, 86.

56. William James, *"The Will to Believe" and Other Essays in Popular Philosophy* (New York, 1956), ix. All further references to this work, abbreviated *W*, will be included in the text.

57. James once more: "No one of us ought to issue vetoes to the other, nor should we bandy words of abuse. We ought, on the contrary, delicately and profoundly to respect one another's mental freedom: then only shall we bring about the intellectual republic; then only shall we have that spirit of inner tolerance without which all our outer tolerance is soulless, and which is empiricism's glory; then only shall we live and let live, in speculative as well as in practical things" (*W*, 30). How far, beyond this, does any postmodern pluralist go?

58. *Journals of Ralph Waldo Emerson*, 1820–1872, ed. Edward Waldo Emerson and Waldo Emerson Forbes, 10 vols. (Boston, 1909–14), 8:79.

Part IV Postlude to Postmodernism

9 Making Sense: The Trials of Postmodern Discourse

Prologue

Making sense: one might take that title, in its strongest sense, as an inquiry into what it means to be human. Prodigious query. I quickly fall back on my subtitle, presumptuous enough, which signals the trials of knowledge, of discourse, in our postmodern moment.

But my text is itself part of that moment. How, then, can I reflect on the crisis of meaning, which my meanings already "reflect," and still make sense of the crisis of sense in our age? As a part-time pragmatist, I want simply to recount seven useful stories. These are plausible intellectual narratives of our situation. Each is partial, inconclusive; yet, taken together, they may make some sense of the predicament of knowledge in our epoch. It is a synoptic way of understanding our fragments, our culture all in pieces.

At the end, in a brief epilogue, I call on some personal beliefs; for they, too, bear on our theories and praxis. Without beliefs we could not make sense, put together those pieces. Reconstruction is what I mean here modestly to explore.

I

I commence with biology. Some million years ago, the brain of *homo sapiens* exploded into evolution—exploding evolution! We do not know exactly how this weird event came about, though freeing the eye, the hand, and the tongue had much to do with it. Internal as well as external selection, the conditions of adaptation on grassy savannahs, yielded somehow the human brain, which empowers some 10^{13} synapses, corresponding to a number of mental states far greater than the total of elementary particles in the universe.[1] Henceforth, the brain, enabling dream, language, imagination, enabling all the cultures we have known—the brain began to bully the genes in the story of evolution.

Yet that old story lives on in the darkness of the thalamus, the limbic system, the primitive stem. Sociobiologists like to remind us to this, and to recall our hereditary selves.[2] Making sense, then, still obeys the atavistic imperatives of evolution, as modernists and postmodernists well know. Yet even sociobiologists grant that the human brain learns to alter the conditions of its own existence. A generalized learner, the big-brained animal carries "a wide range of memories, some of which possess only a low probability of ever proving useful"; he learns, as Edward O. Wilson says, "a perception of history"; and this endows him with a "capacity to generalize from one pattern to another and to juxtapose patterns" in ways that prove adaptively crucial.[3] Thus learning serves as a pacemaker of evolution, leading, in some cases, to higher intelligence.

But how does the brain, ruthless organ of survival, achieve its particular ends? Here we broach inviolate questions concerning the relation of brain to mind. On such questions, neurologists prefer to remain mute, though some of the most eminent—Wilder Penfield, John Eccles, Roger Sperry—indulge sometimes in conjecture. Penfield, for instance, wonders, at "the risk of hollow laughter from the physicists," if the "highest brain-mechanism" can provide mind with a unique, a "changed," form of energy, that "no longer needs to be conducted [electrically] along neuraxones."[4] And Sperry, taking issue with the dualism of both Eccles and Penfield, calls himself a "mentalist," neither idealist nor materialist. Like Eccles, though, Sperry perceives the unity of conscious experience as "provided by the mind and not the neural machinery."[5]

However the enigma of mind may be someday resolved, neurophilosophers concur that mind and brain are marvelously hierarchic, if not tyrannical, structures—therefore nothing postmodern. Integration begins in the thalamus, continues in the cortex; but it is mind that finally commands.

It is possible, of course, that mind may prove mad, and the brain, as Koestler gloomily suggests, a diseased organ of evolution, the ultimate instrument of genocide, perhaps biocide.[6] But here I take my stand with Einstein, who believed that the "mystery of the world is its comprehensibility."[7] This is a stupendous remark, an act of faith, proclaiming the adequacy of mind to the cosmos of which mind remains a part (apart). If "knowledge is destiny" (Bronowski); if "the entire evolutionary record on our planet . . . illustrates a progressive tendency toward intelligence" (Sagan); if "the older noncognitive controls of nature that have regulated events in our biosphere for hundreds of millions of years . . . are no longer in command" (Sperry); if mind resonates mysteriously to the universe (Einstein); and if no nuclear, no final, calamity befalls the human race—if these, may we not then surmise that "making sense" is the biological imperative of evolution, our fragile destiny and gnostic charge among the stars?[8]

II

But the shade of Lord Snow reminds me that humanists suspect sanguine and vatic views. I leave, therefore, the galaxy to its destiny, and come to my second story, that of psychoanalysis and genetic psychology. How do these disciplines clarify the cognitive imperative, quite briefly?

Freud, we know, perceived the drive to knowledge as a sublimation of the erotic instinct. The case is clearest in *Leonardo da Vinci: A Study in Sexuality.* Let us ignore the dubious vulture; our object is Leonardo's universal curiosity, his seamless mind. Freud first quotes Leonardo: "One has no right to love or to hate anything if one has not acquired a thorough knowledge of its nature," and then remarks: "He [Leonardo] only transmuted his passion into inquisitiveness."[9] Da Vinci, who was like a man waking early in the dawn of modern history while others slumbered, read the invisible signatures of God. Learning to depreciate Authority (the Father) and to find in Nature (the Mother) "the source of all wisdom," Freud says, "he only repeated in the highest sublimation attainable to man that which had already obtruded itself on the little boy who surveyed the world with wonder."[10] In Leonardo's case, then, knowledge was a kind of love.

With Jacques Lacan, Freud's French hierophant, the specular displaces the Oedipal in the formation of consciousness. During the "mirror stage," the infant, glimpsing its image—that is, *part* of its body—learns the first alienation; this leads to its discovery of the self. But in this Imaginary phase, the infant has no language or knowledge yet. It is,

Lacan says, "in the *name of the father* [Phallus or Signifier] that we must recognize the support of the Symbolic function which, from the dawn of history, has identified his person with the figure of the law."[11] Thus "language comes forth as the mediating element" of a unique self-consciousness, and the psychoanalytic experience finds "in man the imperative of the *verbe* as the law which has formed him in its image."[12] This means, despite Lacan's genius for obnebulation, that the cognitive imperative acts as a radical power of specular self-constitution within that vast, shifty order of signifiers we call language.

Lacanian psychoanalysis breaks decisively with the Cartesian tradition that extends to Husserl. So does genetic psychology, which, unlike psychoanalysis, explores structural developments of mind beyond childhood. Indeed, for Jean Piaget, no hiatus cleaves biology and knowledge.[13] Learning is a continual transaction between the organism and its environment, a *constructive* exchange both in the phylogenetic and ontogenetic sense. To these transactions, *homo sapiens, homo faber, homo ludens,* or *homo significans* brings a creative disequilibrium, a perpetual openness to existence, a capacity for ceaseless invention, intervention. In so doing, human beings not only play or learn; they also learn to learn. (Piaget tells an anecdote about one of his children who retrieves a big toy through the bars of his playpen by turning it vertically: "not at all satisfied with this chance success," the child "put the toy out again and began all over until he 'understood' what was being done."[14]) Such learning expands, incessantly, the human environment, a progress, Piaget claims, "due to regulations of regulations entailing the exercise of cognitive functions for their own sake. . . . "[15] Thus, for Piaget, knowledge serves as the highest, the most subtle *and* effective, control in our exchanges with reality.

No doubt, one could adduce other cognitive psychologists or information theorists, notably Jerome Bruner, Gregory Bateson, John von Neumann, Ludwig von Bertalanffy, Warren McCullough.[16] But the point, I think, has become obvious. The million and more years of hominid history, the structures of the human brain and urgencies of human desire, decree that we must continually seek to make sense. Others—swamis of deconstruction, satraps of textualism, nabobs of postmodernism—may obey the call of the "freeplay of the world . . . without truth, without origin," and try to "pass beyond man and humanism."[17] But they do so only in comfort, when life makes on them no real demand; for the rest, they are as bound to sense as the rest of us.

III

Sense is destiny. But what specific sense should we make? This brings me to my third story, more equivocal, the story of history, which can illumine only certain parts of our question.[18] The brief account—nothing ineluctable—I want to give of the historical crisis in Western discourse derives from Hans Blumenberg's *The Legitimacy of the Modern Age,* a magisterial opus, muffled in a style that sounds sometimes like metaphysical moans beneath a mattress.

Blumenberg wants to "legitimate" modern history in terms of "human rationality," "theoretical curiosity," "self-assertion," without reference to religious belief. For him, the modern project does not merely "transpose" theological into secular ideas—eschatology into progress, for instance. The modern project emerges, rather, as a genuine historical development, irreducible to medieval or antique precedents. Thus, to defend the modern age against the charge that it represents a "failure of history," Blumenberg traces the crisis of confidence in *this* world back to early Gnostics. "The senselessness of self-assertion was the heritage of the Gnosticism which was not overcome" by Church Fathers, he argues, "but only 'translated.' "[19] We owe this "translation" mainly to Augustine who, eager to exculpate God and His world from the attributes of evil, remanded it to man in Original Sin. Henceforth, man—with a little help from the Devil—carried the crushing weight of sin. It remained for modern self-assertion to overcome both the Gnostic and Christian legacies of worldly refusal.[20] Such self-assertion entails more than physical survival; it implies "an existential program, according to which man posits his existence in a historical situation," in order to realize himself.[21]

Here we approach the crux of our interest in this account. For as Blumenberg concludes, the "man who conceives not only of nature but also of himself as a fact at his disposal has traversed only the first stage of his self-enhancement. . . . The destruction of trust in the world made him for the first time a creatively active being, freed from a disastrous lulling of his activity."[22] This points to a vital paradox: human beings began *to make and discover* sense only when Providence (Design, Purpose) lost its communal sense. With Copernicus, Galileo, Kepler, Bacon, and Newton, with all the philosophers, through the Enlightenment, down to Nietzsche, theoretical curiosity ceased to serve as eudaemonic solace, a guide to happiness. Directed first at nature, that curiosity reached to take all things in its compass.

This is a plausible, indeed persuasive, account. It persuades us that the cognitive imperative, which took many turns since early Gnostics, acquired striking new powers in modern times. Yet Blumenberg's account, I think, fails adequately to render the trials of Western self-assertion since Romanticism, the vicissitudes of modernism itself. It fails, that is, to convey the acute difficulties of secular society, the *aporias* of its knowledge. (Like Habermas, Blumenberg can only apprehend modernism as a product of the *Aufklärung.*) Science, skepticism, objectivity, reason itself, indeed, the very nature of human being in the world, have all suffered great provocations in the last century. These provocations subvert our capacity to share meanings. The arch subversive, dread *provocateur,* was Friedrich Nietzsche, who divined the crisis of postmodern discourse with merciless clarity. I call on him, therefore, to tell my next, a philosophical, story.

IV

In *The Will to Power,* notes written between 1883–88 at the edge of madness, Nietzsche returned, for the last time, to his major theme, which is still ours: "What I relate is the history of the next two centuries. I describe what is coming, what can no longer come differently: the advent of nihilism."[23] A hundred years later, most of us will ruefully admit that God, King, Man, Reason, History, Humanism, the State, have come and gone their way as principles of irrefragable authority; and that even Language, youngest divinity of our intellectual clerisy, threatens to empty itself out, another god that failed. We live in a time of political terrorism, moral improvisation, spiritual *bricolage.* Yet we continue to believe that nihilism is something only others profess.

But what, according to Nietzsche, is this desert of meaning, of value, that we must traverse? I let him speak through his own shards of prophecy, paroxysms of thought:

What does nihilism mean? *That the highest values devaluate themselves.* The aim is lacking; "why?" finds no answer.

> The faith in the categories of reason is the cause of nihilism. We have measured the value of the world according to categories *that refer to a purely fictitious world.*

> If this is not an age of decay and declining vitality, it is at least one of headlong and arbitrary *experimentation*:—and it is probable that a superabundance of bungled experiments should create an overall impression as of decay—and perhaps even decay itself.

> "Modernity" . . . . Sensibility immensely more irritable . . . the abundance of disparate impressions . . . cosmopolitanism in foods, literatures, newspapers, forms, tastes, even landscapes. The tempo of this influx *prestissimo*; the impressions erase each other; one instinctively resists taking in anything . . . deeply. . . . *Profound weakness* of spontaneity: the historian, critic, analyst, the interpreter, the observer, the collector, the reader—all of them *reactive* talents—all science.[24]

Indeed, Nietzsche's perceptions of our moment are nearly preternatural. He recognizes the nihilism in our knowledge, politics, arts; he sees its evidence in vice, addiction, sickliness, celibacy, hysteria, anarchy; and he understands how we narcotize ourselves with spite, resignation, fanaticism, even with mysticism or science. Is there no way out? Clarity, he cries, irony with regard to our own disbelief, recognition of our "will to power," restoration of the life instincts, strength through moderation, perhaps even, some day, the "transvaluation of all values."

Thus Nietzsche, in his implacable confrontation with the modern "destructive element," completes (anachronistically) Blumenberg's historic recital. Nihilism may be the legacy of two thousand years of Christianity, as Nietzsche exorbitantly claims. But nihilism, as he also shows, is the consequence of a more radical disenchantment: the price humanity must pay for its feeble dreams and delusions, for its wishful thinking and "hyperbolic naiveté" since prehistoric times. Precisely here an essential contradiction seems to inform his thought. For if *all* human creations are "lies" or "fictions"—this includes myth, religion, art, science, politics—then surely some "lies" must serve Life. Indeed, though Nietzsche exposes the fictive character of existence, he rejects only weak or pusillanimous fictions, images of our self-solicitude. Hence his celebration of tragic art, which exalts power, heals the will, transfigures the earth. "Ultimately," he explains, "man finds in things nothing but what he himself has imported into them: the finding we call science, the importing—art, religion, love, pride."[25]

We begin to see why Nietzsche is key to any reflection on postmodern discourse: he explodes all notions of absolute Truth and at the same time extols life-enhancing fictions. *Brutally put, nothing has intrinsic sense; a strong sense must be made of everything.*[26] There, in that intolerable dictum, is the kernel of our current afflictions.

As we know Nietzsche casts a hugh shadow on contemporary philosophy and literary theory. Richard Rorty, for instance, places him with William James, Heidegger, Wittgenstein, and Dewey among the great unmakers of metaphysics, destroyers of philosophy as "a foundational discipline which 'grounds' knowledge-claims."[27] Pragmatically, says Rorty, "what ties Dewey and Foucault, James and Nietzsche, together . . . ," is their "sense that there is nothing deep down inside us except what we have put there ourselves, no criterion that we have not created in the course of creating a practice, no standard of rationality that is not an appeal to such a criterion, no rigorous argumentation that is not obedience to our own conventions."[28] As to literary theory, we have heard enough that current debates concerning author, reader, text, trope, representation, displacement, the subject as grammatical fiction, the will to power in signification—concerning these and many other critical issues, advert to Nietzsche.

But the time has come to recover ourselves, recapitulate. I have argued, somewhat breathlessly, that the cognitive imperative is a portentous factor in biological evolution and in human self-mastery, psychic self-creation. Making sense is fatidic. But I have also suggested that this imperative suffers repeated crises in the course of Western history, from ancient Gnosticism to the secular gnosis of our day. The latest crisis we call Nihilism, which is not the name, as J. Hillis Miller reminds us, that Nihilism has chosen for itself; rather is it the mark of odium, of alterity, that metaphysics has given to its enemy in an effort "to cover over the unhealable by annihilating the nothingness hidden within itself."[29] And now we come, at slow last, to postmodern discourse, how to make sense in it, how to make sense of it. How, for instance, to overcome Roland Barthes—surely, the preeminent critical intelligence of our moment, perhaps of our century—when he declares: "It is necessary to attempt to split, not signs, not signifiers on one side and signifieds on the other, but the very idea of a sign: an operation one might call semioclasty. It is

Western discourse as such, in its foundations, its elementary forms, that one might today attempt to split."[30] "Today" is already yesterday. Something, I think, now calls us beyond this "split," beyond semioclasty. To hear that call, however, we need to tell yet another story, the story of postmodern culture, our culture.

V

I have descanted sufficiently on postmodernism to my own and everyone's satiety.[31] I shall not try here to refine or define the concept further. Instead, I want merely to acknowledge the difficulties of making sense in an age of "indetermanence" (indeterminacy lodged in immanence), when signs scatter like so many leaves and authorities wither in the chill autumn of our discontents. I can not hope, of course, to review all these difficulties here—they multiply in a society so diverse as ours. Yet I think they may be exemplified in the controversy between two leading thinkers of our age: I mean the German neo-Marxist, Jürgen Habermas, and the French poststructuralist, Jean-François Lyotard. I will, therefore, end my story of postmodern culture with their dispute.

Interestingly, the dispute has been triangulated, more than arbitrated, by the American pragmatist, Richard Rorty.[32] Rorty quickly perceives the issue: it is consensus (from *consentīre,* to feel, to sense, together) or, more tendentiously, totalization. Lyotard wants to put the masters of suspicion, Freud and Marx, themselves under suspicion; he rejects any politics that will generate yet another metanarrative, another coercive code. Habermas, however, adheres to a universalist concept of reason (the idea of a "better" rather than simply "contextual" argument) in the name of justice, in the name of the Enlightenment. For Lyotard, language is largely conflictual, consensus merely a phase of discourse; for Habermas, language is mainly communicative, consensus the goal of discourse. This brings them, naturally, to different views of knowledge, morality, history.

As to Rorty, he believes it possible to suspend meta-narratives (as Lyotard wishes) *without* yielding to injustice (as Habermas does not wish to yield). But this is precisely what theory can not accomplish, Rorty claims, for theory seeks always "auto-certification." It is rather the task of social praxis, which opens itself to life. Thus Rorty rehabilitates Bacon against Descartes, and dismisses the claims of philosophers to "ground" discourse and of intellectuals to form a political "vanguard." Instead, Rorty accepts the Baconian complicity of knowledge with power, and the Deweyite reenchantment of the world through the familiar, the quotidian, everything useful and near at hand.

But now I must square the triangle, make my own extraneous point. Lyotard's accent on *le différend*—this is not Derrida's *différance*—, on the incommensurable in our realms of discourse, accords with my own sense of postindustrial societies. And his urge to reinsinuate will, desire, metaphor, play, into postmodern rationality conforms to the agility and "*sveltesse*" I, too, would want for our moment.[33] Yet Lyotard has not fully confronted the moral and political consequences of his "minoritarian language games," his paralogies of justice. And his fractions or factions, his *petites histoires,* can prove nearly as much terrorist as Marxist totalities prove tyrannical. With Rorty, however, and even more with William James, I feel on native ground. I shall turn to them presently to make sense of our impasse. But first, another short story, my sixth, concerning literary theory.

VI

It would be unthinkable for me to close this little anthology of stories without reference to literary theory. This is not only because theory interests me personally, ambivalently; it also holds us to our common task as interpreters of culture. Indeed, in the last two decades, theory has become a keystone of the humanities, not of criticism alone.

Many factors have contributed to the key function of literary theory, its readiness to inquire into diverse regions of culture, disciplines of the humanities—art, theater, literature, philosophy, history, psychoanalysis, linguistics, anthropology.[34] Yet theory—I must now mix my metaphor—finally serves less as keystone or capstone to the humanities than as a rogue Keystone Kop who slyly subverts (deconstructs) the very authorities he pretends to defend. Jacques Derrida, our premier Keystone Kop, put it thus: "We are in an implacable political topography . . . one step further toward a sort of original an-archy risks producing the hierarchy. 'Thought' requires *both* the principle of reason and what is beyond the principle of reason, the *arkhe* and an-archy. Between the two, the difference of a breath or an accent . . . ," a " 'wink' or a 'blink.' "[35]

Precisely in that *Augenblick* of reason, theory speaks to us in an echolalia of tongues. But what does it say? It moots and taunts, taunts traditional meaning, moots humanistic sense. I will tersely mention here only three of these crabby issues:

1. The first issue concerns *literariness,* a presumptive quality that transforms words into literature. Does art really possess, as Kant thought, a privileged ontological status, or is its definition merely conventional, consensual? Some critics, like Murray Krieger, discreetly mourn the decline and fall of the "elite object," whereas others, as incongruous as E. D. Hirsch and Paul de Man, rejoice in that same lapse.[36] With literariness gone—actually, it lingers like the smile of the Cheshire Cat—the distinction between literature and criticism also dissolves, infuriating nearly everyone concerned, except those who cried with Barthes: "There are no more critics, only writers."[37] (To this, writers in New Haven quickly assented, as I did, in Milwaukee, for a time.) Furthermore, with literariness gone, the claim for an objective aesthetic structure wobbles. The work itself tilts toward the reader—for the author has "died"—and gives itself to the maddening relativity of human responses.

The loss of literariness, then, destabilizes literature, unmargins it. Without formal or generic constraints, our ability to make specific sense of literature diminishes even as our freedom, as readers, swells.

2. Next is the issue of *hermeneutics.* From Schleiermacher and Dilthey, through Heidegger, Gadamer, Ricoeur, Iser, to Derrida, the "science" of interpretation comes into increasing doubt. As we near the present, hermeneutics becomes prejudicial, uncertain, suspect—after Heidegger, the hermeneutic circle turns, if not vicious, antic. Nowadays, of course, hermeneutics yields to deconstruction, textualism, semiology, rhetoric, "subjective- " or "para-criticism," yields simply to reading which acknowledges no determinate meaning.[38] Thus, for instance, Derrida distinguishes between two interpretations of interpretation: one dreams of deciphering truth, the other merely affirms play.[39] Thus, too, de Man rejects exegesis in favor of rhetoric that "radically suspends logic and opens up vertiginous possibilities of referential aberration"; while Fish conceives interpretation as "the art of constructing," not of "construing."[40]

We are hardly surprised that some critics argue "against interpretation" (Sontag), and others "beyond interpretation" (Culler). For hermeneutics can no longer dis-cover for us any latent, any *necessary,* sense when all its "laws are put in deep abeyance."

3. Last is the issue of *language* itself, our linguistic obsession or logomania. Since Nietzsche's early essay, "Of Truth and Falsity in the Ultramoral Sense," the Western mind has tended to deflect its perennial questions toward language, deflect them toward, and inflect them in, language. With Wittgenstein, the tendency took a decisive turn, though he himself resisted valiantly the "bewitchment of our intelligence by means of language."[41] Logical Positivism, Ordinary Language Philosophy, Speech Act Theory, Structuralism, Stylistics, Deconstruction, all brought their versions of loquacity to our cities of words, towers of babel.[42] The final lessons of Wittgenstein himself, poised austerely at the brink of the unspeakable, seem lost on us. We continue to knock about our "prison-house of language" (Nietzsche), our "fly-bottle" (Wittgenstein), out of which no theory can release us since language seems to have been "always already" (Derrida) everywhere.

Here is the gravamen against theory, then: the immanence of language, the loss of literariness, and the denial of hermeneutics, all three disperse our meanings. We have no way to make sense of our texts or our lives, immersed as they are in an ever-changing sea of signifiers.

Poststructuralist theory, though full of brio and bravura, can only taunt our desire to make sense. It can only tease us into further thought, not anchor our meanings. To this cavil, textualists have ready answers. As Paul de Man put it in his strong essay, "The Resistance to Theory": "Those who reproach literary theory for being oblivious to social and historical (that is to say ideological) reality are merely stating their fear at having their own ideological mystifications exposed by the tool they are trying to discredit"; impartially, de Man then goes on to show that theory "is itself its own resistance," and must inevitably undo itself.[43]

Yet the "ideological mystifications" of one person are the convictions of another. In reaction to the bleached theories of poststructuralism, a number of countertheories now seek to recover the variegated colors of the world. They constrain the freeplay of language and instability of knowledge in the name of history, morality, politics. In doing so, they recall, of course, earlier forms of social criticism—that is, they reinvent continually Ixion's wheel. Of these countertheories, the most genial, perhaps, is critical pluralism, the kind we associate with Meyer Abrams or Wayne Booth.[44] Other critics engage in more singular or truculent advocacies. I have in mind, for instance, Fredric Jameson's "dialectical criticism," Edward Said's "secular criticism," Gerald Graff's "literature as assertion," Frank Lentricchia's "criticism for social change."[45] However distinct, these leftist critics share a passion to recapture the density of historical circumstance, richness of social implication. Lentricchia says it succinctly: "Criticism . . . is the production of knowledge to the ends of power and, maybe, social change."[46]

Will these critics lead us out of the desert? I doubt it for reasons that I can only touch upon here. With their declared, their *general,* intent, I am in earnest accord. Nor am I unduly distracted by their polemics, wounded will to power, or gestures of (unearned) civic virtue. In these velleities, we are all, to various degrees, complicit. But I find phantasmic their tendency to privilege Marxism as the only discourse of dissent, indeed of independent thought, regardless of its theoretical difficulties, economic predicaments, political oppressions, and prophetic failures, regardless of its retreat as a discourse of Hope. (American Marxism, our latest version of bourgeois self-criticism, is most pertinent to postindustrial societies precisely when Marxism least resembles itself.) I find constricting their need to grant politics priority, not merely due significance but *priority,* in the justification of human existence, an "absolute horizon of all reading and all interpretation," as Jameson says.[47] And I find unsettling their concealed social determinism, collectivist bias, distrust of aesthetic pleasure, proclivity to rationalize or "blueprint" human reality, and readiness to confuse their beliefs with universal values and their theories with the irrefutable scheme of things.

Obviously, contentiousness is contagious: I have caught a case of polemics myself. I have simplified the commitments of the new social critics, commitments that I often share, as when Lentricchia untypically says: "The 'active' critical soul in America, from Emerson to Burke, joins parties of one, because it is there, in America, that critical power flourishes."[48] And I have aggravated the differences between social and textual critics, who are all compelled, in our dialogic moment, to heed continually one another.[49] Still, I would maintain that the partisanship of some critics, whether cognitive or political, may limit their imaginative scope, and inhibit that vast sympathy or interdebtedness of life that literature affirms, in its climactic moments, beyond all our facts.

Once more, and for the last time, let me recover, recapture, myself. Whatever powers the cognitive imperative derived from biological evolution and psychogenesis, it suffered the trials of Western history and the crisis of modern philosophical nihilism. That crisis has been further exacerbated by the "indetermanences" of postmodern culture, the taunts of its literary theories. The field of humanistic sense is left open now to a perpetual agon of interpretations, or else to silent dismissals. If we cannot persuade ourselves, like Jameson, that Marxism provides the "ultimate *semantic* precondition of the intelligibility of literary and cultural texts," can we ever hope to make sense in our enterprise?[50]

This brings me to my last story, more pragmatic and, I hope, propitious than the rest.

VII

The time has come—in this paper, in our culture—for provisional reconstructions, pragmatic remythifications.[51] Even in France, the deconstructive mood has turned. Thus Yves Bonnefoy, successor to Roland Barthes at the Collège de France, calls in his Inaugural Address of 1981—so very different from *Leçon,* Barthes' own address of 1977—for a re-turn to being or presence. For Bonnefoy, this implies a reflux of language to human relations.[52] Here is a hint of pragmatism, the kind American thinkers have honored for more than a century now. (Indeed, American Pragmatism is making a comeback to the intellectual scene, making it with clarity and heightened sophistication.) But what is pragmatism? I answer by attending first to Rorty, then to the incomparable William James.

Pragmatism brackets Truth (capitalized), circumvents Metaphysics and Epistemology; it finds no universal "ground" for discourse. As Rorty wryly puts it: "Truth is not the sort of thing one should expect to have a philosophically interesting theory about. For pragmatists, 'truth' is just the name of a property which all true statements have."[53] This is not tautology. What makes statements true (in lower case) is use, context, what I call benevolent consequence in particular circumstance. For human beings possess no mirror to reflect the immutable face of reality.

And though judgments about consequences are themselves debatable, still they remain subject to quotidian mediations, negotiations; they are part of our endless "conversation." This "conversation," Rorty argues, takes the place of knowledge as "the social justification of belief," and becomes our main "edifying" discourse.[54] (Hermeneutics becomes less a way of "knowing" than of "coping." The "conversation" has no end, for its end (goal) is neither closure nor agreement. But this implies no surrender to "relativism." As Rorty insists: "The real issue is not between people who think one view as good as another and people who do not. It is between those who think our culture, or purpose, or intuitions cannot be supported except conversationally, and people who still hope for other sorts of support."[55]

We begin to see the affinity between textualism and Rorty's pragmatism, though he himself sees textualism as "the contemporary counterpart of idealism."[56] We can also recognize their differences in the empiric resolve of pragmatism, its commitment to *beliefs in action rather than ironies of theory.* This commitment invests pragmatism with a moral and social concern that textualism lacks. The commitment further honors the ancient cognitive imperative, which it now translates not into some invariable truth but into effective choices, contexts of desirable action. In short, pragmatism is intimate with all the uncertainties of our postmodern condition without quiescence, sterility, or abdication of judgment.

I admit to some sympathy for the bluff tolerance and optative spirit of American Pragmatism. But I confess also to some discomfort with its penchant to evade or defer crucial issues. How, for instance, should we adjudicate competing claims of short and long range use, conflicting opinions of benevolence, alternate existential acts? What prevents Rorty's endless "conversation" from flaring up into war? And if, with Rorty, we cease to ask, "Is it true?", how do we answer the alternate questions he proposes: "What would it be like to believe that? What would happen if I did? What would I be committing myself to?"?[57] As even philosophers must know, the results of actions or beliefs are no less contingent than notions of truth.

It follows that, though Rorty poses as "the informed dilettante, the polypragmatic, Socratic intermediary between various discourses," he tends finally to scant the role of belief, desire, and power in the "conversations" of postmodern society.[58] At his best he is the dry, lucid, sensible satirist of metaphysics, a little wizened by his contact with analytic philosophy. His favored mood is one of cracker-barrel deprecation.

By contrast, the mood of William James is expansive, celebratory. His mind takes risks, combining rigor with generosity. "I offer the oddly-named thing pragmatism," he says, "as a philosophy that can satisfy both kinds of demand. It can remain religious like the rationalisms, but at the same time, like the empiricisms, it can preserve the richest intimacy with facts."[59] This pragmatism looks away from "*first things, principles, categories, supposed necessities,*" and looks toward "*last things, fruits, consequences, facts,*" and like a corridor in the great mansion of philosophy, it opens on many rooms.[60] Indeed, it opens on rooms that contemporary critics would fain leave forever shut. It engages our *beliefs;* for these, including metaphysical or religious beliefs, inhere in our knowledge as in our actions. Pragmatism "will count mystical experiences if they have practical consequences," and "will take a God who lives in the very dirt of private fact—if that would seem a likely place to find him."[61]

James, then, has no rancorous urge to demystify all beliefs. And though he acknowledges the fecund diversity of truth, a truth "*made,* just as health, wealth, and strength are made, in the course of experience," he invites us to reconstruct our discourse, to ground it even, not on some rock of the Absolute but on resilient concretions of *human desire in their circumstance.*[62] Still, the obdurate question remains, and will endure: can different beliefs, active in their circumstances, abide one another, or will they throw us back on the state of nature, "red in tooth and claw"? The answer calls us to James's "pluralistic universe."

This pluralism derives from a strict philosophic insight, not from some mawkish sentiment of tolerance, an insight into the radical insufficiency of human awareness. We can never know all there is to know, we can never relate all the parts to the whole. "The world," James says as if he were speaking to Lyotard, "is full of partial stories that run parallel to one another, beginning and ending at odd times."[63] There can be, for us, no all-enveloping unity. This makes for "noetic pluralism," a paratactical universe "eternally incomplete, and at all times subject to addition or liable to loss."[64] In this scheme the venerable problem of the One and the Many acquires renewed interest; for it is preeminently the problem of pluralism itself, which must equally abjure monism and relativism. James again: "The world is One just so far as its parts hang together by any definite connexion. It is many just so far as any definite connexion fails to obtain. And finally it is growing more and more unified by those systems of connexion . . . which human energy keeps framing as time goes one."[65] (This last is what I have called the New Gnosticism.)

By his own admission, James struggled with the problem of pluralism for many years—"How can one and the same identical fact experience itself so diversely?"—till, with the aid of Bergson, he broke through the "intellectualistic logic" that created, in the first place, the impasse.[66] Placing himself "at a bound . . . inside of the living, moving, active thickness of the real," he felt "all abstractions and distinctions," all antinomies of reason, dissolve.[67] But that "bound" or leap does not concern us here, our practical concern being to preserve the "multiverse" in our "universe," and so to realize, as James richly realized, the *ethical* commitment that underlies the pluralist stance. It is a commitment to satisfy as many claims as we vitally can; a commitment, otherwise, to mediation, negotiation, rather than to dogmatism or contumacy; and a commitment to a scheme of uncertified possibilities that we can actually trust. It is finally a commitment to recognize beliefs for what they are: rungs in our "faith ladder" on which we climb from "might be true" to "shall be true," and as we climb come to see that life extends farther than conceptual reason.[68]

A pluralistic universe, then, may sustain the abundance of our beliefs, beliefs answerable to their acts and constitutive of our meanings. We take this, of course, on faith. But faith, as James knew, helps to create its own social fact; for society is nothing if not a tough fabric of trusts. "Our faith," he says, "is faith in someone else's faith, and in the greatest matters this is most the case."[69] Our common passion, I might add for him, is the "will to believe," as driving as Nietzsche's "will to power." From that will we create our human world; from that will we make postmodern as archaic sense. Our "willing nature" will not be kept out of the game. It is an earnest, a perilous game, and though deeply inscribed in our particular histories, a game wide as the cosmos. William James has the temerity to perceive it thus:

> In every being that is real there is something external to, and sacred from, the grasp of every other. God's being is sacred from ours. To co-operate with his creation seems all he wants of us. . . . In the silence of our theories we then seem to listen, and to hear something like the pulse of Being beat; and it is

borne in upon us that the mere turning of the character, the dumb willingness to suffer and to serve this universe, is more than all theories about it put together.[70]

I find here balm to the crisis of postmodern discourse, balm enough.

Epilogue

And now, at last, I must abandon my quest for sense, a human quest that can never end so long as mind seeks to know itself. I must also try to resituate my discourse among the many pieces of postmodern knowledge. These pieces are not "fragments to shore up against our ruins" (Eliot); they are what we are and what we know. For in our civic as in our intellectual polity, "more like a federal republic than like an empire or a kingdom," James remarks, "however much may report itself as present at any effective center of consciousness or action," something else always remains, "self-governed and absent and unreduced to unity."[71] Still, our fragments, I suspect, commune with one another, and our knowledge lives in the patterns we make and continually remake.

Perhaps all I have said amounts to no more than what Aristotle said in the first sentence of his *Metaphysics* (not, incidentally, in his *Ethics, Rhetoric, Politics, Physics,* or *Poetics,* but in his *Metaphysics*): "All men, by nature, desire to know." By "nature": this includes human biology, psychology, philosophy, and our second nature, history. Yet in the current climate of discourse, some postmodern writers pretend to forget our primal cognitive imperative, while others, mainly social critics, would supply all our meanings from one totemic system or another. Neither recourse will quite do. I believe American Pragmatism offers us now genuine possibilities of thought and action. For it cheerfully avoids the extremes of philosophic skepticism and ideological dogmatism that, Michael Polanyi believed, once joined to usher political totalitarianism in Continental Europe.[72]

In a crucial sense, then, pragmatism answers to our postmodern condition; more, it brings so many elements of the human condition itself into active choice. Yet pragmatism can not answer all our queries, no more than can any other view, short of mystical revelation. Pragmatism can not finally evade its own evasions as it waits upon the judgment of time on consequences. Pragmatism itself will concede this even as it aspires to a kind of holism in self-healing. Here, for the last time, is William James: "The incompleteness of the pluralistic universe, thus assumed and held as the most probable hypothesis, is also represented by the pluralistic philosophy as being self-reparative through *us*, as getting its disconnections remedied in part by *our* behavior [my italics]."[73]

"Through us": that is where the matter seems finally to rest. Or perhaps not finally, for this "through us" may depend on a faith that no theoretic school, political idea, or professional code can nourish. What faith? I could not really tell anyone that, though in rereading *The Death of Ivan Ilych,* I felt Tolstoy come shatteringly close to it. " 'Why these sufferings?' " Ivan asks on his deathbed. "And the voice [within him] answered, 'For no reason—they just are so.' Beyond and besides this there was nothing"; then, seconds before the end, perhaps during the end itself: "Suddenly some force struck him in the chest and side, making it still harder to breathe, and he fell through the hole and there at the bottom was a light."[74]

Does not all sense filter from just such a region of intuited light? But this is not a question to answer on this occasion, or even to ask, but perhaps only, some day, to dance.[75]

1. Darwinian concepts of evolution have been qualified by new sub-molecular discoveries. See Lancelot Law Whyte, *Internal Factors of Evolution* (New York, 1965). On the number of elementary particles in the universe, see Carl Sagan, *The Dragons of Eden: Speculations on the Evolution of Human Intelligence* (New York, 1977), 42.

See, for instance, Edward O. Wilson, *Sociobiology: The New Synthesis* (Cambridge, Mass., 1975), 3.

3. Ibid., 152.

4. Wilder Penfield, *The Mystery of the Mind: A Critical Study of Consciousness and the Human Brain* (Princeton, 1975), 50. See also pp. 73, 80f.

5. Roger Sperry, *Science and Moral Priority: Merging Mind, Brain, and Human Values* (New York, 1983), 85.

6. Arthur Koestler, *The Ghost in the Machine* (New York, 1967), 239ff.

7. Quoted by Penfield, 90. Sagan also glosses the same remark: "Natural selection has served as a kind of intellectual sieve, producing brains and intelligences increasingly competent to deal with the laws of nature. This resonance, extracted by natural selection, between our brains and the universe may help explain a quandary set by Einstein: The most incomprehensible property of the universe, he said, is that it is so comprehensible." See Sagan, 232ff.

8. Sagan quotes Bronowski, 238; Sagan, 230; Sperry, 8.

9. Sigmund Freud, *Leonardo da Vinci,* trans. A. A. Brill (New York, 1947), 18, 20.

10. Ibid., 96f. Freud attributes here the image of slumbering humanity to Merejkowski.

11. Jacques Lacan, *The Language of the Self: The Function of Language in Psychoanalysis,* trans. Anthony Wilden (Baltimore, 1968), 41. Drawing on D. W. Winnecott as well as Jacques Lacan, Gabriele Schwab gives a perceptive account of "Genesis of the Subject, Imaginary Functions, and Poetic Language," in *New Literary History* 15, no. 3 (Spring 1984):453–74.

12. Ibid., 288f., 86.

13. "Biology must, for its own sake, provide some interpretation of knowledge in its purely organic aspects, these aspects, both phylogenetic and ontogenetic, being very much the field of the biologist," writes Jean Piaget, *Biology and Knowledge: An Essay on the Relations Between Organic Regulations and Cognitive Processes,* trans. Beatrix Walsh (Chicago, 1971), 1

14. Ibid., 350.

15. Ibid., 353.

16. "Cognitive psychology soon found common cause with artificial intelligence, whose heuristic spirit was not in the least constrained by a fixation on the nineteenth century," Jerome Bruner writes, in *On Knowing: Essays for the Left Hand* (Cambridge, Mass., 1979), 172.

17. Jacques Derrida, "Structure, Sign, and Play," in *The Languages of Criticism and the Sciences of Man,* eds. Richard Macksey and Eugenio Donato (Baltimore, 1970), 264. Note, however, that Derrida's sentence runs: "the joyous affirmation of the freeplay of the world and without truth, without origin, *offered to an active interpretation* [italics mine]. . . . " Even here, the cognitive imperative persists.

18. As Hayden White says: "Neither the reality nor the meaning of history is 'out there' in the form of a story awaiting only a historian to discern its outline and identify the plot that comprises its meaning." In "Historical Pluralism," *Critical Inquiry* 12, no. 3 (1986): 487. See also his "Getting Out of History," *Diacritics* 12, no. 3 (Fall 1982), 13.

19. Hans Blumenberg, *The Legitimacy of the Modern Age,* trans. Robert M. Wallace (Cambridge, Mass, 1983), 136.

20. What I have elsewhere called the New Gnosticism refers simply to the crescive intervention of the human mind in reality, the expanding mediations of languages and symbols. See references on p. 184, note 21, above. But note also that medieval Gnosticism, though it directed human attention away from this world, insisted on knowledge rather than faith as the means of salvation. In this, it shares with the New Gnosticism a concern with the noetic capabilities of men and women. See Blumenberg, 290–307.

21. Blumenberg, 138.

22. Ibid., 138. For an account that sometimes parallels, often diverges, from Blumenberg's, see Jeffrey Stout, *The Flight from Authority* (Notre Dame, 1981).

23. Friedrich Nietzsche, *The Will to Power,* trans. Walter Kaufmann and R. J. Hollingdale (New York, 1976), 3.

24. Ibid., 9, 13, 40, 47.

25. Ibid., 327.

26. *"We have need of lies* in order to conquer this reality, this 'truth,' that is, in order to *live,"* writes Nietzsche. Ibid., 451.

27. Richard Rorty, *Philosophy and the Mirror of Nature* (Princeton, 1979), 4.

28. Richard Rorty, *Consequences of Pragmatism* (*Essays: 1972–1980*) (Minneapolis, 1982), xlii. See also pp. xviii, xxi, 40, 161. I might add that the radical perspectivism of Nietzsche has opened the way for pluralist thinkers as diverse as Michael Polanyi, Stephen Pepper, and Nelson Goodman.

29. J. Hillis Miller, "The Critic as Host," in Harold Bloom, et al., *Deconstruction and Criticism* (New York, 1979), 228.

30. Quoted by Josué V. Harari, ed., *Textual Strategies: Perspectives in Post-Structuralism Criticism* (Ithaca, N.Y., 1979), 30.

31. See pp. 168–73 above.

32. Richard Rorty, "Habermas, Lyotard, et la Postmodernité," *Critique* 442 (mars 1984):181–97, which also appeared, in English, in *Praxis International* 4, no. 1 (April 1984):32–44. Rorty takes as his main texts the lectures of Jürgen Habermas, delivered at the Collège de France in March 1983, published as *Habermas and Modernity,* ed. Richard Bernstein (Cambridge, Mass., 1985), and Jean-François Lyotard, *The Postmodern Condition,* trans., Geoff Bennington and Brian Massumi (Minneapolis, 1984), though he recognizes that the debate also refers to earlier works.

33. "Il faut donc accorder l'infini de la volonté avec la sveltesse: beaucoup moins 'travailler,' beaucoup plus apprendre, savoir, inventer, circuler," in Jean-François Lyotard, *Le Tombeau de l'intellectuel et autres papiers* (Paris, 1984), 86f. See also pp. 79–83.

34. See Ralph Cohen, "Literary Theory as a Genre," *Centrum* 3, no. 7 (Spring 1975), 57; and Evan Watkins, "Conflict and Consensus in the History of Recent Criticism," *New Literary History* 12, no. 2 (Winter 1981), 350–54.

35. Jacques Derrida, "The Principle of Reason: The University in the Eyes of its Pupils," *Diacritics* 13, no. 3, (Fall 1983), 18f., 20.

36. See Murray Krieger, *Arts on the Level: The Fall of the Elite Object* (Knoxville, 1981), 10–19; E. D. Hirsch, *The Aims of Interpretation* (Chicago, 1972), 108; Paul de Man, *Blindness and Insight: Essays in the Rhetoric of Contemporary Criticism* (New York, 1971), 12.

37. Roland Barthes, "Theory of the Text," in *Untying the Text: A Post-Structuralist Reader,* ed. Robert Young (Boston & London, 1981), 44.

38. For a lucid discussion of this question, see Paul B. Armstrong, "The Conflict of Interpretation and the Limits of Pluralism," *PMLA* 98, no. 3 (May 1983):341–52. See also the articles in *New Literary History* 14, no. 1 (Autumn 1982) and 15, no. 2 (Winter 1984), devoted to problems on meaning, creativity, and interpretation.

39. Jacques Derrida, *L'Écriture et la différence* (Paris, 1967), 427.

40. Paul de Man, *Allegories of Reading: Figural Language in Rousseau, Nietzsche, Rilke, and Proust* (New Haven, 1979), 10; Stanley Fish, *Is There a Text in This Class? The Authority of Interpretive Communities* (Cambridge, Mass., 1980), 327. Less immoderate, Wolfgang Iser recognizes that interpretation "though a cognitive operation, has to bridge a gulf between cognition and the incommensurable." For Iser, too, interpretation is "basically pragmatic" in its nature; and when we forget this, we imprison ourselves within our interpretive

frameworks. "That is, reification," he concludes in "The Interplay Between Creation and Interpretation," *New Literary History* 15, no. 2 (Winter 1984), 394, 395.

41. Ludwig Wittgenstein, *Philosophical Investigations*, trans. G. E. M. Anscombe (Oxford, 1968), 47[e].

42. For some leading philosophical issues of language, see Richard Rorty, ed., *The Linguistic Turn: Recent Essays in Philosophical Method* (Chicago, 1967); for literary issues, see Barbara Herrnstein Smith, *On the Margins of Discourse: The Relations of Literature to Language* (Chicago, 1978), and George Steiner, *After Babel: Aspects of Language and Translation* (New York, 1975).

43. Paul de Man, "The Resistance to Theory," in *The Pedagogical Imperative: Yale French Studies* 63, ed. Barbara Johnson, pp. 11, 20. Murray Krieger would deny this, and argue that deconstructionists inescapably thematize their "pristine instrument of verbal analysis." See Murray Krieger, "In the Wake of Morality: The Thematic Underside of Recent Theory," *New Literary History* 15, no. 1 (Autumn 1983), 130f.

44. Abrams predicts: "For a while the diverse modes for disestablishing the intelligibility of literary language will flourish. But in the course of time, the way of reading that we have in common with our critical precursors will assimilate what the new ways have to offer." M. H. Abrams, "Literary Criticism in America," in M. H. Abrams and James Ackerman, *Theories of Criticism: Essays in Literature and Art* (Washington, D. C., 1984), 29. See also Wayne Booth, *Critical Understanding: The Limits of Critical Pluralism* (Chicago, 1979). For other "intermediate" positions, arguing that texts are mediated but not constructed, see Walter A. Davis, "The Fisher King: *Wille zur Macht* in Baltimore," *Critical Inquiry* 10, no. 4 (June 1984), and James Phelan, "Data, Danda, and Disagreement," *Diacritics* 13, no. 2 (Summer 1983).

45. Fredric Jameson, *The Political Unconscious: Narrative as a Socially Symbolic Act* (Ithaca, N.Y.: 1981); Edward W. Said, *The World, the Text, and the Critic* (Cambridge, Mass., 1983); Gerald Graff, *Literature Against Itself: Literary Ideas in Modern Society* (Chicago, 1979), and "Literature as Assertion," in *American Criticism in the Poststructuralist Age,* ed. Ira Konigsberg (Ann Arbor, 1981); Frank Lentricchia, *Criticism and Social Change* (Chicago, 1983).

46. Lentricchia, 11.

47. Jameson, 7.

48. Lentricchia, 6.

49. " 'Ironic' is not a bad word to use along with 'oppositional,' " Said says of his "secular criticism," and this is not altogether alien to de Man: "Irony is no longer a trope but the undoing of the deconstructive allegory of all tropological cognitions, the systematic undoing, in other words, of understanding." See Said, 29, and de Man, *Allegories,* 301. Congruously, Jameson remarks: "Interpretation is not an isolated act, but takes place within a Homeric battlefield, on which a host of interpretive opinions are either openly or implicitly in conflict," p. 13.

50. Jameson, 75.

51. Jacques Derrida is always aware of the inescapable urge for presence, remythification, even if other critics view that urge more positively than he does; see, for instance, Krieger, *Arts,* 42f., and Ralph Cohen, "The Statements Literary Texts Do Not Make," *New Literary History* 13, no. 3 (Spring 1982), 389f.

52. Yves Bonnefoy, "Image and Presence: Yves Bonnefoy's Inaugural Address at the Collège de France," *New Literary History* 15, no. 3 (Spring 1984):447.
53. *Consequences,* xiii.
54. Rorty, *Philosophy,* 170, 210, 370–73.
55. *Consequences,* 167.
56. Ibid., 139–59.
57. Ibid., 163.
58. *Philosophy,* 317.
59. William James, *Pragmatism* (New York, 1955), 33.
60. Ibid., 47. James prefers Papini's figure of a hotel corridor.
61. Ibid., 61.
62. Ibid., 143.
63. Ibid., 98.
64. James's statement, which uncannily previsions postmodern styles, runs as follows: "It *may* be that some parts of the world are connected so loosely with some other parts as to be strung along by nothing but the copula *and.* They might even come and go without those other parts suffering any internal change. This pluralistic view, of a world of *additive* constitution, is one that pragmatism is unable to rule out from serious consideration. But this view leads one to the farther hypothesis that the actual world, instead of being complete 'eternally,' as the monists assure us, may be eternally incomplete, and at all times subject to addition or liable to loss" (ibid., 112). Note also the "philosophical pluralism," consonant with James's, which Robert Nozick attractively expounds in *Philosophical Explanations* (Cambridge, Mass., 1981), 18–24; 643–47.
65. Ibid., 105.
66. William James, *A Pluralistic Universe* (Cambridge, Mass., 1977), 94f.
67. Ibid., 116.
68. Ibid., 148.
69. William James, *The Will to Believe and Human Immortality* (New York, 1956), 9. See also pp. 18f, 25, 28f., 52–58, 92–110.
70. Ibid., 141.
71. *A Pluralistic,* 145.
72. Michael Polanyi and Harry Prosch, *Meaning* (Chicago, 1975), 10f.
73. *A Pluralistic,* 148.
74. *The Short Novels of Tolstoy,* ed. Philip Rhav, trans. Aylmer Maude (New York, 1949), 463, 468.
75. "It is surprising to find ourselves emerging from Nonsense into the dance. . . .," says Elizabeth Sewell, trying marvelously to make all kinds of sense from Nonsense in *The Field of Nonsense* (London, 1952), 192.

10 Prospects in Retrospect

I

A third of our century has elapsed since postmodernism began to intrude on our awareness, and all the conundrums continue unresolved. This is in part because the questions before us are questions that postmodernism itself has taught us to raise about itself. But have we had now enough? *That* question, suggesting supervention, *dépassement,* may not be postmodern. Nonetheless, the mere fact that we ask it betrays our impatience, our need for some larger sense of the moment.

Once more, I see in Jamesian pragmatism—it will not abolish all our afflictions—something ready and available to our current condition. This perception may become more persuasive if I review, one last time, the condition of postmodernism itself, now a cultural field of brilliant dreck and jocose rubble. Such a review may also hint, if not preview, a future so near as to appear almost present.

II

The first impulse of every critic of postmodernism is still to relate it to the semanteme it contains: namely, modernism. This often leads to intellectual miseries, and sometimes to critical conceits.[1] The degree to which modernism and postmodernism seem continuous or discontinuous, and indeed both at the same time, will always depend on historical presuppositions; probably, that degree will remain perpetually moot. There is clearer consensus on the modernist break with *its* tradition, a consensus voiced by such diverse figures as Herbert Read, C. S. Lewis, Geoffrey Barraclough, David Jones, Alan Bullock, George Steiner. The point is most recently and tersely made by Ricardo J. Quinones: "Post-Modernists do not define themselves by a counter-Modernity in the way the Modernists defined themselves by a counter-Romanticism."[2] This, of course, assumes a linear scheme of time that poststructuralists deplore.[3] In any event the geopolitical changes that postmodernism previsions may finally prove more momentous than any modernist revolution in style and sensibility—unless, of course, we attribute these changes to modernism itself.

If critics fail to agree on the breadth or depth of the modernist/postmodernist break, they do so in part because they share no theory of cultural transformation. Some may adhere to a conventional idea of literary history whereas others adopt René Thom's "catastrophe theory" which describes discontinuities without destruction, radical alterations in systems without their annihilation.[4] Others, still, may argue for coexisting paradigms, palimpsests of change, "soft" theories.[5] For the time being, we may have to settle for a concept of postmodernism that simply polemicizes modernism, revalues it in a polychronic scheme of history, a form of cultural intertemporality. As Matei Calinescu put it: "Postmodernism . . . has had the merit of reopening for us the problem of history as a field . . . as a process in which irreversibility penetrates what appears as repetition and vice versa, in short, as a multiplicity of continuous/discontinuous knowledges and know-hows, practices and counter-practices, as a variety of traditions and *not* as the imaginary Tradition against which the modernists revolted in the name of a no less imaginary Lost Unity."[6] This is the dialogical postmodern way to work our way through postmodernism, to habituate ourselves to our own models of change.

Having made these models, we begin to discern, and sometimes impose, family resemblances between discrepant phenomena: for example, concrete poetry, the *roman nouveau,* Latin American fiction, happenings, deconstruction, the works of Laurie Anderson, Andy Warhol, John Barth, the OULIPO and L-A-N-G-U-A-G-E groups—discern resemblances and differences too. That discernment, as I have argued throughout *The Postmodern Turn,* is neither arbitrary nor perverse. Indeed, it has already shaped Western discourse as the term postmodernism migrates between continents: to Germany, to Italy, to England, and lately to France. This migration suggests that the energizing matrix of postmodernism, if not its origin, may have been the sixties in America, with all their liberationist and countercultural tendencies.

There is no benefit in recounting once more the history of postmodernism, a history, or rather story, told well enough by others, if told always a little differently.[7] Perhaps I need only recall that the postmodern impulse, in America, was positive as well as negative, was utopian, not only antinomian, not only delegitimizing as French critics have recently claimed. Certainly the impulse found sustenance in prophecies of Marshall McLuhan, Buckminster Fuller, John Cage, Norman O. Brown, Carlos Casteneda, Herbert Marcuse, in the projects of futurists and ecologists, feminists and civil rightists, consumer movements and activists of every kind. Dissent was part of the postmodern motive; another part was visionary. Hence the swerve toward Blake in the sixties, toward Emerson recently.

The point needs emphasis today because deconstruction threatens to engulf postmodernism in its ironies, threatens to neutralize its utopian will. This will, though, has learned pragmatism, eschewing impatient—"Freedom *Now*!"—and comprehensive claims. It has learned to find freedom, or at least play, in anomalies of power and vagrancies of desire, in dreams of popular culture, mysteries of new technologies, inquinations of codes, disinhibitions of every kind, in old insistencies of the heart. Thus postmodernism seems to avoid, more than modernism, both the heroics of revolt and the agonies of acquiescence. In doing so, however, it opens itself to rival ideologies that nearly overwhelm it as they struggle to appropriate contemporary change.

Yet postmodernism itself has also changed. A cool, diffuse avant-gardist strain pervaded the earlier stages of postmodernism, manifest in the works of John Cage, Merce Cunningham, Robert Rauschenberg, Nam June Paik, Robert Wilson, Donald Barthelme. In that stage, of course, postmodernism wrested its own peculiar style, its distinctive multitemporal and fragmentary awareness, from modernism. Later, its reflexive, parodic bent, no less essential to its disengagement from modernism, became the ruling strain in divers metafictional writers, from Nabokov to Coover and Barth. (Both strains had met, half a century earlier, in Marcel Duchamp, master of both dadaist and reflexive enigmas, reborn as the ironic apostle of postmodernism.) Later still, toward the end of the seventies, postmodernism dispersed into various eclectic tendencies: some—in music, art, and architecture—neoromantic, others kitsch, camp, pop, deconstructionist, neodadaist, hermetically reflexive, or simply otiose.[8]

III

In the last decade, I have noted, various ideologies began to contest, and sometimes contend for, postmodernism. These ideologies include neoconservatism, neo-Marxism, poststructuralism, and neopragmatism, not to mention such diatribes as Charles Newman's *The Post-Modern Aura,* a work that makes Gerald Graff's *Literature Against Itself* appear almost winsome.[9]

A specter haunts neoconservatives—the specter is, more than Communism, decadence. This clouds their perceptions of postmodern change. Their arguments, however, lack neither urgency nor subtlety. Thus Daniel Bell declares:

> I believe we are coming to a watershed in Western society: we are witnessing the end of the bourgeois idea—that view of human action and social relations, particularly of economic exchange—which has molded the modern era for the last 200 years. And I believe that we have reached the end of the creative impulse and ideological sway of modernism, which, as a cultural movement, has dominated all the arts, and shaped our symbolic expressions, for the last 125 years.[10]

Bell's declaration is rich in regret. Disjunctions between the realms of economy, polity, and culture; the crisis of the Protestant ethic, of middle-class values in general; the advent, beyond rising expectations, of a politics of entitlement and envy; syncretism and the jumbling of styles in our world; the increasing permeability of all society to novelty, without discrimination or resistance; the confusions of fact and fantasy in public as in private life; the enervation of the postmodern self, if not its evacuation, a self nourished on hedonism, consumption, febrile affluence—all these, Bell fears, have undermined the Western order of things.

There is yet more cause for alarm. For Bell identifies the main culprit as culture itself, the entire symbolic universe, managed more and more by postmodern vanguards. Art changes life as the "post-modernist temper demands that what was previously played out in fantasy and imagination must be acted out in life as well. . . . Anything permitted in art is permitted in life."[11] Thus cultural vanguards come to shape society as a whole, affecting its manners, morals, and ultimately politics. This assimilation, this "democratization," of the old, agonistic avant-gardes, Bell believes, now imperils the very idea of a society.

Bell, of course, exaggerates the influence of postmodern vanguards; and though he writes with acumen, he writes also as a sociologist who finds lamentable that the contemporary imagination should disconfirm our polity. (I wonder what he thinks of classic American literature and its terrible power of darkness.) Like most neoconservatives, his view of postmodernism is dire: the exhaustion of modernism has left behind it a desiccated self and a depleted *civitas*. Postmodern culture turns that exhaustion into an "onslaught" on the values of ordinary behavior, on bourgeois liberalism really. Where, then, may legitimacy, may a "normative" order, reside? Perhaps only a "return in Western society of some conception of religion," Bell supposes, can resolve our crisis of belief, ground us in reality again.[12] This harks back to Eliot, in "Thoughts After Lambeth," predicting the failure of a non-Christian civilization.

The rhetoric of decadence characterizes the neoconservative stance; time brings only woes; nothing very good can come of postmodernism. This is also Hilton Kramer's melancholy refrain. Kramer wants to undo the sixties, reverse all their "insidious assaults." He wants to reclaim modernism, a modernism that preserves clear distinctions between high and low culture, a modernism—ascetic, rigorous, unmenacing—that may help us to stem the "fateful collapse" in critical standards. This is a political project that assumes an easy relation between culture and capitalism: "It is now only in a democratic society like ours that the values of high art can be expected to survive and prosper."[13] Indeed, as Kramer asks, why should the Left alone be given the privilege to politicize art?

In Kramer's account, modernism ended by denying itself in postmodernism which evokes nostalgically nineteenth century bourgeois art. This postmodern evocation, though, is not merely nostalgic; it is also camp, ironic, retro, substituting pop facetiousness for the high seriousness of modernist art. Thus postmodernism, Kramer ingeniously argues, constitutes the "revenge of the philistines" on their old, intransigent enemy, modernism itself. But all is not yet lost: the revenge remains incomplete since modernism survives as a "vital tradition," the only tradition, really, that our arts can claim. As for postmodernism, in a "purely negative way, it has placed the modernist heritage in dramatic historical relief, and thus helped to redefine its importance to us."[14]

The yearning of neoconservatives for modernism is understandable if mildly pathetic. It is, of course, a yearning for the past generally, more specifically, for an entirely safe, docile version of modernism, a "mainline modernism" without terror, agony, or provocation. Indeed, modernism becomes the sign for "the good, old days," for "moral grandeur" and "high purpose," for qualities one might as well impute to the Victorian era. For this "mainline modernism" has become "deeply integrated" into middle class culture, and stands in noble contrast with a postmodernism indistinguishable from "a grievous and sometimes nihilistic academicism serving a variety of aesthetic and political interests."[15]

IV

On interesting points the neoconservative view accords perfectly with that of neo-Marxists, though the latter approach postmodernism with greater theoretical brio. They do so, ignoring that Marxist theory without Marxist praxis is no Marxism at all; "theory" becomes a high-minded illusion meant to save Marxism from its history, save ideas from their consequences. In short, neo-Marxists ignore Marx's most fundamental thesis on Feuerbach, which insists on the task of philosophy to *change* the world, not merely to understand it. This evasion, one among others, allows neo-Marxist philosophy to persist in America—precisely where it has never been "tried"—as a "dialectical immaterialism," an omnibus of grievances, a theology of hope—and beyond that, as an intellectual exercise, conferring on its practitioners moral superiority with total immunity.[16]

Marxist theoretical chic is, of course, part of our condign ("bourgeois") self-criticism, our genuine malaise, mid lingering poverty, racism, sexism, in an affluent and pluralist society. Marxism, let us also avow, offers the most densely articulated sociohistorical discourse we possess, and thus provides a ballast to the airy *aporias* of rife textualism. Yet neither the redemptive myth of Marxism nor its historical rhetoric can conceal from us, beyond its illiberal ethos, its inadequacy as a critical discourse in Western societies.

None of this, of course, has prevented neo-Marxists from giving postmodernism their fierce attention. Some welcome postmodernism as evidence of degeneration in "late capitalism." Others, however, seek regeneration of their own theories in the historical challenges of postmodernism, challenges they can no longer ignore if they are to recover their "progressive" image. Invariably, though, they all come to postmodernism in search of its "adversary" role; that is, having defined art as a category of social emancipation, they need only to ascertain if that emancipation now conforms to Marxist thought. This relieves them of the burden of an aesthetic sense, a disencumbrance manifest in a long line of thinkers from Marx himself to Habermas, with the signal exceptions of Adorno and Benjamin.

An example in point is Hal Foster's anthology, *The Anti-Aesthetic.* The tone is set by the editor from the start. After restating many earlier notions of postmodernism, Foster distinguishes between two kinds, the good and the bad: "A postmodernism of resistance, then, arises as a counterpractice not only to the official culture of modernism but also to the 'false normativity' of a reactionary postmodernism."[17] No doubt, postmodernism now displays much kitsch and camp, displays also the recycled dreck of our culture, returned to it as counters of its complacencies. Yet so far as postmodernism expresses anything vital, it must still resist facile judgments on its historic (reactionary or progressive) intent. For such judgments assume a degree of cultural rationalization we have yet to attain. Andreas Huyssen, a saner neo-Marxist, puts it thus:

> Postmodernism . . . operates in a field of tension between tradition and innovation, conservation and renewal, mass culture and high art, in which the second terms are no longer automatically privileged over the first; a field of tension which can no longer be grasped in categories such as progress vs. reaction, Left vs. Right, present vs. past, modernism vs. realism, abstraction vs. representation, avant-garde vs. kitsch. The fact that such dichotomies, which after all are central to the classical account of modernism, have broken down is part of the shift. . . .[18]

Indeed, the "progressive element" in our culture is no longer—nor was it ever—self-evident in terms of preemptive ideologies. Nor 'is power, in use or misuse, always other, always exploitative.[19] How, then, can "resistance" be so transparent? The Marxist model has become very nearly obsolete; it assumes defiance or alienation, smells of gunpowder at the barricades or sour, sooty streets. But postmodern life, at its worst, moves silently through the "ob-scenity," the empty scene, of our representations; its glazed stupefactions require more ingenious tactics of opposition.[20]

A powerful historical preconception also marks Fredric Jameson's contribution to *The Anti-Aesthetic.* For him, postmodernism effaces the past; it is the schizophrenia of signs, "an alarming and pathological symptom of a society that has become incapable of dealing with time and history."[21] Thus nostalgia and pastiche prevail: "In a world in which stylistic innovation is no longer possible, all that is left is to imitate dead styles, to speak through masks and with the voices of the styles in the imaginary museum"; this guarantees "the necessary failure of art and the aesthetic, the failure of the new, the imprisonment in the past."[22] But surely this perception remains, at best, partial; it bends postmodernism to older, in some ways reactionary, presuppositions. That is, the judgment *both* defines and critiques innovation in modernist, even Edwardian, terms, applicable to a society very different in its modes of self-representation, its immanent procedures.[23]

All this does not mean that postmodernism exempts itself from our judgments; the dissatisfactions that Bell and Kramer, Foster and Jameson vent are real. Such dissatisfactions, though, call for something more than oppugnancy or dismissal. They call for imaginative assessments, call for truly radical reflections on our interpretive frames. For the world, I suspect, may be no more or less baneful than our perception of its bane.

Just so, Baudrillard's contribution to Foster's volume strikes me as (poetically) radical. "Something has changed," he says, "and the Faustian, Promethean (perhaps Oedipal) [would he add Marxian?] period of production and consumption gives way to the 'proteinic' era of networks, to the narcissistic and protean era of connections, contact, contiguity, feedback and generalized interface that goes with the universe of communication."[24] In this universe, "the body, landscape, time all progressively disappear as scenes. And the same for public space: the theater of the social and theater of politics are both reduced more and more to a large soft body with many heads."[25] The message no longer exists; only media impose themselves as pure circulation. "One has only to prolong this Marxist analysis, or push it to the second or third power, to grasp the transparence and obscenity [literally, off-scene, without scene] of the universe of communication, which leaves far behind it those relative analyses of the universe of commodity. . . . That's the ecstasy of communication," Baudrillard concludes.[26]

Here we see hints of a genuinely post-Marxist (not simply neo-Marxist) analysis that serves to problematize the postmodern condition in terms more adequate to itself. The terms, in any case, are more consequent than Habermas's in his celebrated essay on modernity, which inaugurates *The Anti-Aesthetic.* The reverberations of that essay, I believe, attest less to its intellectual force than to its moral demand, attest, above all, to the growing vigor of the postmodern debate. We need, therefore, to review the main themes of that debate that bring to focus postmodern rationality, gathering arguments in its polemic light.

V

Beginnings are always dim; we know only that the postmodern debate drifted from America to Europe.[27] In France, Lyotard, congenial to indetermanences, surveyed information societies and epitomized postmodernism as an "incredulity toward metanarratives." He then went on to add:

> Where, after the metanarratives, can legitimacy reside? The operativity criterion is technological; it has no relevance for judging what is true or just. Is legitimacy to be found in consensus obtained through discussion, as Jürgen Habermas thinks? Such consensus does violence to the heterogeneity of language games. And invention is always born of dissension. Postmodern knowledge is not simply a tool of the authorities; it refines our sensitivity to differences and reinforces our ability to tolerate the incommensurable. Its principle is not the expert's homology, but the inventor's paralogy.[28]

The emergence of new technologies and the redeployment of liberal capitalism, since the last world war, both played a decisive role in the desuetude of master codes. So did the reshaping of scientific boundaries, itself part of a larger dissemination in all language games. Thus Lyotard takes issue with the "belief that still underlies Habermas's research, namely, that humanity as a collective (universal) subject seeks its common emancipation through the regularization of the 'moves' permitted in all languages games and that the legitimacy of any statement resides in its contributing to that emancipation."[29]

The stricture merits our attention. But Lyotard is on dubious ground—witness recent political trends in both developed and undeveloped societies—when he states: "Most people have lost the nostalgia for the lost narrative. It in no way follows that they are reduced to barbarity. What saves them from it is their knowledge that legitimation can only spring from their own linguistic practice and communicational interaction."[30] He is on treacherous ground as well when he claims that "recognition of the heteromorphous nature of language games" leads to "a renunciation of terror, which assumes that they are isomorphic and tries to make them so."[31] "Nostalgia"—crushing exprobation in the current idiom—may also convey active desires, a principle of futurity and hope. And terror is rarely "renounced" by rational perceptions of any kind. Let us also recall that these "language games" commit genocide, despoil the earth, vaporize cities.

The adamant issues all theoreticians of postmodernism face is incommensurability, irrepresentability; that is, in postmodern society, how preserve, overcome, or mediate differences? In happily preserving them, Lyotard lends himself to a certain blitheness, though his adherents might call it pagan gaity. In trying to overcome them, Habermas makes a larger claim for reason than our history permits. But these are brutal simplifications that their own thought, meeting sensibly in pragmatism would disavow.[32]

In the case of Habermas, disavowal serves his greater purpose: to rehabilitate Marxist rationality in our world. This places him, he believes, in the tradition of the Enlightenment, to which so many postwar German intellectuals crowd. In its luminous name, Habermas defends modernity, conceived as an unfinished nisus of emancipation—that is, once again, discounting its dark and savage side—against the "reactions" of postmodern culture. Rhetorically, Habermas asks: "Should we try to hold on to the *intentions* of the Enlightenment, feeble as they may be, or should we declare the entire project of modernity a lost cause?"[33] The answer is never in doubt. For Habermas, much remains at stake in this "unfulfilled project": namely, the role of art in the world, the "relinking of modern culture with an everyday praxis," the ability of the "life-world . . . to develop institutions out of itself which set limits to the internal dynamics and to the imperatives of an almost autonomous economic system and its administrative complements." [34] Given this apprehension of modernity, it is not altogether bizarre that Habermas should distinguish the "antimodernism of the young conservatives" (in France, "the line from Bataille via Foucault to Derrida"), from the "premodernism of the old conservatives" (Leo Strauss, Hans Jonas, Robert Spaemann), and from "the postmodernism of the neoconservatives" (in Germany, "the early Wittgenstein, Carl Schmitt of the middle period, and Gottfried Benn of the late period").[35]

Within his concrete circle of assumptions, then, Habermas feels free to rescind postmodernism no less than Daniel Bell, if for entirely other motives. Having defined Marxism once and for all as "progressive," he has no choice but to label any other ideology as reactionary or conservative, regardless of what it might offer. And having experienced in his youth the Third Reich, he has no alternative but to look anxiously on *anything*—Myth, Romanticism, Wagner, Nietzsche, Heidegger, Derrida, Postmodernism, all capitalized in a certain slant of History—that may revive old nightmares. But all this, of course, does not suffice to make his arguments unobjectionable.

Objections have been made to Habermas's ideas of reason, history, art, consensus, the subject, modernity, and postmodernity, made by Marxists and non-Marxists alike. I can advert here only to a few, starkly essential points regarding the last two topics. As Lyotard reminds us, modernity it not merely the rediscovery of *"les Lumières tout court"*; modernity also reinsinuates will and desire into reason, and reinvests *"l'infini de la volonté"* in language itself.[36] (Thus innovations, whether modern or postmodern, continually play on the irreconcilability of verbal regimes, *"régimes des phrases."*) Nor is modernity itself, understood *historically* if not Marxistically, but an interpretation many times revised, a tale many times retold. This is all to say, as Martin Jay put it, that "Habermas owes us a more explicit explanation of the nature of the aesthetic-practical rationality he wants to defend in modernism."[37] He owes us also a subtler account of postmodernism, one that may find no need to label Foucault and Derrida "young conservatives."

But in a dialogical moment, minds press upon minds and pragmatism sometimes wins the day. Habermas seems to have already modified, or at least clarified, his position on the postmodern debate. He finds now certain affinities between the negative dialectics of Adorno, the archaeologies of Foucault, and the deconstructions of Derrida, and finds even greater affinities between himself and Rorty.[38] Moreover, Habermas acknowledges his long-standing discovery of American pragmatism as "the third productive reply to Hegel," after Marx and Kierkegaard. "Ever since," he admits, "I have relied on this American version of the philosophy of praxis when the problem arises of compensating for the weaknesses of Marxism with respect to democratic theory."[39] He even welcomes pragmatic compromise. "This is why I do not have any difficulties with the pluralism of interests," he adds. "After all, we anticipate that the pluralism of life-forms and the individualism of life-styles would increase at an exponential rate in a society which deserves the name socialist."[40] Here Habermas's ideological imperative points to the utopian promise of postmodernism, the promise of a society, if and when its time comes, that we will certainly call neither capitalist nor socialist.

It is finally this ideological imperative that distinguishes various conceptions and valuations of postmodernism, distinguishing them also from the pragmatism they partly share. Thus Habermas, though kindly to pragmatism, can not renounce the role of philosophy as "the guardian of reason." He can not concede, as Rorty does or Lyotard, that justified beliefs rest less on "good reasons" than on "life-habits that enjoy social currency in some places and not in others."[41] Such concessions, Habermas fears, would cripple philosophy and nurture political reaction. And though he is eager, like all postmodern thinkers, to weaken "claims of totality," he is finally more concerned to join such claims "with the stronger statements about general structures."[42]

VI

American pragmatism chooses another way. The real issue, for Rorty say, is not one of theory but of praxis—a task, I would add, of ceaseless, uncertified negotiations between wholes and parts. In the end Rorty must distance himself from both Lyotard and Habermas: from artistic as from political vanguardism, from both "the sublime" and "communicative rationality." Instead, Rorty would follow Dewey whom he quotes: "When philosophy shall have cooperated with the force of events and made clear and coherent the meaning of the daily detail, science and emotion will interpenetrate, practice and imagination will embrace."[43] "Splitting the difference" between Lyotard and Habermas, Rorty would seek a "de-theoreticized sense of community," a form "of social life, in which society as a whole asserts itself without bothering to ground itself."[44]

The tilt of postmodernism—not only in America—toward various pragmatisms reveals itself in another controversy, one "Against Theory." So far, the debate has concerned mainly literary theoreticians, provoked by the initial statement of Steven Knapp and Walter Benn Michaels. Yet the debate raises an issue of wider cultural reference: namely, if postmodern knowledge is essentially narrative, provisional, "groundless," then how can theory define or authorize practise (behavior, values, norms)? Knapp and Michaels, of course, would deny any such authorizing role. As they put it bluntly in a later response: "Our arguments from the start have taken the form of showing that whatever positions people think they hold on language, interpretation, and belief, in practice they are all pragmatists."[45]

But the authors touch on the crucial question of belief rather casually, as do in fact most neopragmatists. Thus, for instance, Stanley Fish remarks on postmodern or "antifoundationalist" thought: "Antifoundationalist theory tells us that no such justification [of grounded truth] will ever be available and that therefore there is no way of testing our beliefs against something whose source is not a belief."[46] Granted, we are never free of beliefs. But *which* belief? *How* do beliefs actually mediate *particular* practices? Are there *degrees* of beliefs, of mediation? And what happens when the beliefs of a person conflict with another's, or conflict with *other* beliefs that *same* person holds? About such crucial, if punishing, queries, most pragmatists nowadays seem insouciant, though similar queries disturbed Peirce, Dewey, and especially William James.

Beliefs, I have argued earlier, are crux to the postmodern condition precisely because that condition is pluralist, conflictual, indetermanent; consciously or unconsciously, they inform all our labors of legitimation, let alone our fanaticisms. I shall finally return to that argument after noting how the pervasive procedures of postmodern society, its ambiguous immanences, exacerbate all questions of belief.

VII

The theory of postmodernism, I repeat, retains its sundry difficulties and evasions. Many of these difficulties revert to ambiguities in Western societies themselves. We call these societies by many names—postindustrial, mass media, consumer, information societies—and these tags express both our intuition and our bafflement about their emergent character. We draw on Marx or Weber, on Durkheim or Gehlen, on Bell or Parsons, to help us conceptualize that character. Yet clearly we remain without a rational model, sometimes even without empiric comprehension, of our politics, economics, cultures, of our societies in the large. We have only mirrors of our ideologies, shattered continually by reality, only to be remade in the image of our desires.

Perhaps nothing, after all, has changed in our social theories since the Enlightenment except their candidly ideological quality. But perhaps, too, contemporary social theories fail to account for the novelty, perversity, cunning, the sheer fugaciousness of new technological realities. We sense, at least, the need for a new vocabulary when Foucault speaks of "the unthought," Deleuze of "rhizomes," Lyotard of "little Miss Marx," in trying to limn the dispositions of knowledge and power in our time.[47] We sense the same thing when Baudrillard announces the end of *"le social,"* all accountable social relations, or when he speaks of "the shadow of power," a "force of absorbtion or implosion," a "black whole in space," in contemporary Western societies. "The masses and their involuntary temper will introduce us to a pataphysics of the social that will finally rid us of all this metaphysics of the social that encumbers us," he remarks.[48]

I am not quite convinced that "the masses" defy all understanding, or that cognitive dispersals meet urgent demands of the age. This negative attitude or presumption ignores the adhesive instinct, indeed the survival imperative of our world. The same presumption, furthermore, rests on a verbal model of political interactions that continually tropes, renders metaphoric, the "substance" of our lives, including pain, torture, death. Still, I do believe that the terms of our social discourse, its silent, constitutive metaphors, may now require reinvention.

Surely such terms as left and right, base and superstructure, production and reproduction, materialist (very macho these days) and idealist, objective and subjective, society and self, even heredity and environment, such terms and all the indurations they imply, have become nearly unserviceable, except to perpetuate prejudice. In a cybernetic, semiotic society, a society of constant exchange, mediation, displacement, blockage, flow, would not a *transactive model,* one that keeps traditional distinctions in abeyance, that sublates or transumes or even forgets them *provisionally*—would not such a transactive model prove more proximate to our ends, our lives? Such a transactive model, in any case, would come nearer our ambiguous immanences, our pervasive interventions, our dubious "New Gnosticism."[49]

These immanences, nothing "religious," have not escaped the attention of incongruent thinkers. Daniel Bell, for instance, remarks on "the exponential growth and branching of science, the rise of a new intellectual technology, the creation of systematic research through R & D budgets, and, as the calyx of all this, the codification of theoretical knowledge."[50] As a result reality, no longer natural or artifactual, becomes symbolic, transactive, "experienced through the reciprocal consciousness of self and other," and indeed, society itself becomes "a web of consciousness, a form of imagination to be realized as a social construction."[51] Jameson, from a different perspective, hints at the same phenomenon when he speaks of the "technological sublime," or "high tech paranoia," which assumes some "immense communicational and computer network" that provides distorted figurations of "present-day multinational capitalism."[52] And from another perspective still, Lyotard represents reality, as in his eerie, ingenious, and disputed exhibition at the Centre Georges Pompidou, "Les Immatériaux," as a set of shifting messages in which our own five senses disappear. Walking through this (almost) dematerialized electronic environment—a space of invisible codes, artistic concepts, inaudible whispers—the visitor senses himself also disappear into disembodied sensations, states of mind. The semiotic model replaces the model of matter and/or spirit. We are left only with forms of energy and their flux of transactions, with *les immatériaux.* "One day, who knows," Lyotard murmurs in our earphones, in one of the mental zones of the show, "we will have inhabited the existence, and men will have lodged in their stories, in the same way the bodies of the solar system are traveling in the middle of galaxies."[53] Meanwhile, of course, we inhabit ubiquitous simulacra.

Or we inhabit "the hyperreal," as Baudrillard says in *Simulations,* a word "henceforth sheltered from the imaginary, and from any distinction between the real and the imaginary, leaving room only for the orbital recurrence of models and the simulated generation of differences."[54] This is a gnostic world wherein maps may precede their territories because map and territory have become the same. It is a world of simulations rather than representations, intolerable to both rightists and leftists because it renounces the fiction of concealed truth, because it undermines the exercise of power—how does one punish or reward simulations of crime or virtue? Thus it becomes "*now impossible to isolate the process of the real,* or to prove the real."[55] Consequently, Baudrillard says, we surrender to a "hysteria of production and reproduction of the real"; and instead of producing goods and commodities, those vestiges of "*la belle époque* of political economy," we disseminate the hyperreal.[56]

At times, of course, one has the impression that advanced thinkers are just discovering French McLuhan, as they discovered French Nietzsche and French Freud before. Yet Baudrillard's elliptic, tropic insights into contemporary society, like the insights of Lyotard in "Les Immatériaux," take us far toward recognizing the immanent character of postmodern society, its semiotic fata morgana, its cheery or dreary or deadly Disneylands. No wonder, then, that in our vertigo of reality, "ecstasy of communication," "hysteria of the hyperreal," we find it futile to apply our habitual distinctions, literary or political, to postmodernism.

VIII

Change occurs, recurs, on many levels. As a cultural if not global, transformation, postmodernism has proven remarkably cool and jokey, sometimes hokey.

"Les Immatériaux" signaled, quite after the fact, profound changes in the human condition, perhaps in the future conditions of being human. But a few months after this noetic exhibit closed at the Centre Pompidou, another opened at the Grand Palais in Paris. There, under the banner of "Styles 85"—the banner portrayed Einstein's head with tongue waggishly thrust out—, a hundred hectares of postmodern designs, ranging from thumbtacks to yachts, displayed another aspect of postmodernism. Walking through the bright farrago, hectares of *esprit*, parody, persiflage, I began to feel the smile on my lips freeze; it never became scowl or snarl, only an approximate leer. I realized then that postmodernism, *that* sort of postmodernism, had become arrested wit, wit waiting on disbelief. Unlike the immense glass space of the Grand Palais, postmodern design was a kind of small *belle époque* drained of heroism, illusion, faith.

But men and women have never done very long without some bracing, some enabling faith. Neither the indeterminacies of postmodernism nor its ghostly immanences will deter the Jamesian "will to believe." If postmodernism points at all any way, it points now to something beyond mourning or nostalgia for old faiths, points, in many directions at once, to belief itself, if not renewed beliefs. The time for sterility is past, grateful as we must remain to the masters of demystification. Derrida's *carte postale* does have both destiny and destination: it is the universe, a universe movingly informed by human will, mind, belief, whatever else may have formed it. Without some radiancy, wonder, wisdom, we all risk, in this postmodern clime, to become barren.

I speak of faith, belief. What belief or faith? Between skepticism and caducity, what commitment enhances life, avails? Once more, I turn to William James whom I have invoked thrice now, in *The Postmodern Turn,* to open for us a window on the near future.

Even before our time, a time parlous with nihilist *and* religious frenzies, James knew that no touchstone of reason will help us distinguish between too much and too little faith. Hence our constant struggle, perpetual trial, in a "half-wild, half-saved" universe. But James also knew how the will to believe can become knowledge or act:

> A conception of the world arises in you somehow, no matter how. Is it true or not? you ask.
>
> It *might* be true somewhere, you say, for it is not self-contradictory.
>
> It is *fit* to be true, it would be *well if it were true,* it *ought* to be true, you presently feel.
>
> It *must* be true, something persuasively in you whispers next; and then—as a final result—
>
> It shall be *held for true,* you decide; it *shall be* as if true, for *you.*
>
> And your acting thus may in certain special cases be a means of making it securely true in the end.
>
> Not one step in this process is logical, yet it is the way in which monists and pluralists alike espouse and hold fast to their visions. It is life exceeding logic, it is the practical reason for which the theoretic reason finds arguments after the conclusion is once there. In just this way do some of us hold to the unfinished pluralistic universe; in just this way do others hold to the timeless universe eternally complete.[57]

This "unfinished pluralism" is not mellow but exigent, harsh. Without dogmatism, it continually demands moral, political, cognitive engagements on our part. If it "rests" on anything at all, it surely rests on answerable belief, some ultimate trust in a universe gravid and stubborn with its differences. So long as two minds seek to apprehend that universe, no overwhelming force or sweet seduction, no theory whatever, will reduce it to one. Pragmatic pluralism, then, is no philosophical system: it seems the very condition of our existence in the world, to which postmodernism reawakens us in history—this side of unanimous night.

Let postmodernism now work itself out as it might. Perhaps all we have learned from it is what the gods have taught us in both myth and history: that even in their own omnivorous eyes, the universe is not single, but still One and Many as it shows itself to our sight.

1. "The 'post' of 'postmodernism' would therefore suggest not 'after' so much as an extension of modernism and a reaction to it," writes Linda Hutcheon in *Narcissistic Narrative: The Metafictional Paradox* (Waterloo, Ontario, 1980), 2. Updike, quoting John Barth, puts it more esculently: "The good postmodernist . . . 'has the first half of our century under his belt, but not on his back.' The moderns digested, he looks relatively plump," in John Updike, "Modernist, Postmodernist, What Will They Think of Next?", *New Yorker*, 10 September 1984, 142. This is, of course, a version of an ancient conceit that Robert K. Merton traces riotously in *On the Shoulders of Giants: A Shandean Postscript* (New York, 1965).

2. Ricardo J. Quinones, *Mapping Literary Modernism: Time and Development* (Princeton, 1985), 254. See also Timothy J. Reiss, *The Discourse of Modernism* (Ithaca, N.Y., 1982), 5, 585.

3. Thus, for instance, the late Paul de Man: "The difficulty for me is that the 'postmodern approach' seems a somewhat naively historical approach. . . . It is a bottomless pit that does attempt to define the literary movement in terms of its increased modernity (this happens in the work of Hassan, too)." See Stefano Rosso, "An Interview with Paul de Man," *Nuova Corrente* (1984), 310. But was it not de Man himself who taught superbly that "bottomless pits" lurk in all rhetorical schemes?

4. See René Thom, "The Rational and the Intelligible," and Horia Bratu, "Vocabulary of Crisis: Catastrophes," both in *Krisis*, no. 2 (1984):120–26 and 127–36.

5. Many of these issues are very usefully reviewed in Douwe W. Fokkema, *Literary History, Modernism, and Postmodernism* (Amsterdam, 1984) and in Douwe W. Fokkema and Hans Bertens, eds., *Approaching Postmodernism* (Amsterdam, 1986). See also footnote 42 below on "soft" or "weak" thought.

6. Matei Calinescu, "Postmodernism and Some Paradoxes of Periodization," in *Approaching Postmodernism*, 252.

7. See Michael Köhler, " 'Postmodernismus': Ein begriffsgeschichtlicher Überblick," *Amerikastudien* 22, no. 1 (1977):8–18; Andreas Huyssen, "Mapping the Postmodern," *New German Critique* 33 (Fall 1984):5–52; and Hans Bertens, "The Postmodern Weltanschauung and its Relation with Modernism," in *Approaching Postmodernism*. I might also note three academic events which helped to disseminate the postmodern debate: a conference on "Postmodernity and Hermeneutics" sponsored by *Boundary 2* in Binghamton, N.Y., in 1976; a symposium on "Postmodern Performance" held at the University of Wisconsin-Milwaukee in 1976; and a Modern Language Association Forum on "The Question of Postmodernism" held at the Annual Convention in New York in 1978. Three publications ensued: *Boundary 2* 4, no. 2 (Winter 1976); Michel Benamou and Charles Caramello, eds., *Performance in Postmodern Culture* (Madison, Wis., 1977); and Harry R. Garvin, ed., *Romanticism, Modernism, Postmodernism* (Lewisburg, Pa., 1980).

8. Christopher Butler also distinguishes between two tendencies of postmodernism: an aleatory and a rule-dominated method of composition. He further recognizes the antiexistential, anti-ideological ethos of postmodernism in general, a new, abstract aestheticism, he says, all its "arts poised between theoretical rigour and ecclecticism." See *After the Wake: An Essay on the Contemporary Avant-Garde* (Oxford, 1980), 116, also ix, 132, 159.

9. See Charles Newman, *The Post-Modern Aura* (Evanston, Ill., 1985); and various responses to it, including mine, in *Salmagundi* 67 (Summer 1985):163–97.

10. Daniel Bell, *The Cultural Contradictions of Capitalism* (New York, 1976), 7.

11. Ibid., 53f.

12. Ibid., 29. See also 278–82.

13. "A Note on *The New Criterion*," editorial for the first issue of *The New Criterion* 1, no. 1 (September 1982), 5. The style suggests Hilton Kramer to be its author.

14. Hilton Kramer, *The Revenge of the Philistines: Art and Culture, 1972–1984* (New York, 1985), 11.

15. Ibid., xiii.

16. See Frederick Crews, "Dialectical Immaterialism," *The American Scholar* 54, no. 4 (Autumn 1985):449–66, for a sound, sometimes supercilious, always amusing critique of contemporary Marxism. But see also, for a more thorough and equable critique, Martin Jay, *Marxism and Totality: The Adventures of a Concept from Lukács to Habermas* (Berkeley, 1984).

17. Hal Foster, ed., *The Anti-Aesthetic: Essays on Postmodern Culture* (Port Townsend, Wash., 1983), xii. Foster alters this dichotomy in another essay, "(Post)Modern Polemics," *New German Critique* 33 (Fall 1984):67–78, where a postmodernism of textuality and another of pastiche are shown to be finally "symptoms of the same 'schizophrenic' collapse of the subject and historical narrativity—signs of the same process of reification and fragmentation under late capitalism," p. 76. For a different, an ampler, view of postmodern tendencies, see Charles Russell, *Poets, Prophets, and Revolutionaries: The Literary Avant-Garde from Rimbaud through Postmodernism* (New York, 1985), especially 236–70. For probing, recent studies of literary postmodernism, see Charles Caramello, *Silverless Mirrors: Book, Self, and Postmodern Fiction* (Tallahassee, Fla., 1983) and Carl Darryl Malmgren, *Fictional Space in the Modernist and Postmodernist Novel* (Lewisburg, Pa., 1985).

18. Andreas Huyssen, "Mapping the Postmodern," 48.

19. As Umberto Eco puts it: "I would consider postmodernism the orientation of anyone who has learned the lesson of Foucault [he might have added Lyotard or Baudrillard], i.e., that power is not something unitary that exists outside us." See Stefano Rosso, "A Conversation with Umberto Eco," *Boundary 2* 12, no. 1 (Fall 1983), 4.

20. See Jean Baudrillard, "What Are You Doing After the Orgy?", *Artforum*, October 1983, 43.

21.Fredric Jameson, "Postmodernism and Consumer Society," in *The Anti-Aesthetic*, 117.

22. Ibid., 115f.

23. In a longer essay, impressive in its cultural range as well as in some of its architectural analysis, Jameson attempts dialectically to "hold to the truth of postmodernism." But these attempts remain largely intentional; sooner or later, the iron yoke of ideology presses down: "this whole global, yet American, postmodern culture is the internal and superstructural expression of a whole new wave of American military and economic domination throughout the world: in this sense, as throughout class history, the underside of culture is blood, torture,

death, and horror." See Fredric Jameson, "Postmodernism, or The Cultural Logic of Late Capitalism," *New Left Review* 146 (July–August 1984), 57; but see also, for more modulated statements, 56, 58, 86, 92. In any case for Jameson, postmodernism permits no "critical distance"; inevitably, it coopts. This makes for great gloom: "What we must now affirm is that it is precisely this whole extraordinarily demoralizing and depressing original new global space which is the 'moment of truth' of postmodernism," he writes (ibid., 88).

24. Jean Baudrillard, "The Ecstasy of Communication," in *The Anti-Aesthetic*, 127.

25. Ibid., 129.

26. Ibid., 131.

27. The Milwaukee and New York City conferences on postmodernism were attended, respectively, by Jean-François Lyotard and Julia Kristeva (see note 7). Lyotard then published *La Condition postmoderne* (Paris, 1979). Indirectly, Jürgen Habermas replied in "Die Moderne: Ein unvollendetes Projekt," *Die Zeit*, no. 39, 26 September 1980, first delivered as the Theodor W. Adorno Prize Lecture in Frankfurt that year, and reprinted as "Modernity versus Postmodernity," trans. by Seyla Benhabib, *New German Critique* 22 (Winter 1981):3–14, and as "Modernity—an Incomplete Project," in *The Anti-Aesthetic*. Thereafter, the controversy expands. A few crucial references would include: Jean-François Lyotard, "Answering the Question: What is Postmodernism?" in Ihab Hassan and Sally Hassan, eds., *Innovation/Renovation: New Perspectives on the Humanities* (Madison, Wis., 1983), reprinted as appendix to Jean-François Lyotard, *The Postmodern Condition*, trans. Geoff Bennington and Brian Massumi (Minneapolis, Minn., 1984); Jean-François Lyotard, "Règles et Paradoxes *et* Appendice Svelte," *Babylone* 1 (Hiver 1982–1983): 67–80; Richard Rorty, "Habermas and Lyotard on Postmodernity," *Praxis International* 4, no. 1 (April 1984): 32–44; Jürgen Habermas, "Habermas: Questions and Counter-Questions," *ibid.*, 229–49; Jurgen Habermas, "A Philosophico-Political Profile: Interview," *New Left Review* 151 (May–June 1985):75–105; Albrecht Wellmer, "On the Dialectic of Modernism and Postmodernism," *Praxis International* 4, no. 4 (January 1985):337–62, a particularly balanced and perceptive essay; as well as the articles in three special issues, *New German Critique* 33 (Fall 1984), *Theory, Culture and Society* 2, no. 3 (Spring 1985), and *Critique*, no. 456 (1985). Many of these essays are also collected in Richard J. Bernstein, ed., *Habermas and Modernity* (Cambridge, Mass.: MIT Press, 1985).

28. Lyotard, *The Postmodern Condition*, xxivf.

29. Ibid., 66.

30. Ibid., 41.

31. Ibid., 66.

32. See particularly Jean-François Lyotard, *Le Différend* (Paris, 1983) and Jürgen Habermas, *Theory of Communicative Action*, v. 1, trans. Tom McCarthy (Boston, 1983).

33. Habermas, "Modernity versus Postmodernity," 9.

34. Ibid., 13.

35. Ibid. But see also the more elaborate "*combinatoire*" that Fredric Jameson constructs in "The Politics of Theory: Ideological Positions in the Postmodernism Debate," *New German Critique* 33 (Fall 1984):53–65.

36. Lyotard, "Règles et Paradoxes *et* Appendice Svelte," 77–79.

37. Martin Jay, "Habermas and Modernism," *Praxis International* 4, no. 1 (April 1984), 12. See also Wellmer, "The Dialectic of Modernism and Postmodernism," 357–60.

38. Jürgen Habermas, "A Philosophico-Political Profile," 81, 82, 93.

39. Ibid., 77.

40. Ibid., 96.

41. Jürgen Habermas, "Habermas: Questions and Counter-Questions," 231.

42. Ibid., 248. See also Pier Aldo Rovatti and Gianni Vattimo, eds., *Il Pensiero Debole* (Milano, 1983), on "weak thought," more anthropological than systematic in character—thus more pragmatic.

43. Rorty, "Habermas and Lyotard on Postmodernity," 42.

44. Ibid., 41, 43. Hence Vattimo's conclusion that Rorty, more than Habermas, would dissolve hermeneutics into anthropology. See Gianni Vattimo, "Difference and Interference: On the Reduction of Hermeneutics to Anthropology," *Res* 4 (Autumn 1982), 87.

45. Steven Knapp and Walter Benn Michaels, "A Reply to Rorty: What is Pragmatism?" *Critical Inquiry* 11, no. 3 (March 1985), 472. All essays in this controversy are collected in W. J. T. Mitchell, ed., *Against Theory: Literary Studies and the New Pragmatism* (Chicago, 1985).

46. Stanley Fish, "Consequences," *Critical Inquiry* 11, no. 3 (March 1985), 440.

47. See pp. 158–63 above.

48. Jean Baudrillard, *À L'Ombre des majorités silencieuses ou la fin du social* (Fontenay-sous-Bois, 1978), 52f. The quotation is in my translation.

49. I have used this expression throughout this work, though I document the phenomenon more fully in Ihab Hassan, "The New Gnosticism," *Paracriticisms: Seven Speculations of the Times* (Urbana, Ill., 1975).

50. Daniel Bell, *The Coming of Post-Industrial Society: A Venture in Social Forecasting* (New York, 1973), 44.

51. Ibid., 488.

52. Jameson, "Postmodernism, or The Cultural Logic of Late Capitalism," 79f.

53. Jean-François Lyotard, "Site of Stellar Crucibles," trans. Ali and Mary Chokri, in *Immaterials,* pamphlet of the Centre Georges Pompidou Exhibition: 28 March—15 July, 1985, 12. See also associated publications of the exhibition, particularly Jean-François Lyotard and Thierry Chaput, "La Raison des Épreuves," *Épreuves d'écriture* (Paris, 1985), 6f., and Élie Théofilakis, ed., *Modernes, et après? "Les Immatériaux"* (Paris, 1985), especially 4–14.

54. Jean Baudrillard, *Simulations,* trans. Paul Foss, Paul Patton, and Philip Beitchmann (New York, 1983), 4.

55. Ibid., 41.

56. Ibid., 44.

57. William James, *A Pluralistic Universe* (Cambridge, Mass., 1977), 148.

Bibliography

A "selected bibliography" on a subject so amorphous as postmodernism entails many hidden judgments, decisions. Implicitly, it reflects the compiler's bias and knowledge—in this case, my own sense of postmodernism, its scope and limits. Still, in compiling this bibliography, I have tried to keep in mind the interests of a general student of postmodernism. More specifically, I have adopted the following practical principles:

1. The bibliography addresses postmodernism as a cultural, not simply literary, field. It therefore includes, very selectively, references to pertinent works in other disciplines.

2. Though the bibliography centers on postmodernism, it also lists a number of works on modernism; these may help clarify the main concern of this book.

3. In the case of major influences on postmodern culture and thought—Marx, Nietzsche, William James, Freud, Wittgenstein, Heidegger, etc.—the bibliography contains only a few suggestive works, works particularly germane to the postmodern debate.

4. The bibliography lists more books than articles because the latter often find their way into the former. In the case of a few historically significant articles, the bibliography lists both the article's first place and date of publication and the later volume in which the article appeared.

5. The bibliography lists only works published in, or translated into, English, and gives preference to American over British editions for the convenience of American readers.

* * *

Abbas, M.A. "Photography/Writing/Postmodernism." *Minnesota Review, n.s.* 23 (1984):91–111.

Ackroyd, Peter. *Notes for a New Culture: An Essay on Modernism.* New York: Barnes and Noble, 1976.

Albright, Daniel. *Representation and the Imagination: Beckett, Kafka, Nabokov, and Schoenberg.* Chicago, Ill.: University of Chicago Press, 1981.

Alpert, Barry. "Post-Modern Oral Poetry: Buckminster Fuller, John Cage, and David Antin." *Boundary 2* 3 (1975):665–82.

Alter, Robert. *Partial Magic: The Novel as a Self-Conscious Genre.* Berkeley and Los Angeles, Calif.: University of California Press, 1975.

———. "The Self-conscious Moment: Reflections on the Aftermath of Modernism." *TriQuarterly* 33 (1975):209–30.

Altieri, Charles. "From Symbolist Thought to Immanence: The Ground of Postmodern American Poetics." *Boundary 2* 1 (1973):605–41.

Amerikastudien 22, no. 1 (1977). Issue on Postmodernism.

Andre, Linda. "The Politics of Postmodern Photography." *Minnesota Review,* n.s. 23 (1984):17–35.

Antin, David. "Modernism and Postmodernism: Approaching the Present in American Poetry." *Boundary 2* 1 (1972):98–113.

———. *Talking at the Boundaries.* New York: New Directions, 1976.

Arac, Jonathan, ed. *Postmodernism and Politics.* Minneapolis, Minn.: University of Minnesota Press, 1986.

Arac, Jonathan, Wlad Godzich, and Wallace Martin, eds. *The Yale Critics: Deconstruction in America.* Minneapolis, Minn.: University of Minnesota Press, 1983.

Armstrong, Paul B. "The Conflict of Interpretation and the Limits of Pluralism." *PMLA* 98 (1983):341–52.

Arnheim, Rudolph. *Entropy and Art: An Essay on Disorder and Order.* Berkeley and Los Angeles, Calif.: University of California Press, 1971.

Artaud, Antonin. *The Theatre and Its Double.* Translated by Mary Caroline Richards. New York: Grove Press, 1958.

Bakhtin, Mikhail M. *The Dialogic Imagination: Four Essays.* Edited by Michael Holquist. Translated by Caryl Emerson and Michael Holquist. Austin, Tex.: University of Texas Press, 1981.

———. *Problems of Dostoyevsky's Poetics.* Edited and translated by Caryl Emerson. Minneapolis, Minn.: University of Minnesota Press, 1984.

———. *Rabelais and His World.* Translated by Helena Iswolsky. Cambridge, Mass.: Harvard University Press, 1968.

Barth, John. "The Literature of Exhaustion." *Atlantic Monthly,* August 1967, 29–34.

———. "The Literature of Replenishment: Postmodernist Fiction." *Atlantic Monthly,* January 1980, 65–71.

Barthes, Roland. *Critical Essays.* Translated by Richard Howard. Evanston, Ill.: Northwestern University Press, 1972.

———. *Image–Music–Text.* Translated by Stephen Heath. New York: Hill and Wang, 1977.

———. *A Lover's Discourse: Fragments.* Translated by Richard Howard. New York: Hill and Wang, 1978.

———. *The Pleasure of the Text.* Translated by Richard Miller. New York: Hill and Wang, 1975.

Baudrillard, Jean. *In the Shadow of the Silent Marjorities: or, the End of the Social and Other Essays.* Translated by Paul Foss, Paul Patton, and John Johnston. New York: Semiotext(e), 1983.

———. *The Mirror of Production.* Translated with an Introduction by Mark Poster. St. Louis, Mo.: Telos Press, 1975.

———. *Simulations.* Translated by Paul Foss, Paul Patton, and Philip Beichtman. New York: Seimiotext(e), 1983.

Beebe, Maurice. "What Modernism Was." *Journal of Modern Literature* 3 (1974):1065–84.

Bell, Daniel. *The Coming of Post-Industrial Society.* New York: Basic Books, 1973.

———. *The Cultural Contradictions of Capitalism.* New York: Basic Books, 1976.

Bellamy, Joe David, ed. *The New Fiction: Interviews with Innovative American Writers.* Urbana, Ill.: University of Illinois Press, 1974.

Benamou, Michel, and Charles Caramello, eds. *Performance in Postmodern Culture.* Madison, Wis.: Coda Press, 1977.

Benstock, Shari. "From the Editor's Perspective." *Tulsa Studies in Women's Literature* 3 (1984):5–28.

Bergonzi, Bernard, ed. *Innovations: Essays on Art and Ideas.* London: Macmillan, 1968.

Berman, Marshall. *All That is Solid Melts Into Air: The Experience of Modernity.* New York: Simon & Schuster, 1982.

Bernstein, Richard J., ed. *Habermas and Modernity.* Cambridge, Mass.: M.I.T. Press, 1985.

Bersani, Leo. *A Future for Astyanax: Character and Desire in Literature.* Boston, Mass.: Little, Brown, 1976.

Blau, Herbert. *Blooded Thought: Occasions of Theatre.* New York: Performing Arts Journal Publications, 1982.

———. *Take Up the Bodies: Theater at the Vanishing Point.* Urbana, Ill.: University of Illinois Press, 1982.

Bleich, David. *Subjective Criticism.* Baltimore, Md.: Johns Hopkins University Press, 1978.

Bloom, Harold. *The Anxiety of Influence: A Theory of Poetry.* New York: Oxford University Press, 1975.

———, et al. *Deconstruction and Criticism.* New York: Seabury Press, 1979.

———. *Kabbalah and Criticism.* New York: Seabury Press, 1975.

———. *A Map of Misreading.* New York: Oxford University Press, 1975.

———. *Poetry and Repression: Revisions from Blake to Stevens.* New Haven, Conn.: Yale University Press, 1976.

Bolin, Brent. *The Failure of Modern Architecture.* New York: Van Nostrand Reinhold, 1976.

Bonito Oliva, Achille. *The International Trans-Avant Garde.* Milan: Giancarlo Politi Editore, 1982.

Bonnefoy, Yves. " 'Image and Presence': Yves Bonnefoy's Inaugural Address at the Collège de France." *New Literary History* 15 (1984):433–51.

Boorstin, Daniel. *The Image: A Guide to Pseudo-Events in America.* Magnolia, Mass.: Peter Smith, 1985. Originally published under the title: *The Image: or, What Happened to the American Dream.* New York: Atheneum, 1962.

Booth, Wayne. *Critical Understanding: The Powers and Limits of Critical Pluralism.* Chicago, Ill.: University of Chicago Press, 1979.

Borges, Jorge Luis. *Other Inquisitions, 1937–1952.* Translated by Ruth L. C. Simms. Austin, Tex.: University of Texas Press, 1964.

Bornstein, George. "Beyond Modernism." *Michigan Quarterly Review* 12 (1973):278–84.

Boulding, Kenneth. *The Meaning of the Twentieth Century: The Great Transition.* New York: Harper and Row, 1964.

Boundary 2 3, 1 (1981). Issue on "Why Nietzsche Now? A Boundary 2 Symposium." Published also as *Why Nietzsche Now?* Edited by Daniel T. O'Hara. Bloomington, Ind.: Indiana University Press, 1985.

Boundary 2 4, 2 (1976). Issue on "The Destructionist Program." Published as *Martin Heidegger and the Question of Literature.* Edited by William V. Spanos. Bloomington, Ind.: Indiana University Press, 1979.

Bradbury, Malcolm, and James McFarlane, eds. *Modernism: 1890–1930.* London: Penguin Books, 1976.

Brooke-Rose, Christine. *A Rhetoric of the Unreal: Studies in Narrative and Structure, Especially of the Fantastic.* Cambridge: Cambridge University Press, 1981.

Brown, Curtis F. *Star-Spangled Kitsch: An Astounding and Tastelessly Illustrated Exploration of the Bawdy, Gaudy, Shoddy Mass-Art Culture in this Grand Land of Ours.* New York: Universe Books'. 1975.

Brown, Norman O. *Love's Body.* New York: Random House, 1966.

Bürger, Peter. *Theory of the Avant-Garde.* Translated by Michael Shaw. Minneapolis, Minn.: University of Minnesota Press, 1984.

Burke, Kenneth. *Language as Symbolic Action: Essays on Life, Literature, and Method.* Berkeley and Los Angeles, Calif.: University of California Press, 1966.

Burnham, Jack. *Great Western Salt Works: Essays on the Meaning of Post-Formalist Art.* New York: George Braziller, 1974.

Butler, Christopher. *After the Wake: An Essay on the Contemporary Avant-garde.* Oxford: Clarendon Press, 1980.

———. *Interpretation, Deconstruction, and Ideology: An Introduction to Some Current Issues in Literary Theory.* Oxford: Clarendon Press, 1984.

———. "The Pleasures of the Experimental Text." In *Criticism and Critical Theory.* Edited by Jeremy Hawthorn. London: Edward Arnold, 1984.

Butor, Michel. *Inventory: Essays.* New York: Simon and Schuster, 1968.

Butterick, George F. "Editing Postmodern Texts." *Sulfur* 11 (1984):113–40.

Cage, John, *Empty Words.* Middletown, Conn.: Wesleyan University Press, 1979.

———. *For the Birds.* Boston, Mass.: Marion Boyars, 1981.

———. *Silence: Lectures and Writings.* Middletown, Conn.: Wesleyan University Press, 1961.

———. *A Year From Monday: New Literature and Writings.* Middletown, Conn.: Wesleyan University Press, 1967.

Caliban 12 (1975). Issue on Postmodernism.

Calinescu, Matei. "Avant-Garde, Neo-Avant-Garde, Post-Modernism: The Culture of Crisis." *Clio* 4 (1975):317–40.

———. " 'Avant-Garde': Some Terminological Considerations." *Yearbook of Comparative and General Literature* 23 (1974):67–78.

———. *Faces of Modernity: Avant-Garde, Decadence, Kitsch.* Bloomington, Ind.: Indiana University Press, 1977. 2d ed., rev. Durham, N.C.: Duke University Press, forthcoming.

Calvino, Italo. "Notes Toward a Definition of the Narrative Form as a Combinative Process." *Twentieth Century Studies* 3 (1970): 93–101.

Capra, Fritjof. *The Tao of Physics: An Exploration of the Parallels Between Modern Physics and Eastern Mysticism.* 2nd. ed., rev. Boulder, Colo.: Shambhala Press, 1983.

Caramello, Charles. *Silverless Mirrors: Book, Self, and Postmodern American Fiction.* Tallahassee, Fla.: University Presses of Florida, 1983.

Caws, Mary Ann. *The Eye in the Text: Essays on Perception, Mannerist to Modern.* Princeton, N.J.: Princeton University Press, 1981.

Chefdor, Monique; Ricardo Quinones; and Albert Wachtel, eds. *Modernism: Challenges and Perspectives.* Urbana, Ill.: University of Illinois Press, 1986.

Chiari, Joseph. *The Aesthetics of Modernism.* London: Vision, 1970.

Chicago Review 33, nos. 2 and 3 (1983). Issues on Postmodern Literature and Criticism.

Clarke, Arthur C. *Profiles of the Future: An Inquiry into the Limits of the Possible.* New York: Bantam Books, 1964.

Cohen, Ralph. "A Propadeutic for Literary Change." *Critical Exchange* 13 (1983):1–17.

———, ed. *New Directions in Literary History.* Baltimore, Md.: Johns Hopkins University Press, 1974.

Cohn, Ruby. *Currents in Contemporary Drama.* Bloomington, Ind.: Indiana University Press, 1969.

Cooper, David Graham. *The Death of the Family.* New York: Pantheon, 1970.

Couturier, Maurice, ed. *Representation and Performance in Postmodern Fiction.* Montpellier: Delta, Presses de l'Imprimerie de Recherche, Université Paul Valéry, 1983.

Cox, Harvey G. *The Feast of Fools: A Theological Essay on Festivity and Fantasy.* Cambridge, Mass.: Harvard University Press, 1969.

Crimp, Douglas. "The Photographic Activity of Postmodernism." *October* 15 (1980):91–101.

Croyden, Margaret. *Lunatics, Lovers, and Poets: The Contemporary Experimental Theatre.* New York: McGraw Hill, 1974.

Culler, Jonathan. *On Deconstruction.* Ithaca, N.Y.: Cornell University Press, 1982.

———. *The Pursuit of Signs: Semiotics, Literature, Deconstruction.* Ithaca, N.Y.: Cornell University Press, 1981.

Cullum, J. W. "Nathan Scott and the Problem of a Postmodern Ethic." *Boundary 2* 4 (1976):965–72.

Daiches, David. "What Was the Modern Novel?" *Critical Inquiry* 1 (1975):813–19.

Danto, Arthur C. *The Transfiguration of the Commonplace: A Philosophy of Art.* Cambridge, Mass.: Harvard University Press, 1981.

Davidson, Michael. "Languages of Post-Modernism." *Chicago Review* 27 (1975):11–22.

Davis, Douglas. *Art and the Future: A History/Prophecy of the Collaboration Between Science, Technology, and Art.* New York: Praeger, 1973.

———. *Artculture: Essays on the Post-Modern.* New York: Harper and Row, 1977.

Deleuze, Gilles, and Félix Guattari. *Anti-Oedipus: Capitalism and Schizophrenia.* Translated by Robert Hurley, Mark Seem, and Helen R. Lane. New York: Viking Press, 1977.

———. *Nietzsche and Philosophy.* New York: Columbia University Press, 1983.

de Man, Paul. *Allegories of Reading: Figural Language in Rousseau, Nietzsche, Rilke, and Proust.* New Haven, Conn.: Yale University Press, 1979.

———. *Blindness and Insight: Essays in the Rhetoric of Contemporary Criticism.* New York: Oxford University Press, 1971.

Depew, Wally. *Nine Essays on Concrete Poems.* Alamo, Calif.: Holmgangers Press, 1974.

Derrida, Jacques. *Dissemination.* Translated, with an Introduction, by Barbara Johnson. Chicago, Ill.: University of Chicago Press, 1981.

———. *Margins of Philosophy.* Translated, with notes, by Alan Bass. Chicago, Ill.: University of Chicago Press, 1982.

———. *Of Grammatology.* Translated by Gayatri Chakravorty Spivak. Baltimore, Md.: Johns Hopkins University Press, 1976.

———. "The Principle of Reason: The University in the Eyes of its Pupils." *Diacritics* 13 (1983):3–21.

———. "Structure, Sign, and Play." In *The Languages of Criticism and the Sciences of Man."* Edited by Richard Macksey and Eugenio Donato. Baltimore, Md.: Johns Hopkins University Press, 1970.

———. *Writing and Difference.* Translated, with an Introduction and additional notes, by Alan Bass. Chicago, Ill.: University of Chicago Press, 1978.

Donadio, Stephen. *Nietzsche, Henry James, and the Artistic Will.* New York: Oxford University Press, 1978.

The Drama Review 19, no. 1 (1975). Issue on Post-Modern Dance.

Doubrovsky, Serge. *The New Criticism in France.* Translated by Derek Coltman. Chicago, Ill.: University of Chicago Press, 1973.

Ebert, Teresa L. "The Convergence of Postmodern Innovative Fiction and Science Fiction." *Poetics Today* 1 (1980):91–104.

Eco, Umberto. *The Role of the Reader: Explorations in the Semiotics of Texts.* Bloomington, Ind.: Indiana University Press, 1979.

———. *A Theory of Semiotics.* Bloomington, Ind.: Indiana University Press, 1976.

Ehrmann, Jacques. "The Death of Literature." *New Literary History* 3 (1971): 31–48.

———. "Introduction: Games, Play, Literature." *Yale French Studies* 41 (1968):5.

Ellmann, Richard, ed. *The Artist as Critic: Critical Writings of Oscar Wilde.* New York: Random House, 1969.

———, and Charles Feidelson, eds. *The Modern Tradition: Backgrounds of Modern Literature.* New York: Oxford University Press, 1965.

Enzensberger, Hans Magnus. *The Consciousness Industry: On Literature, Politics, and the Media.* New York: Seabury Press, 1974.

Esslin, Martin. *The Age of Television.* San Francisco, Calif.: Freeman, 1982.

———. *The Theatre of the Absurd.* 3d ed., rev. and enl. Harmondsworth, Middlesex, England and New York: Penguin, 1980.

Fanon, Frantz. *The Wretched of the Earth.* Preface by Jean Paul Sartre. Translated by Constance Farrington. New York: Grove Press, 1968.

Federman, Raymond. "Fiction Today or the Pursuit of Non-Knowledge." *Humanities in Society* 1 (1978):115–31.

———. "Imagination as Plagiarism [an unfinished paper . . .]" *New Literary History* 7 (1976):563–78.

Felperin, Howard. *Beyond Deconstruction: The Uses and Abuses of Literary Theory.* Oxford: Clarendon Press, 1985.

Ferkiss, Victor. *The Future of Technological Civilization.* New York: George Braziller, 1974.

Fiedler, Leslie. *Collected Essays.* 2 volumes. New York: Stein and Day, 1971.

———. "Cross the Border—Close the Gap." *Playboy,* December 1969: 151, 230, 252–54, 256–58. Also in *Collected Essays,* vol. 2.

———. "The New Mutants." *Partisan Review* 32 (1965):505–25. Also in *Collected Essays,* vol. 2.

———, and Houston A. Baker, Jr., eds. *Opening Up the Canon: Selected Papers from the English Institute,* New Series, no. 4. Baltimore, Md.: Johns Hopkins University Press, 1981.

Fish, Stanley. *Is There a Text in This Class? The Authority of Interpretive Communities.* Cambridge, Mass.: Harvard University Press, 1980.

Fokkema, Douwe, and Hans Bertens, eds. *Approaching Postmodernism.* Amsterdam: John Benjamins, 1986.

Fokkema, Douwe, and Matei Calinescu, eds. *Exploring Postmodernism.* Amsterdam: John Benjamins, forthcoming.

Fokkema, Douwe. *Literary History, Modernism, and Postmodernism.* Amsterdam: John Benjamins, 1984.

Foster, Hal, ed. *The Anti-Aesthetic: Essays on Postmodern Culture.* Port Townsend, Wash.: Bay Press, 1983.

Foster, John Burt. *Heirs to Dionisus: A Nietzschean Current in Literary Modernism.* Princeton, N.J.: Princeton University Press, 1981.

Foster, Stephen C., ed. *Lettrisme: Into the Present.* University of Iowa Musuem of Art Catalogue. Special Issue of *Visible Language* 17, no. 3 (1983).

Foucault, Michel. *Language, Counter-Memory, Practice: Selected Essays and Interviews.* Edited by Donald F. Bouchard. Translated by Donald F. Bouchard and Sherry Simon. Ithaca, N.Y.: Cornell University Press, 1977.

———. *The Order of Things: An Archeology of the Human Sciences.* Translation of *Les Mots et les choses.* New York: Pantheon, 1970.

———. *Power/Knowledge: Selected Interviews and Other Writings, 1972–1977.* Edited by Colin Gordon. Translated by Colin Gordon, Leo Marshall, John Mepham, and Kate Soper. New York: Pantheon, 1980.

Frank, Joseph. *The Widening Gyre: Crisis and Mastery in Modern Literature.* New Brunswick, N.J.: Rutgers University Press, 1963.

Freud, Sigmund. *Beyond the Pleasure Principle.* Translated by James Strachey. New York: Liveright, 1950.

———. *Civilization and Its Discontents.* Translated and edited by James Strachey. New York: W. W. Norton, 1962.

———. *The Interpretation of Dreams.* Translated and edited by James Strachey. New York: Basic Books, 1955.

Friedan, Betty. *The Feminine Mystique.* New York: Norton, 1963.

Fuller, R. Buckminster, in collaboration with E. J. Applewhite. *Synergetics: Explorations in the Geometry of Thinking.* New York: Macmillan, 1975.

Fuller, R. Buckminster. *Utopia or Oblivion: The Prospects for Humanity.* New York: Overlook Press, 1972.

Gablik, Suzi. *Progress in Art.* New York: Rizzoli, 1977.

Gadamer, Hans Georg. *Philosophical Hermeneutics.* Translated and edited by David E. Linge. Berkeley and Los Angeles, Calif.: University of California Press, 1976.

———. *Truth and Method.* Translation edited by Garrett Barden and John Cumming. New York: Seabury Press, 1975.

Gallie, W. B. *Philosophy and the Historical Understanding.* 2d ed. New York: Schocken Books, 1968.

Gallop, Jane. *The Daughter's Seduction: Feminism and Psychoanalysis.* Ithaca, N.Y.: Cornell University Press, 1982.

Galloway, David. "Postmodernism." *Contemporary Literature* 14 (1973):398–405.

Gans, Herbert J. *Popular Culture and High Culture: An Analysis and Evaluation of Taste.* New York: Basic Books, 1975.

Garvin, Harry R., ed. *Romanticism, Modernism, Postmodernism. Bucknell Review Annual* 25. Lewisburg, Pa.: Bucknell University Press, 1980.

Gass, William H. "The Death of the Author." *Salmagundi* 65 (1984):3–26.

———. *Fiction and the Figures of Life.* New York: Alfred A. Knopf, 1970.

———. *Habitations of the Word: Essays.* New York: Simon and Schuster, 1985.

Gayle, Addison, ed. *The Black Aesthetic.* Garden City, N.Y.: Doubleday, 1971.

Gehlen, Arnold. *Man in the Age of Technology.* Translated by Patricia Lipscomb. New York: Columbia University Press, 1980.

Genette, Gérard. *Figures of Literary Discourse.* Translated by Alan Sheridan. New York: Columbia University Press, 1982.

———. *Narrative Discourse: An Essay in Method.* Translated by Jane E. Lewin. Ithaca, N.Y.: Cornell University Press, 1980.

Gillespie, Gerald. "New Apocalypse for Old: Kermode's Theory of Modernism." *Boundary 2,* 3 (1975):307–23.

Gilman, Richard. "The Idea of the Avant-Garde." *Partisan Review* 39 (1972): 382–96.

Goffman, Erving. *Frame Analysis: An Essay on the Organization of Experience.* New York: Harper and Row, 1974.

Goldmann, Lucien. *Cultural Creation in Modern Society.* Translated by Bart Grahl. Oxford: Basil Blackwell, 1977.

Gombrich, E. H. *Art and Illusion: A Study in the Psychology of Pictorial Representation.* 2d ed., rev. New York: Pantheon, 1961.

Goodman, Nelson. "Realism, Relativism, and Reality." *New Literary History* 14 (1983):269–72.

———. *Ways of Worldmaking.* Indianapolis, Ind.: Hackett Publishing Co., 1978.

Graff, Gerald. "Babbitt at the Abyss: the Social Context of Postmodern American Fiction." *TriQuarterly* 33 (1975):305–37.

———. *Literature Against Itself: Literary Ideas in Modern Society.* Chicago, Ill.: University of Chicago Press, 1979.
———. "The Myth of the Postmodernist Breakthrough." *TriQuarterly* 26 (1973):383–417.
Greenberg, Clement. "Modern and Postmodern." *Arts Magazine* 54 (1980):64–66.
Grossvogel, David. *Four Playwrights and a Postscript: Brecht, Ionesco, Beckett, Genet.* Ithaca, N.Y.: Cornell University Press, 1962.
Habermas, Jürgen. "The French Path to Postmodernity: Bataille between Eroticism and General Economics." *New German Critique* 33 (1984):79–102.
———. *Legitimation Crisis.* Translated by Thomas McCarthy. Boston, Mass.: Beacon Press, 1975.
———. "Modernity versus Postmodernity." *New German Critique* 22 (1981):3–14.
———. *Theory of Communicative Action,* vol. 1. Translated by Thomas McCarthy. Boston, Mass.: Beacon Press, 1984.
Hafrey, Leigh. "The Gilded Cage: Postmodernism and Beyond." *TriQuarterly* 56 (1983):126–36.
Harari, Josué V., ed. *Textual Strategies: Perspectives in Post-Structuralist Criticism.* Ithaca, N.Y.: Cornell University Press, 1979.
Harman, Willis W. *An Incomplete Guide to the Future.* San Francisco, Calif.: San Francisco Book Co., 1976.
Harskamp, J. T. "Contemporaneity, Modernism, Avant-garde." *British Journal of Aesthetics* 20 (1980):204–14.
Hartman, Geoffrey H. *Criticism in the Wilderness: The Study of Literature Today.* New Heaven, Conn.: Yale University Press, 1980.
———. *Saving the Text: Literature/Derrida/Philosophy.* Baltimore, Md.: Johns Hopkins University Press, 1981.
Hassan, Ihab. "Abstractions." *Diacritics* 2 (1975):13–18.
———. "Culture, Indeterminacy, and Immanence: On the Margins of the (Postmodern) Age." *Humanities in Society* 1, no. 1 (1978): 51–85. Reprinted in *The Right Promethean Fire.*
———. "Desire and Dissent in the Postmodern Age." *Kenyon Review* 5 (1983):1–18.
———. *The Dismemberment of Orpheus: Toward a Postmodern Literature.* 2d ed., rev. Madison, Wis.: University of Wisconsin Press, 1982.
———. "Joyce, Beckett, and the Postmodern Imagination." *TriQuarterly* 34 (1975):179–200.
———, ed. *Liberations: New Essays on the Humanities in Revolution.* Middletown, Conn.: Wesleyan University Press, 1971.
———. *The Literature of Silence: Henry Miller and Samuel Beckett.* New York: Alfred A. Knopf, 1967.
———. *Paracriticisms: Seven Speculations of the Times.* Urbana, Ill.: University of Illinois Press, 1975.
———. *The Postmodern Turn: Essays in Postmodern Theory and Culture.* Columbus: Ohio State University Press, 1987.
———. "POSTmodernISM: A Paracritical Bibliography." *New Literary History* 3, no. 1 (Autumn 1971):5–30. Reprinted in *Paracriticisms.*

———. *The Right Promethean Fire: Imagination, Science, and Cultural Change.* Urbana, Ill.: University of Illinois Press, 1980.

———, and Sally Hassan, eds. *Innovation/Renovation: New Perspectives on the Humanities.* Madison, Wis.: University of Wisconsin Press, 1983.

Hayman, David. "Double-Distancing: An Attribute of the 'Post-Modern' Avant-Garde." *Novel* 12 (1978):33–47.

Heidegger, Martin. *Being and Time.* Translated by John Macquarrie and Edward Robinson. New York: Harper and Row, 1962.

———. *On the Way to Language.* Translated by Peter D. Hertz. New York: Harper and Row, 1971.

———. *Poetry, Language, Thought.* Translated by Albert Hofstadter. New York: Harper and Row, 1971.

Heilbrun, Carolyn G. *Toward a Recognition of Androgyny.* New York: Alfred A. Knopf, 1973.

Heisenberg, Werner. *Across the Frontiers.* Translated by Peter Heath. New York: Harper and Row, 1974.

———. *Physics and Beyond: Encounters and Conversations.* Translated by Arnold J. Pomerans. New York: Harper and Row, 1971.

Heller, Erich. *The Artist's Journey into the Interior and Other Essays.* New York: Random House, 1965.

———. *The Disinherited Mind: Essays in Modern German Literature and Thought.* New York: Farrar, Straus, and Cudahy, 1957.

Hertz, Richard. *Theories of Contemporary Art.* Englewood Cliffs, N.J.: Prentice-Hall, 1985.

Higgins, Dick. *A Dialectic of the Centuries: Notes Toward a Theory of the New Arts.* New York: Printed Editions, 1978.

———, and Wolf Vostell. *Fantastic Architecture.* New York: Something Else Press, 1971.

———. *Horizons: The Poetics and Theory of the Intermedia.* Carbondale, Ill.: Southern Illinois University Press, 1984.

Hoffmann, Gerhard. "The Fantastic in Fiction: Its 'Reality' Status, its Historical Development and its Transformation in Postmodern Narration." *REAL* (*Yearbook of Research in English and American Literature*) 1 (1982):267–364.

———, ed. *Making Sense* (forthcoming).

———; Alfred Horning; and Rüdiger Kunow. " 'Modern,' 'Postmodern,' and 'Contemporary' as Criteria for the Analysis of 20th Century Literature." *Amerikastudien* 22 (1977):19–46.

———. "Social Criticism and the Deformation of Man: Satire, the Grotesque, and Comic Nihilism in the Modern and Postmodern American Novel." *Amerikastudien* 28 (1983):141–203.

Holland, Norman H. *The Dynamics of Literary Response.* New York: W. W. Norton, 1968.

———. "The New Paradigm: Subjective or Transactive?" *New Literary History* 7 (1976):335–46.

———. *Poems in Persons: An Introduction to the Psychoanalysis of Literature.* New York: W. W. Norton, 1973.

Howe, Irving. *The Decline of the New.* New York: Harcourt, Brace, and World, 1970.

———. "Mass Society and Post-Modern Fiction." *Partisan Review* 26 (1959): 420–36. Also in *The Decline of the New.*

Hughes, Robert. *The Shock of the New: Art and the Century of Change.* New York: Alfred A. Knopf, 1981.

Hutcheon, Linda. *A Theory of Parody: The Teachings of Twentieth-Century Art Forms.* New York: Methuen, 1985.

———. *Narcissistic Narrative: The Metafictional Paradox.* Waterloo, Ontario: Wilfrid Laurier University Press, 1980.

Huyssen, Andreas. "Mapping Postmodernism." *New German Critique* 33 (1984):5–52.

———. "The Search for Tradition: Avant-Garde and Postmodernism in the 1970s." *New German Critique* 22 (1981):23–40.

Illich, Ivan. *Deschooling Society.* New York: Harper and Row, 1971.

Iser, Wolfgang. *The Act of Reading: A Theory of Aesthetic Response.* Baltimore, Md.: Johns Hopkins University Press, 1978.

———. *The Implied Reader: Patterns of Communication in Prose Fiction from Bunyan to Beckett.* Baltimore, Md.: Johns Hopkins University Press, 1974.

———. "Indeterminacy and the Reader's Response in Prose Fiction." In *Aspects of Narrative: Selected Papers from the English Institute.* Edited by J. Hillis Miller. New York: Columbia University Press, 1971.

———. "The Interplay Between Creation and Interpretation." *New Literary History* 15 (1984):387–95.

James, William. *A Pluralistic Universe.* Cambridge, Mass.: Harvard University Press, 1977.

———. *Pragmatism.* New York: Meridan Books, 1955.

———. *"The Will to Believe" and Other Essays in Popular Philosophy.* New York: Dover, 1956.

Jameson, Fredric. *The Political Unconscious: Narrative as a Socially Symbolic Act.* Ithaca, N.Y.: Cornell University Press, 1981.

———. "Postmodernism, or the Cultural Logic of Late Capitalism." *New Left Review* 146 (July–August 1984):53–92.

Jardine, Alice, and Hester Eisenstein, eds. *The Future of Difference.* Boston, Mass.: G. K. Hall; New York; Barnard College Women's Center, 1980.

Jauss, Hans Robert. *Toward an Aesthetics of Reception.* Translated by Timothy Bahti. Introduction by Paul de Man. Minneapolis, Minn.: University of Minnesota Press, 1985.

Jay, Martin. "Habermas and Modernism." *Praxis International* 4, no. 1 (1984):1–14.

Jefferson, Ann. *The Nouveau Roman and the Poetics of Fiction.* Cambridge and New York: Cambridge University Press, 1980.

Jencks, Charles, ed. *The Language of Post-Modern Architecture.* 4th ed., rev. and enl. New York: Rizzoli, 1984.

———, ed. *Post-Modern Classicism: The New Synthesis.* London: *Architectural Design* 5/6, 1980.

Johnson, Ellen H. *American Artists on Art: From 1940 to 1980.* New York: Harper and Row, 1982.

Journal of Modern Literature 3, 5 (1974). Issue on "From Modernism to Postmodernism."

Kafalenos, Emma. "Fragments of a Partial Discourse on Roland Barthes and the Postmodern Mind." *Chicago Review* 35 (1985):72–94.

Kahn, Herman, and Anthony J. Wiener. *The Year 2000: A Framework for Speculation on the Next Thirty-Three Years.* New York: Macmillan, 1967.

Kearney, Richard. *Dialogues with Contemporary Continental Thinkers: The Phenomenological Heritage: Paul Ricoeur, Emmanuel Levinas, Herbert Marcuse, Stanislas Breton, Jacques Derrida.* Manchester, U.K. and Dover, N.H.: Manchester University Press, 1984.

Kennard, Jean E. *Number and Nightmare: Forms of Fantasy in Contemporary Fiction.* Hamden, Conn.: Archon Books, 1975.

Kenner, Hugh. *The Pound Era.* Berkeley and Los Angeles, Calif.: University of California Press, 1971.

———. *The Stoic Comedians: Flaubert, Joyce, and Beckett.* Boston: Beacon Press, 1962.

Kermode, Frank. *Continuities.* New York: Random House, 1968.

———. "Modernisms Again: Objects, Jokes, and Art." *Encounter* 26, 4 (1966):65–74. Expanded and reprinted as "Modernisms" in *Continuities.*

Kirby, Michael. *The Art of Time: Essays on the Avant-Garde.* New York: E. P. Dutton, 1969.

———. *Happenings: An Illustrated Anthology.* Scripts and productions by Jim Dine and others. New York: Dutton, 1965.

———. "Post-Modern Dance Issue: An Introduction." *Drama Review* 19 (1975):3–4.

Klinkowitz, Jerome. *The Life of Fiction.* Urbana, Ill.: University of Illinois Press, 1977.

———. *Literary Disruptions: The Making of a Post-Contemporary American Fiction.* 2d ed., rev. Urbana, Ill.: University of Illinois Press, 1980.

———. *The Self-Apparent Word: Fiction as Language/Language as Fiction.* Carbondale, Ill.: Southern Illinois University Press, 1984.

Knapp, Steven, and Walter Benn Michaels. "Against Theory." *Critical Inquiry* 8 (1982):723–42.

Koestler, Arthur, and J. R. Smythies, eds. *Beyond Reductionism: New Perspectives in the Life Sciences.* Alpbach Symposium, 1968. New York: Macmillan, 1970.

Köhler, Michael. " 'Postmodernismus': Ein begriffsgeschichtlicher Überblick." *Amerikastudien* 22 (1977):8–18.

Kostelanetz, Richard, ed. *The Avant-Garde Tradition in Literature.* Buffalo, N.Y.: Prometheus Books, 1982.

———. *The End of Intelligent Writing: Literary Politics in America.* New York: Sheed and Ward, 1974.

———, ed. *Essaying Essays: Alternative Forms of Exposition.* New York: Out of London Press, 1975.

———. *Master Minds: Portraits of Contemporary American Artists and Intellectuals.* New York: Macmillan, 1969.

Kramer, Hilton. *The Age of the Avant-Garde: An Art Chronicle of 1956–1972.* New York: Farrar, Straus, and Giroux, 1973.

———. *The Revenge of the Philistines: Art and Culture, 1972–1984.* New York: Free Press, 1985.

Krauss, Rosalind E. *The Originality of the Avant-Garde and Other Modernist Myths.* Cambridge, Mass.: M.I.T. Press, 1985.

Krieger, Murray. *Arts on the Level: The Fall of the Elite Object.* Knoxville, Tenn.: University of Tennessee Press, 1981.

———, and L. S. Dembo, eds. *Directions for Criticism: Structuralism and Its Alternatives.* Madison, Wis.: University of Wisconsin Press, 1977.

———. "In the Wake of Morality: The Thematic Underside of Recent Theory." *New Literary History* 15 (1983):119–36.

———. *Poetic Presence and Illusion.* Baltimore, Md.: Johns Hopkins University Press, 1979.

Krísis 2 (1984). Issue on Negative Thinking, Crisis, Postmodernism. See especially articles by: René Thom, "The Rational and the Intelligible", 120–26; Horia Bratu, "Vocabulary of Crisis: Catastrophes", 127–36; Richard Palmer, "Expostulations on the Postmodern Turn", 140–49; Robert Solomon, "Beyond Postmodernism", 151–53.

Krísis 3–4 (1985). Issue on "Postmodernism: Search for Criteria." Articles and papers from the Cérisy-la-Salle Conference on Postmodernism.

Kristeva, Julia. *Desire in Language: A Semiotic Approach to Literature and Art.* Translated by Thomas Gora, Alice Jardine, and Leon S. Roudiez. New York: Columbia Unviersity Press, 1980.

———. *Powers of Horror: An Essay on Abjection.* Translated by Leon S. Roudiez. New York: Columbia University Press, 1982.

Kuhn, Thomas. *The Structure of Scientific Revolutions.* 2d. ed., enl. Chicago, Ill.: University of Chicago Press, 1970.

Kutnik, Jerzy. *The Novel as Performance: The Fiction of Ronald Sukenick and Raymond Federman.* Carbondale, Ill.: Southern Illinois University Press, 1986.

Lacan, Jacques. *The Language of the Self: The Function of Language in Psychoanalysis.* Translated by Anthony Wilden. Baltimore, Md.: Johns Hopkins University Press, 1968.

Laing, Ronald David. *The Divided Self: An Existential Study in Sanity and Madness.* London: Pelican, 1969.

———. *The Politics of Experience.* New York: Pantheon, 1967.

———. *The Politics of the Family and Other Essays.* New York: Pantheon, 1969.

Laplanche, Jean. *Life and Death in Psychoanalysis.* Translated by Jeffrey Mehlman. Baltimore, Md.: Johns Hopkins University Press, 1976.

Lasch, Christopher. *The Culture of Narcissism: American Life in an Age of Diminishing Expectations.* New York: Norton, 1978.

Leavitt, Ruth, ed. *Artist and Computer.* New York: Harmony Books, 1976.

LeClair, Tom, and Larry McCaffery, eds. *Anything Can Happen: Interviews with Contemporary American Novelists.* Urbana, Ill.: University of Illinois Press, 1983.

Lentricchia, Frank. *After the New Criticism.* Chicago, Ill.: University of Chicago Press, 1980.

———. *Criticism and Social Change.* Chicago, Ill.: University of Chicago Press, 1983.

Levin, Harry. "What Was Modernism?" *The Massachusetts Review* 1, 4 (1960):609–30. Reprinted in *Refractions: Essays in Comparative Literature.* New York: Oxford University Press, 1966.

Lévi-Strauss, Claude. *The Savage Mind.* Chicago, Ill.: University of Chicago Press, 1966.
———. *A World on the Wane.* Translated by John Russell. New York: Criterion Books, 1961.
LeVot, André. "Disjunctive and Conjunctive Modes in Contemporary American Fiction." *Forum* 14 (1976):44–55.
Lodge, David. *The Modes of Modern Writing: Metaphor, Metonymy, and the Typology of Modern Literature.* Ithaca, N.Y.: Cornell University Press, 1977.
Lukacs, John A. *The Passing of the Modern Age.* New York: Harper and Row, 1970.
Lunn, Eugene. *Marxism and Modernism; An Historical Study of Lukács, Brecht, Benjamin, and Adorno.* Berkeley and Los Angeles, Calif.: University of California Press, 1982.
Lyotard, Jean-Francois, and Jean-Loup Thébaud. *Just Gaming.* Translated by Wlad Godzich and Brian Massumi. Minneapolis, Minn.: University of Minnesota Press, 1985.
———. *The Postmodern Condition: A Report on Knowledge.* Translated by Geoff Bennington and Brian Massumi. Minneapolis, Minn.: University of Minnesota Press, 1984.
Mailer, Norman. *Advertisements for Myself.* New York: Putnam, 1959.
———. *Armies of the Night: History as Novel, the Novel as History.* New York: New American Library, 1968.
McCaffery, Larry. *The Metafictional Muse: The Works of Robert Coover, Donald Barthelme, and William H. Gass.* Pittsburgh, Pa.: University of Pittsburgh Press, 1982.
McConnell, Frank. "The Corpse of the Dragon: Notes on Postromantic Fiction." *TriQuarterly* 33 (1975):273–304.
McHale, Brian. "Writing About Postmodern Writing." *Poetics Today* 3 (1982): 211–27.
Macksey, Richard, and Eugenio Donato, eds. *The Languages of Criticism and the Sciences of Man.* Baltimore, Md.: Johns Hopkins University Press, 1970.
McLuhan, Marshall; Kathryn Hutchon; and Eric McLuhan. *City as Classroom: Understanding Language and Media.* Agincourt, Ont.: Book Society of Canada, 1977.
McLuhan, Marshall. *Understanding Media: The Extensions of Man.* New York: McGraw-Hill, 1964.
McLuhan, Marshall, and Quentin Fiore. *War and Peace in the Global Village.* New York: McGraw-Hill, 1968.
Malcolm X. *The Autobiography of Malcolm X.* With the Assistance of Alex Haley. New York: Grove Press, 1965.
Malmgren, Carl Darryl. *Fictional Space in the Modernist and Postmodernist American Novel.* Lewisburg, Pa.: Bucknell University Press, 1985.
Marcuse, Herbert. *An Essay on Liberation.* Boston, Mass.: Beacon Press, 1969.
———. *Eros and Civilization: A Philosophical Inquiry into Freud.* Boston, Mass.: Beacon Press, 1955.
———. *One Dimensional Man: Studies in the Ideology of Advanced Industrial Society.* Boston, Mass.: Beacon Press, 1964.

Marks, Elaine, and Isabella de Courtivron, eds. *New French Feminisms.* New York: Schocken Books, 1981.

Marx, Karl. *Capital.* 3 volumes. Edited by Frederick Engels. New York: International Publishers, 1967.

———. *Economic and Philosophical Manuscripts of 1844.* Edited with an Introduction by Dirk J. Struik. Translated by Martin Milligan. New York: International Publishers, 1964.

Marx, Karl, and Frederick Engels. *The German Ideology.* Part One with selections from Parts Two and Three, together with Marx's "Introduction to a Critique of Political Economy." Edited with an Introduction by C. J. Arthur. New York: International Publishers, 1970.

Matson, Floyd W. *The Broken Image: Man, Science, and Society.* Garden City, N.Y.: Doubleday, 1966.

Mauriac, Claude. *The New Literature.* Translated by Samuel I. Stone. New York: George Braziller, 1959.

Mazzaro, Jerome. *Postmodern American Poetry.* Urbana, Ill.: University of Illinois Press, 1980.

Megill, Allan. *Prophets of Extremity: Nietzsche, Heidegger, Foucault, Derrida.* Berkeley and Los Angeles, Calif.: University of California Press, 1985.

Mellard, James M. *The Exploded Form: The Modernist Novel in America.* Urbana, Ill.: Unviersity of Illinois Press, 1980.

Mercier, Vivian. *The New Novel from Queneau to Pinget.* New York: Farrar, Straus, and Giroux, 1971.

Meyer, Leonard B. "The End of the Renaissance?" *Hudson Review* 16 (1963): 169–86. Reprinted in *Music, the Arts, and Ideas.*

———. *Music, the Arts, and Ideas: Patterns and Predictions in Twentieth Century Culture.* Chicago, Ill.: University of Chicago Press, 1967.

Meyer, Ursula. *Conceptual Art.* New York: Dutton, 1972.

Miller, David LeRoy. *The New Polytheism: Rebirth of the Gods and Goddesses.* New York: Harper and Row, 1974.

Miller, J. Hillis. "The Critic as Host." In *Deconstruction and Criticism.* Edited by Harold Bloom et al. New York: Seabury Press, 1979.

———. *The Linguistic Moment: From Wordsworth to Stevens.* Princeton, N.J.: Princeton University Press, 1985.

———. *Poets of Reality: Six Twentieth-Century Writers.* Cambridge, Mass.: The Belknap Press of the Harvard University Press, 1965.

Mink, Louis O. "History and Fiction as Modes of Comprehension." *New Literary History* 1 (1970):541–58.

Minnesota Review, n.s. 23 (Fall 1984). Issue on "The Politics of Postmodernism."

Mitchell, W. J. T., ed. *Against Theory: Literary Studies and the New Pragmatism.* Chicago, Ill.: University of Chicago Press, 1985.

Morrissette, Bruce. "Post-Modern Generative Fiction: Novel and Film." *Critical Inquiry* 2 (1975):253–62.

Morson, Gary Saul. *The Boundaries of Genre: Dostoevsky's "Diary of a Writer" and the Traditions of Literary Utopia.* Austin, Tex.: University of Texas Press, 1981.

Nagele, Rainer. "Modernism and Postmodernism: The Margins of Articulation." *Studies in Twentieth Century Literature* 5 (1980):5–25.

Nelson, Benjamin. "Art and Technology: A Dialogue Between Harold Rosenberg and Benjamin Nelson." *Salmagundi* 27 (1974):40–56.

Neumann, John von. *The Computer and the Brain.* New Haven, Conn.: Yale University Press, 1958.

New German Critique 22 (1981). Issue on Habermas and Postmodernism.

New German Critique 33 (1984). Issue on Postmodernism. See especially essays by: Andreas Huyssen, "Mapping the Postmodern"; Hal Foster, "(Post)-Modern Polemics"; Jürgen Habermas, "The French Path to Postmodernism"; Seyla Benhabib, "Epistemologies of Postmodernism."

New Literary History 3, 1 (1971). Issue on "Modernism and Postmodernism: Inquiries, Reflections, and Speculations."

New Literary History 7, 1 (1975). Issue on "Critical Challenges: The Bellagio Symposium."

Newman, Charles. *The Post-Modern Aura: The Act of Fiction in an Age of Inflation.* Evanston, Ill.: Northwestern University Press, 1985.

Nietzsche, Freidrich. *The Gay Science.* Translated by Walter Kaufmann. New York: Random House, 1974.

———. "Truth and Falsity in an Ultramoral Sense." In *The Philosophy of Nietzsche.* Edited by Geoffrey Clive. New York: New American Library, 1965.

———. *Untimely Meditations.* Translated by R. J. Hollingdale. New York: Cambridge University Press, 1983.

———. *The Will to Power.* Translated by Walter Kaufmann and R. J. Hollingdale. New York: Random House, 1967.

Norris, Christopher. "Philosophy as a Kind of Narrative: Rorty on Postmodern Liberal Culture." *Enclitic* 7 (1983):144–59.

Nozick, Robert. *Philosophical Explanations.* Cambridge, Mass.: Harvard University Press, 1981.

O'Doherty, Brian. "What is Post-Modernism?" *Art in America* 59 (1971):19.

O'Hara, Daniel T., ed. *Why Nietzsche Now?* Bloomington, Ind.: Indiana University Press, 1985.

Olderman, Raymond M. *Beyond the Waste Land: A Study of the American Novel in the Nineteen-Sixties.* New Haven, Conn.: Yale University Press, 1972.

Olson, Charles. "The Act of Writing in the Context of Post-Modern Man." *Olson: The Journal of the Charles Olson Archives* 2 (1974):28. (Written in 1952.)

———. *Additional Prose: A Bibliography on America, Proprioception, and Other Notes and Essays.* Edited by George F. Butterick. Bolinas, Calif.: Four Seasons, 1974.

Ortega y Gasset, José. *The Dehumanization of Art and Notes on the Novel.* Translated by Helene Weyl. New York: Peter Smith, 1951.

Owens, Craig. "The Allegorical Impulse: Toward a Theory of Postmodernism." Part 1: *October* 12 (1980):67–86. Part 2: *October* 13 (1980):59–80.

Paine, Sylvia. *Beckett, Nabokov, Nin: Motives and Modernism.* Port Washington, N.Y.: Kennikat Press, 1981.

Palmer, Richard. *Hermeneutics: Interpretation Theory on Schleiermacher, Dilthey, Heidegger, and Gadamer.* Evanston, Ill.: Northwestern University Press, 1969.

———. "Postmodernity and Hermeneutics." *Boundary 2* 5 (1977):363–93.

———. "The Postmodernity of Heidegger." *Boundary 2* 4 (1976):411–32.
Par Rapport 2, 2 (1979). Issue on Postmodernism.
Paz, Octavio. *Children of the Mire: Modern Poetry from Romanticism to the Avant-Garde.* Cambridge, Mass.: Harvard University Press, 1974.
Pearce, Joseph Chilton. *The Crack in the Cosmic Egg: Challenging Constructs of Mind and Reality.* New York: Julian Press, 1971.
Peckham, Morse. *Man's Rage for Chaos: Biology, Behavior, and the Arts.* Philadelphia, Pa.: Chilton Books, 1965.
Pepper, Stephen C. *World Hypotheses: A Study in Evidence.* Berkeley and Los Angeles, Calif.: University of California Press, 1942.
Perloff, Marjorie. *The Dance of the Intellect: Studies in the Poetry of the Pound Tradition.* Cambridge: Cambridge University Press, 1985.
———. *The Poetics of Indeterminacy: Rimbaud to Cage.* Princeton, N.J.: Princeton Unviersity Press, 1981.
Phelan, James. "Data, Danda, and Disagreement." *Diacritics* 13 (1983):39–50.
Pinsker, Sanford. "*Ulysses* and the Post-Modern Temper." *Midwest Quarterly* 15 (1974):406–16.
Pinsky, Robert. *The Situation of Poetry: Contemporary Poetry and Its Traditions.* Princeton, N.J.: Princeton University Press, 1976.
Pirsig, Robert. *Zen and the Art of Motorcycle Maintenance.* New York: William Morrow, 1974.
Poggioli, Renato. *The Theory of the Avant-Garde.* Translated by Gerald Fitzgerald. Cambridge, Mass.: Belknap Press of Harvard University Press. 1968.
Poirier, Richard. "The Aesthetics of Radicalism." *Partisan Review* 41 (1974): 176–96.
———. "The Difficulties of Modernism and the Modernism of Difficulty." In *Images and Ideas in American Culture: The Function of Criticism. Essays in Memory of Philip Rahv.* Edited by Arthur Edelstein. Hanover, N.H.: Brandeis University Press, 1979.
———. *The Performing Self: Compositions and Decompositions in the Languages of Contemporary Life.* New York: Oxford University Press, 1971.
Polanyi, Michael. *Personal Knowledge: Towards a Post-Critical Philosophy.* Rev. ed. Chicago, Ill.: University of Chicago Press, 1962.
Portoghesi, Paolo. *After Modern Architecture.* Translated by Meg Shore. New York: Rizzoli, 1982.
Pratt, Mary Louise. *Toward a Speech Act Theory of Literary Discourse.* Bloomington, Ind.: Indiana University Press, 1977.
Pütz, Manfred. "The Struggle of the Postmodern: Books on a New Concept in Criticism." *Kritikon Litterarum* 2 (1973):225–37.
Pütz, Manfred, and Peter Freese, eds. *Postmodernism in American Literature: A Critical Anthology.* Darmstadt: Thesen Verlag, 1984.
Radhakrishnan, R. "The Post-Modern Event and the End of Logocentrism." *Boundary 2,* 12 (1983):33–60.
Ricoeur, Paul. *Freud and Philosophy: An Essay on Interpretation.* New Haven, Conn.: Yale University Press, 1970.
———. *The Rule of Metaphor: Multi-disciplinary Studies of the Creation of Meaning in Language.* Translated by Robert Czerny with Kathleen McLaughlin and John Costello. Toronto and Buffalo: University of Toronto Press, 1977.

Riesman, David. *The Lonely Crowd: A Study of the Changing American Character.* New Haven, Conn.: Yale University Press, 1950.

Robbe-Grillet, Alain. *For a New Novel: Essays on Fiction.* Translated by Richard Howard. New York: Grove Press, 1965.

Rorty, Richard. *Consequences of Pragmatism (Essays: 1972–1980).* Minneapolis, Minn.: University of Minnesota Press, 1982.

———. "Habermas and Lyotard on Post-Modernity." *Praxis International* 4, 1 (1984):32–44.

———. *Philosophy and the Mirror of Nature.* Princeton, N.J.: Princeton University Press, 1979.

Rose, Margaret A. *Parody // Meta-Fiction: An Analysis of Parody as a Critical Mirror to the Writing and Reception of Fiction.* London: Croom Helm, 1979.

Rosenberg, Harold. *The Anxious Object: Art Today and Its Audience.* New York: Horizon Press, 1966.

———. "Art and Technology: A Dialogue Between Harold Rosenberg and Benjamin Nelson." *Salmagundi* 27 (1974):40–56.

———. *The De-definition of Art: Action Art to Pop to Earthworks.* New York: Horizon Press, 1972.

———. *The Tradition of the New.* New York: Grove Press, 1961.

Roszak, Theodore. *The Making of a Counter Culture: Reflections on the Technocratic Society and its Youthful Oppositions.* Garden City, N.Y.: Doubleday, 1969.

Rother, James. "Parafiction: The Adjacent Universes of Barth, Barthelme, Pynchon, and Nabokov." *Boundary 2,* 5 (1976):21–43.

Russell, Charles, ed. *The Avant-Garde Today: An International Anthology.* Urbana, Ill.: University of Illinois Press, 1981.

———. *Poets, Prophets, and Revolutionaries: The Literary Avant-garde from Rimbaud through Postmodernism.* New York: Oxford University Press, 1985.

Said, Edward W. *Beginnings: Intention and Method.* New York: Basic Books, 1975.

———. "An Ideology of Difference. *Critical Inquiry* 12, 1 (1985):38–58.

———. "Travelling Theory." *Raritan* 1 (1982):41–67.

———. *The World, the Text, and the Critic.* Cambridge, Mass.: Harvard University Press, 1983.

Salmagundi 67 (1985):163–97. Responses to Charles Newman's *The Post-Modern Aura* by various critics.

Sandler, Irving. "Modernism, Revisionism, Pluralism, and Post-Modernism." *Art Journal* 40 (1980):345–47.

Sarraute, Nathalie. *The Age of Suspicion: Essays on the Novel.* Translated by Maria Jolas. New York: George Braziller, 1963.

Sartre, Jean-Paul. *Being and Nothingness: An Essay on Phenomenological Ontology.* Translated by Hazel E. Barnes. New York: Philosophical Library, 1956.

———. *What is Literature?* Translated by Bernard Frechtman. New York: Harper and Row, 1965.

Schechner, Richard. "The Decline and Fall of the (American) Avant-Garde." *Performing Arts Journal* 14 & 15 (1981):9–19.
Schevill, James. *Break Out! In Search of New Theatrical Environments.* Chicago, Ill.: Swallow Press, 1973.
Schmidt, Siegfried J. "Perspectives on the Development of Post-Concrete Poetry." *Poetics Today* 3 (1982):101–36.
Schmitz, Neil. "Gertrude Stein as Post-Modernist: The Rhetoric of *Tender Buttons.*" *Journal of Modern Literature* 3 (1974):1203–18.
Scholes, Robert. *Fabulation and Metafiction.* Urbana, Ill.: Unviersity of Illinois Press, 1979.
———, and Eric Rabkin. *Science Fiction: History-Science-Vision.* New York: Oxford University Press, 1977.
———. *Semiotics and Interpretation.* New Haven, Conn.: Yale University Press, 1982.
———. *Structural Fabulation: An Essay on Fiction of the Future.* Notre Dame, Ind.: University of Notre Dame Press, 1975.
———. *Structuralism in Literature: An Introduction.* New Haven, Conn.: Yale University Press, 1974.
Schwab, Gabriele. "Genesis of the Subject, Imaginary Functions, and Poetic Language." *New Literary History* 15 (1984):453–74.
Schwartz, Sanford. *The Matrix of Modernism: Pound, Eliot, and Early 20th Century Thought.* Princeton, N.J.: Princeton University Press, 1985.
Scott, Nathan A., Jr. *Negative Capability: Studies in the New Literature and the Religious Situation.* New Haven, Conn.: Yale University Press, 1969.
Searle, John R. *Speech Acts: An Essay in the Philosophy of Language.* Cambridge: Cambridge University Press, 1969.
Sears, Sallie, and Georgina W. Lord, eds. *The Discontinuous Universe.* New York: Basic Books, 1972.
Seidenberg, Roderick. *Post-Historic Man: An Inquiry.* Chapel Hill, N.C.: University of North Carolina Press, 1950.
Sewell, Elizabeth. *The Field of Nonsense.* Darby, Pa.: Arden Library, 1978.
Shattuck, Roger. "After the Avant-Garde." *New York Review of Books,* 12 March 1970, 41–47.
———. *The Banquet Years: The Origins of the Avant-Garde in France, 1885 to World War I: Alfred Jarry, Henri Rousseau, Erik Satie, Guillaume Apollinaire.* Rev. ed. New York: Random House, 1968.
Simard, Rodney. *Postmodern Drama: Contemporary Playwrights in America and Britain.* Landham, Md.: University Press of America, 1984.
Singer, Alan. *A Methaphorics of Fiction: Discontinuity and Discourse in the Modern Novel.* Tallahassee, Fla.: Florida State University Press, 1984.
Skinner, B. F. *Beyond Freedom and Dignity.* New York: Alfred A. Knopf, 1971.
Sontag, Susan. "The Aesthetics of Silence." *Aspen* 5 & 6 (1967): section 3 (no pagination). Reprinted in *Styles of Radical Will.*
———. *Against Interpretation and Other Essays.* New York: Farrar, Straus, and Giroux, 1966.
———. *On Photography.* New York: Farrar, Straus, and Giroux, 1977.
———. *Styles of Radical Will.* New York: Dell, 1969.

Spanos, William V., ed. *A Casebook on Existentialism 2.* New York: Thomas Y. Crowell, 1976.

———. "The Detective and the Boundary: Some Notes on the Postmodern Literary Imagination." *Boundary 2,* 1 (1972):147–68. Reprinted in *A Casebook on Existentialism 2.*

———. "Heidegger, Kierkegaard, and the Hermeneutic Circle: Towards a Postmodern Theory of Interpretation as Dis-closure." *Boundary 2,* 4 (1976): 455–88.

———, ed. *Martin Heidegger and the Question of Literature: Toward a Postmodern Literary Hermeneutics.* Bloomington, Ind.: Indiana University Press, 1979.

———; Paul Bové; and Daniel T. O'Hara. *The Question of Textuality: Strategies of Reading in Contemporary American Criticism.* Bloomington, Ind.: Indiana University Press, 1982.

Spencer, Sharon. *Space, Time, and Structure in the Modern Novel.* New York: New York University Press, 1971.

Spender, Stephen. *The Struggle of the Modern.* Berkeley and Los Angeles, Calif.: University of California Press, 1963.

Stark, John O. *The Literature of Exhaustion: Borges, Nabokov, and Barth.* Durham, N.C.: Duke University Press, 1974.

Steiner, George. *Extra-Territorial: Papers on Literature and the Language Revolution.* New York: Atheneum, 1971.

———. *In Bluebeard's Castle: Some Notes Towards the Redefinition of Culture.* New Haven, Conn.: Yale University Press, 1971.

———. *Language and Silence: Essays on Language, Literature, and the Inhuman.* New York: Atheneum, 1967.

———. "The Retreat From the Word." *Kenyon Review* 23 (1961):187–216. Reprinted in *Language and Silence.*

Stevick, Philip. *Alternative Pleasures: Postrealist Fiction and the Tradition.* Urbana, Ill.: University of Illinois Press, 1981.

———. "Scheherezade Runs Out of Plots, Goes on Talking; the King, Puzzled, Listens: An Essay on New Fiction." *TriQuarterly* 26 (1973):332–62.

Sukenick, Ronald. *In Form: Digressions on the Art of Fiction.* Carbondale, Ill.: Southern Illinois University Press, 1985.

Suleiman, Susan R., and Inge Crosman, eds. *The Reader in the Text: Essays on Audience and Interpretation.* Princeton, N.J.: Princeton University Press, 1980.

Sypher, Wylie. *Literature and Technology: The Alien Vision.* New York: Random House, 1968.

———. *Loss of the Self in Modern Literature and Art.* New York: Random House, 1962.

Szabolcsi, Miklos. "Avant-Garde, Neo-Avant-Garde, Modernism: Some Questions and Suggestions." *New Literary History* 3 (1971):49–70.

Tani, Stefano. *The Doomed Detective: The Contribution of the Detective Novel to Postmodern American and Italian Fiction.* Carbondale, Ill.: Southern Illinois University Press, 1984.

Tanner, Tony. *City of Words: American Fiction, 1950–1970.* New York: Harper and Row, 1971.

Tatham, Campbell. "Correspondence/Notes/Etceteras." *Chicago Review* 26 (1975):112–32.

———. "Critical Investigations: Language Games: (Post)Modern(Isms)." *Sub-Stance* 10 (1974):67–80.

Thiher, Allen. *Words in Reflection: Modern Language Theory and Postmodern Fiction.* Chicago, Ill.: University of Chicago Press, 1984.

Thompson, John B. *Critical Hermeneutics: A Study in the Thought of Paul Ricoeur and Jürgen Habermas.* Cambridge and New York: Cambridge University Press, 1981.

Thompson, William Irwin. *At the Edge of History: Speculations on the Transformation of Culture.* New York: Harper and Row, 1971.

———. *Passages About Earth: An Exploration of the New Planetary Culture.* New York: Harper and Row, 1974.

Todorov, Tzvetan. *The Fantastic: A Structural Approach to a Literary Genre.* Translated by Richard Howard. Cleveland, Ohio: Case Western Reserve University Press, 1973.

———. *The Poetics of Prose.* Translated by Richard Howard. Ithaca, N.Y.: Cornell University Press, 1977.

Toffler, Alvin. *Future Shock.* New York: Random House, 1970.

Tomkins, Calvin. *The Bride and the Bachelors: The Heretical Courtship in Modern Art.* New York: Viking Press, 1965.

———. *The Scene: Reports on Post-Modern Art.* New York: Viking Press, 1976.

Tompkins, Jane P., ed. *Reader-Response Criticism: From Formalism to Post-Structuralism.* Baltimore, Md.: Johns Hopkins University Press, 1980.

Toulmin, Stephen E. *Human Understanding: The Collective Use and Evolution of Concepts.* Princeton, N.J.: Princeton University Press, 1972.

Trilling, Lionel. *Beyond Culture: Essays on Literature and Learning.* New York: Viking Press, 1965.

———. *Mind in the Modern World.* New York: Viking Press, 1973.

TriQuarterly 26, (1973), 30 (1974), 32 (1975), 33 (1975). Issues on Postmodern Art, Literature, and Criticism.

Turner, Frederick. "Escape from Modernism: Technology and the Future of the Imagination." *Harper's Magazine,* November 1984, 47–55.

Turner, Victor. *Dramas, Fields, and Methaphors: Symbolic Action in Human Society.* Ithaca, N.Y.: Cornell University Press, 1974.

Ulmer, Gregory L. *Applied Grammatology: Post(e)-Pedagogy from Jacques Derrida to Joseph Beuys.* Baltimore, Md.: Johns Hopkins University Press, 1985.

Updike, John. "Modernist, Postmodernist, What Will They Think of Next?" *New Yorker,* 10 September 1984, 136–42.

Venturi, Robert; Denise Scott Brown; and Steven Izenour. *Learning from Las Vegas: the Forgotten Symbolism of Architectural Form.* Cambridge, Mass.: M.I.T. Press, 1977.

Vernon, John. *The Garden and the Map: Schizophrenia in Twentieth Century Literature and Culture.* Urbana, Ill.: University of Illinois Press, 1973.

Wallace Stevens Journal 7 (1983). Issue on "Stevens and Postmodern Criticism."

Wasson, Richard. "From Priest to Prometheus: Culture and Criticism in the Post-Modernist Period." *Journal of Modern Literature* 3 (1974):1188–1202.

———. "Notes on a New Sensibility." *Partisan Review* 36 (1969):460–77.

Watkins, Evan. "Conflict and Consensus in the History of Recent Criticism." *New Literary History* 12 (1981):345–65.

Weightman, John. *The Concept of the Avant-Garde: Explorations in Modernism.* London: Alcove Press, 1973.

Weinberg, Helen A. *The New Novel in America: The Kafkan Mode in Contemporary Fiction.* Ithaca, N.Y.: Cornell University Press, 1970.

Wellmer, Albrecht. "On the Dialectic of Modernism and Postmodernism." *Praxis International* 4 (1985):337–62.

White, Hayden. *Metahistory: The Historical Imagination in Nineteenth-Century Europe.* Baltimore, Md.: Johns Hopkins University Press, 1973.

———. "The Politics of Historical Interpretation: Discipline and De-Sublimation." *Critical Inquiry* 9 (1982):124–28.

———, and Margaret Brose, eds. *Representing Kenneth Burke: Selected Papers from the English Institute.* New Series, No. 6. Baltimore, Md.: Johns Hopkins University Press, 1982.

———. *Tropics of Discourse.* Baltimore, Md.: Johns Hopkins University Press, 1978.

Wiener, Norbert. *The Human Use of Human Beings: Cybernetics and Society.* Boston, Mass.: Houghton Mifflin, 1954.

Wilde, Alan. *Horizons of Assent: Modernism, Postmodernism, and the Ironic Imagination.* Baltimore, Md.: Johns Hopkins University Press, 1981.

———. "Modernism and the Aesthetics of Crisis." *Contemporary Literature* 20 (1979):13–50.

———. "Strange Displacements of the Ordinary: Apple, Elkin, Barthelme, and the Problem of the Excluded Middle." *Boundary 2,* 10 (1982):177–99.

Wilson, Edmund. *Axel's Castle: A Study of the Imaginative Literature of 1870–1930.* New York: Charles Scribner, 1931.

Wittgenstein, Ludwig. *The Blue and Brown Books.* Oxford: Basil Blackwell and Mott, 1958.

———. *Philosophical Investigations.* Translated by G. E. M. Anscombe. Oxford: Oxford University Press, 1968.

———. *Zettel.* Translated by G. E. M. Anscombe. Berkeley and Los Angeles, Calif.: University of California Press, 1967.

Yale French Studies 36 & 37 (1966). Issue on Structuralism.

Zavarzadeh, Mas'ud. *The Mythopoeic Reality: The Postwar American Nonfiction Novel.* Urbana, Ill.: University of Illinois Press, 1976.

Ziolkowski, Theodore. "Toward a Post-Modern Aesthetics?" *Mosaic* 2, 4 (1969):112–19.

Index of Names and Titles